Hemingway a

Hemingway and Pound

A Most Unlikely Friendship

JOHN COHASSEY

Best Wishes
John Cohassey

McFarland & Company, Inc., Publishers
Jefferson, North Carolina

ALSO OF INTEREST

American Cultural Rebels: Avant-Garde and Bohemian Artists, Writers and Musicians from the 1850s through the 1960s by Roy Kotynek and John Cohassey (McFarland, 2008)

LIBRARY OF CONGRESS CATALOGUING-IN-PUBLICATION DATA

Cohassey, John, 1961– author.
    Hemingway and Pound : a most unlikely friendship /
John Cohassey.
        p.   cm.
    Includes bibliographical references and index.

    ISBN 978-0-7864-7640-4 (softcover : acid free paper) ∞
    ISBN 978-1-4766-1647-6 (ebook)

    1. Hemingway, Ernest, 1899–1961—Friends and associates.
2. Pound, Ezra, 1885–1972—Friends and associates.   I. Title.
PS3515.E37Z584626 2014
813'.52—dc23
[B]

                                                    2014020828

BRITISH LIBRARY CATALOGUING DATA ARE AVAILABLE

On the cover: *left to right* Ezra Pound (clipart.com); Ernest Hemingway, ca. 1920 (Photofest); background image and texture (© iStock/Thinkstock)

Printed in the United States of America

McFarland & Company, Inc., Publishers
  Box 611, Jefferson, North Carolina 28640
  www.mcfarlandpub.com

To Roy Kotynek,
a unique friend, mentor
and all-around good guy

Contents

Acknowledgments

Reprinted with the permission of Scribner Publishing Group from *The Sun Also Rises* by Ernest Hemingway. Copyright © 1926 by Charles Scribner's Sons; copyright renewed © 1954 by Ernest Hemingway. All rights reserved.

Reprinted with the permission of Scribner Publishing Group from *Death in the Afternoon* by Ernest Hemingway. Copyright © 1932 by Charles Scribner's Sons; copyright renewed © 1960 by Ernest Hemingway. All rights reserved.

Reprinted with the permission of Scribner Publishing Group from *To Have and Have Not* by Ernest Hemingway. Copyright © 1937 by Ernest Hemingway; copyright renewal © 1965 by Mary Hemingway. All rights reserved.

Reprinted with the permission of Scribner Publishing Group from *For Whom the Bell Tolls* by Ernest Hemingway. Copyright © 1964 by Ernest Hemingway; copyright renewed © 1940 by Ernest Hemingway. Copyright renewed © 1968 by Mary Hemingway. All rights reserved.

Reprinted with the permission of Scribner Publishing Group from *A Moveable Feast* by Ernest Hemingway. Copyright © 1964 by Ernest Hemingway; copyright renewed © 1992 by John H. Hemingway, Patrick Hemingway, and Gregory Hemingway. All rights reserved.

Reprinted with the permission of Scribner Publishing Group from *True at First Light* by Ernest Hemingway. Copyright © 1999. All rights reserved.

Reprinted with the permission of Scribner Publishing Group from *Ernest Hemingway, Selected Letters 1917–1961* by Carlos Baker. Copyright ©. All rights reserved.

Letters from Ernest Hemingway to Sherwood Anderson and letter from Sherwood Anderson to Lewis Galantiere (Midwest MS Anderson Box 21 Folder 1068; Box 7 Folder 261) quoted courtesy Newberry Library, Chicago.

Letters of Ernest Hemingway and Ezra Pound (Pound mss II, Pound mss III and Hemingway mss III) quoted courtesy Lilly Library, Indiana University, Bloomington, Indiana.

"Canto XVI" by Ezra Pound, from *The Cantos of Ezra Pound,* copyright © 1934 by Ezra Pound. Copyright © 2013 by the Estate of Omar S. Pound and Mary de Rachewiltz. Reprinted by permission of New Directions Publishing Corp.

Preface

Friendships did not last long in Ernest Hemingway's turbulent life. Hemingway's admiration for poet Ezra Pound, however, survived fiery temperaments and divergent political outlooks. Bonds of friendship between unique individuals are never easily understood. Sharp-tongued critics, both Hemingway and Pound lashed out at enemies, real and perceived. During their short time together in 1920s Paris, Pound edited Hemingway's early work. Over decades Hemingway considered Pound a major poet and read *The Cantos* as they appeared in little magazines and published volumes. Although Hemingway found both strengths and weaknesses in this epic work, he considered it a formidable arrangement of words. In turn, Pound praised Hemingway's prose as having the fine "touch of the chisel." Hemingway never forgot his friend's commission-free promotion of his work and that of numerous writers, artists, and musicians. He most likely last saw Pound in Paris in 1933, and two decades later when receiving the Nobel Prize suggested it be awarded to the aging poet. In a posthumously published tribute Hemingway lauded Pound as "a sort of saint," an irascible artistic visionary, a flawed genius, who in later years saw the world through prison bars and madhouse windows.

Pound once wrote: "A new acquaintance is an experiment, a new friend a peril. The acquisition of either means a derangement of one's system of life. It means rearranging one's time to admit the intruder." Showing up at Pound's Paris apartment in the winter of 1922, Hemingway was neither an intruder nor a peril. Born in Idaho—the state where Hemingway ended his life nearly half a century later—Pound mocked American country rubes and politicians in a way that no doubt greatly entertained Hemingway, who was given to nicknaming his friends and wives and brutally satirizing others. For decades Hemingway and Pound's friendship survived by correspondence, in which the latter addressed his friend as "Hem" or "Hembo," and signed off as "Yr fexshunate unkl." Hemingway considered Pound's letters in response to his troubles as "life preservers." Long after this early mentor-pupil relationship had ended, these writers tested the limits of friendship as Pound, the former fencer, and Hemingway, the amateur boxer, jabbed at one another with words.[1]

A year before Hemingway met Pound, New York lawyer and famous art patron John Quinn wrote his poet friend: "You and I can swear in writing at each other, and talk and write straight from the shoulder, whereas some of these younger fellows don't understand it." Nearly fourteen years younger than Pound, Hemingway well understood the poet's temperament and eccentricities, establishing a lasting friendship. Their correspondences did not always reflect their public comments about each other. As literary scholar James Mellow asserted: "Hemingway could be ambivalent, both generous and yet wary of crediting too much to Pound's influence on his writing. It depended on the impression he wanted to make with a particular correspondent." But Hemingway always tried to avoid harsh words about his old friend, or if so, worded them carefully. Even if Hemingway at times privately questioned Pound's ability to write first-rate poetry over time, he stuck by him—always giving credit to his contribution to twentieth century literature.[2]

Many-sided in personality and temperament, Hemingway and Pound made impressions so diverse that they seemed to be different men at different times. There was the garrulous Pound, the "village explainer," the avuncular promoter of young artists, the economic crank, the irrational anti–Semite, the kind poet feeding stray cats. On the other hand, there was Hemingway the sportsman, the accident-prone bully drunkard, the vindictive writer easily roused by the slightest criticism, the witty storyteller with the slow Midwestern grin—charming in youth, sad-eyed and disheveled in later years.

To understand these two literary figures it is important to contrast their adoptive countries. After meeting in Paris, each went his own way—Pound to Italy, where he lived out his life following his twelve-year American imprisonment. Hemingway's attending the bullfights in Pamplona in 1923 began a deep affinity with Spain and its culture, also influencing a twenty-year stay among Cuba's Spanish-speaking fishermen and working people. Meanwhile, Pound pronounced Italy's heralding a new age of art through Social Credit economics. As Pound defended Mussolini's invasion of Ethiopia and his aiding Franco's Nationalists during the Spanish Civil

War, Hemingway took up with fervor the Republican cause in a United Front against fascism.

Aware of Pound's wartime Radio Rome broadcasts that urged the Allies to end the conflict peaceably and that conspiratorially accused President Roosevelt as a tool of Jewish world finance, Hemingway still did not end his friendship. When leading figures struggled to free Pound from St. Elizabeths Hospital for the Criminally Insane, he became a major contributor to Pound's release. During World War II, Hemingway privately branded Pound "a stupid traitor" and thought him mentally unstable. But Hemingway judged Pound's best work, *The Cantos,* marred by "several stale jokes, and quite a lot of crap," but containing "some Christwonderful poetry that no one can better."[3]

In reference to F. Scott Fitzgerald and Hemingway, literary biographer Matthew J. Bruccoli wrote: "The mortality rate among literary friendships is high. Writers tend to be bad risks as friends—probably for much the same reasons they are bad matrimonial risks. They save the best parts of themselves for their work." This may have been true of Pound, but he also spent decades finding pleasure in disagreeing and arguing with friends Yeats and Eliot, while asserting: "The fun of an intellectual friendship is that you diverge on something or other and agree on a few points."[4]

More than an intellectual friendship, Hemingway and Pound's bond rested upon the fine crafting of words—a memorable affection first shared in cramped Parisian Left Bank apartments and editing offices.

CHAPTER 1

Crossing Paths in Paris

While living in Chicago in January 1921, Hemingway met acclaimed novelist Sherwood Anderson in a life-changing event, one of many that would occur over the next several years. Twenty-one years old and a little-known journalist, Hemingway had set his sights on writing stories for popular magazines. At the time of Hemingway's meeting Anderson, the writer's book *Winesburg, Ohio* (1919), though considered sexually scandalous by many readers, was lauded by leading critics such as H.L. Mencken and Van Wyck Brooks. It became a force among the country's leading modernists, including the circle of the New York photographer and impresario Alfred Stieglitz, who hailed Anderson as setting a new literary standard. Leading critics of Stieglitz's circle—Waldo Frank and Paul Rosenfeld—enthusiastically embraced the Ohio-born writer.

Having broken with his religious parents, Hemingway found in Anderson a kind mentor twenty-five years his senior who thought him a gifted writer. Invited to live in a large apartment house at 63 East Division Street by Y.K. Smith—the older brother of family friends—Hemingway shared quarters with other aspiring writers. Nearby, on East Division, lived Anderson, who often stopped by Y.K.'s apartment, telling and retelling stories by the hour. "For the most part," explains Anderson's biographer Walter Rideout, "Hemingway listened quietly and admiringly, though not uncritically, since he was already far more bent on realism in his writing than Anderson was."[1]

Though he later denied Anderson's influence, Hemingway took away valuable lessons in literature and visual art. Anderson's biographer David D. Anderson discerned similarities between these two Mid-American writers' romantic idealism "whose people, hurt spiritually by a hostile world ...

embarked on a search for meaning in spite of the fact that there is none. Eventually both of them point out in their works that the end of the search is not important; that what matters is the way in which the search is carried out."[2]

In May 1921, Anderson and his wife took a trip to Europe funded by art critic Paul Rosenfeld. In Paris, Anderson encountered Sylvia Beach, American owner of the Shakespeare and Company bookshop. Beach, immediately charmed by Anderson, recalled, "I saw him as a mixture of poet and evangelist (without the preaching), with perhaps a touch of the actor. Anyhow, he was a most interesting man." Beach introduced Anderson to James Joyce and accompanied him to Gertrude Stein's apartment at 27 rue de Fleurus.[3]

In late May Pound called upon Anderson at the Hotel Jacob et l'Angleterre. In response to his meeting, Pound wrote Margaret Anderson, the publisher of the *Little Review*, that "Sherwood Anderson is here, and promises something for coming year." Pound had taken notice of Anderson's writing and, in 1918, noted that there "is something ... to Sherwood <A.> [Anderson]" and often suggested that the *Little Review*'s editor include more of his work in her magazine. Anderson, on the other hand, came away from meeting Pound with an unfavorable impression. In a letter to a friend, he wrote, "Pound seems to be an empty man without fire." Anderson also expressed this view in his Paris Notebook, writing that the poet was "empty with nothing to give." Despite this assessment, Anderson was well aware of Pound's connections in the literary world and his willingness to promote young talent and, for the next several years, still suggested young writers meet Pound while visiting Paris.[4]

Back in Chicago during the fall of 1921, Anderson encountered Hemingway, who had recently married to Hadley Richardson of St. Louis. Taken to dinner by Anderson and his wife, the Hemingways were urged to make Paris their new home, where they could live cheaply and encounter a vibrant art and literary scene. In his eastward gravitation towards Europe, Hemingway diverged from the typical path of most 1920s young writers from the American hinterlands, who first tried their luck in New York City before moving on to Paris. Having served with the Red Cross in Italy during World War I, Hemingway considered returning there, until Anderson piqued his interest in Paris.

Ernest and Hadley arrived in Paris in late December 1921. Provided with several of Anderson's letters of introduction, Hemingway was at first cautious in using these words of praise that described him as a "young fellow of extraordinary talent" destined to "get somewhere." These letters of introduction were mailed once Ernest was in Paris. Not long before Anderson wrote Stein: "I am writing this note to make you acquainted with my friend Ernest Hemingway, who with Mrs. Hemingway is going to Paris to live, and will ask him to drop it in the mails when he arrives there. Mr. Hemingway is an American writer instinctively in touch with everything worth while going on here and I know you will find Mr. and Mrs. Hemingway delightful people to know."[5]

Despite Hemingway's excitedly writing Sherwood Anderson in late December that he would immediately send his letters of introduction, he waited a bit. After a skiing trip to Switzerland, Hemingway first called upon Pound in February and, in the following month, made use of another letter of introduction to visit Stein. Before his meeting Pound, Hemingway had a limited knowledge of Pound's work, and what he did know most likely came from Anderson, who urged his meeting the poet. But this may have not been too flattering if judged by Anderson's unfavorable personal impression of Pound. At this time, according to Hadley, Ernest was aware only of Pound's landmark poem "Hugh Selwyn Mauberley," three *Cantos* of his modern epic, and several Asian poetic translations, which had been poorly received by the critics.

Hemingway met Pound at the poet's studio at 70 bis rue Notre Dame des Champs. This "meandering" street, wrote an American in his Parisian guidebook, probably "shelters more genius, more artistic and intellectual cults and movements, than any other street of similar length in the world." Located on a hill near the river, Pound's studio was separated by two garden courtyards that made for quieter living quarters. The large open interior of the stove-heated studio had a kitchen, a small dressing room, and an upstairs bedroom. On the studio's "mud-green" were displayed Japanese paintings. In bohemian fashion, fencing foils—relics of Pound's student days of studying fencing at University of Pennsylvania—decorated the main room. Guests sat on Pound's brightly painted homemade furniture. In December 1921, Pound wrote his father that he had already constructed "two armchairs, kitchen table, Chinese dinning table—wash stand and stool plus shelves."[6]

Pound's English friend, painter and writer Wyndham Lewis, immediately noticed the livelier atmosphere of the studio as compared to Pound's London residence. "First sight of him in his Paris studio," observed Lewis, "was for me a great change from the dark Kensington quarters." American writer John Peale Bishop visited Pound's studio "in back of the courtyard, under the high window that cast no shadow until twilight, with Pound lolling in his homemade armchair, with an air of weariness, like a strong man worn out by the stupidities of the world, his mind unwearied, his soul unbelieving but still his own." Pound talked of "strange tongues he had learned"—his "mind was his Mediterranean, whose shores are alive with antiquity."[7]

A lifelong apartment dweller, Pound lived simply, even if at times he was supported by his upper-middle-class English-born wife, Dorothy Shakespear. Pound once told his American patron friend John Quinn that "NO artist needs more than 2,000 dollars per year ... 30,000 dollars would feed a whole little art world for five years." Because Dorothy refused to cook—something her well-to-do London family never required—Pound prepared meals by gas lamp in the main room and saved money by doing the cleaning. Singer Yves Tinayre and his wife, calling on the Pounds, had tea served on a cloth-covered packing case. The two couples shared a single spoon, and Tinayre described Pound's homemade chairs as Renaissance-like, being "stiff and ungainly, with hard pillows." When William Carlos Williams visited, he ate a meal cooked over an "alcohol lamp."[8]

These were the comforts of the Pound household when Ernest and Hadley first called upon them in 1922. Ernest intently listened, while Ezra's beautiful, soft-spoken wife, Dorothy, served tea from a large silver pot. Hadley later recalled Ernest's reverent behavior towards Pound as irritating, while another of her accounts claims that Pound expounded on "big ideas" of civilization, its ills and triumphs, avoiding the literary advice and insight that interested Hemingway. If Ernest did appear a wide-eyed new apostle, this behavior most likely masked his aversion to Pound's artsy pretense—the poet's open Byronic collar and fin de siècle–style clothes and thick, unruly red hair. In his classic work, *Exile's Return*, Malcolm Cowley describes visiting Pound's studio and seeing the excited poet "walking back and forth in his red dressing gown, while his red beard jutted out like that of an archaic Greek soldier (or, as I afterward thought, like a fox's muzzle)." Pound's Whistler-like look matched that of his studio, with its fencing foils and Japanese art. In reaction, Hemingway wrote a satiric sketch of Pound, mocking his dandy pose popularized by the 1894 novel *Trilby*.[9]

Pound had long played at looking the poet. During his college days, his odd attire earned him the reputation as a "Latin Quarter type." Pound's fellow University of Pennsylvania student William Carlos Williams thought his friend's attire and unruly hair as emulating the sixteenth-century French poet Pierre de Ronsard—whose fencing displays recalled Dumas's D'Artagnen. With his cane-carrying boulevardier look, Pound appeared like his poetic personification of Hugh Selwyn Mauberley, being "out of key with his time." In London, Rebecca West fondly remembered

Pound as "resolutely acting the dandy after the prescription of Baudelaire, but Baudelaire born again as an innocent child."[10]

Intended for the *Little Review*, Hemingway's Pound satire never saw publication. Sherwood Anderson's Chicago journalist friend Lewis Galantière, then serving as Paris secretary for the International Chamber of Commerce, talked Hemingway out of publishing something that would jeopardize a vital literary connection. Months before, Galantière had received a letter from Anderson praising Hemingway as a "very delightful friend ... a young fellow of extraordinary talent and, I believe, will get somewhere." Anderson noted Hemingway's ability as a journalist and that he and his wife were to live in Paris for a time, and promised that Galantière would find the couple "great playmates. As I understand it, they will not have that much money, so that they will have to live in the Latin Quarter." After their staying at the Hôtel Jacob, Gallantière helped Ernest and Hadley find an apartment in a working-class neighborhood at 74 rue du Cardinal Lemoine.[11]

Knowing Pound's artistic stature and predilection for the promoting young talent, Gallentière further warned Hemingway that his parody of Pound would not be printed because Margaret Anderson and Jane Heap—editors of the influential New York–based *Little Review*—were friends of the poet and owed much to his contributions to their magazine and solicitation of vital contributors.

Whatever the circumstances surrounding the Pound sketch, Hemingway destroyed it and quickly befriended him. Despite Pound's out-of-date, dandy look, the poet shared Hemingway's dislike for young American visitors who aped the image of Greenwich Village bohemians. At the same time, Pound lived simply and, in the dandy tradition, acquired an aristocratic bearing while disliking the Parisian "lost generation" types who dressed in French workingman's garb and made cafes their second home. Several years before, in London, Pound received a letter from his friend, the famous and influential New York lawyer and patron John Quinn, containing a scathing denouncement of Green Village bohemians. Pound replied that he, too, was "suspicious of Washington Sq." In the *Little Review*, Pound summed up his opinion of this 1920s counterculture: "Because of amalgams, Bohemians are worth avoiding, the poor ones are like pools full of frogs eggs, and hordes of these globules perish annually. I mean they merge into suburbias." A decade later Pound still spoke out against the unproductive colonies of so-called artists "who form chapels wherever there can be gathered together a few hundred of a few dozen idle people who are emphatically NOT artists."[12]

When Hemingway encountered these Americans aboard, he responded by writing the article "American Bohemians in Paris a Weird Lot" for *The Toronto Star*, excoriating them as Greenwich Village scum who spent entire days engaged in café chatter and idleness. In his *Toronto Star* article Hemingway mentions the poet Charles Baudelaire, whom he wrongly attributes to walking a leashed lobster in the Latin Quarter, the actual habit of the poet Gérard de Nerval. In his famous 1863 essay "Painter of Modern Life," Baudelaire defined the Parisian dandy and elements of bohemian life. Hemingway disdained the precious, pretentious artist—Baudelaire's "aristocratic superiority of the mind." No doubt he found a living example in Pound.[13]

Unlike Gertrude Stein, whose contribution to Hemingway's early work he would later disingenuously deny, or at least downplay, Pound—fourteen years his senior—was not only a literary mentor but spirited company, whom Hemingway called "a good game guy," an enthusiastic tennis player and willing boxing student. If descriptions of Pound's tennis games with Ford Maddox Ford are indicative of the poet's style on the court ("zany and enthusiastic affairs in which scoring was likely to be haphazard and hotly disputed"), his games with Hemingway may have been unorthodox contests as well. Hemingway's friend Harold Loeb thought Ernest "a lousy tennis player." Hampered by his war-injured knee and a near-blind eye, Hemingway fumed when missing a shot, slashing his racket until recovering his temper with a laugh. In matches against Pound, Hemingway later told how he invented what he called a "pigball"—a bounceless serve "stroked heavily on top with a very violent but caressing motion" that drove the ball to a dead stop. If the pigball succeeded only once, it was for Hemingway a feat of unique execution—a demonstration of "superprofessional skill" in a sport he played rather poorly.[14]

Like his boyhood hero Theodore Roosevelt, Hemingway was an amateur boxer. Robert McAlmon remembered Hemingway shadowboxing in front of Parisian cafes with "his lips moving, calling his imaginary opponent's bluff." Always looking for a willing sparring partner, Hemingway taught Pound the basics of boxing. Stripped to waist in his apartment, Pound went rounds with Hemingway, who initially thought his pupil as having all the grace of a crawfish, but later disingenuously asserted that the poet had developed a "terrific wallop."[15]

An American reporter exposed to the tough streets of Kansas City and Chicago, Hemingway had a beat reporter's thirst for alcohol, a habit that Pound occasionally partook in Europe when offered a glass of wine. James "Jimmy the Barman" Charters recalled Pound in Paris as being, what he called "a white winer," an elegant and light drinker, never out of control.

William Carlos Williams remembered Pound the university student as a sober product of a Presbyterian family and "gingerly temperate." This remained true during Pound's days as instructor at Wabash College, when putting on bohemian airs and smoking cigarettes. Pound asserted that "booze was no river to enlightenment," and "a pest" to literature; during the twenties, he stated, "We owe its resurgence in contemporary letters to our autochthonous imbecility and to its expression in one of the worst legal outrages of all time"—that of Prohibition. Coming of age in pre–World War I English salon society, Pound—who claimed to have been drunk only three times in his life—established a friendship with Hemingway that never slipped into a contentious fog of alcoholism that plagued Ernest and F. Scott Fitzgerald.[16]

Pound occasionally frequented Parisian nightspots. *Paris Herald* reporter Al Laney recalled Pound at Emile's, an Alsatian restaurant "near the Bal Bullinger, that large dancehall opposite of the Closerie des Lilas, where the boulevard Montparnasse meets the St. Michel." Bookstore owner Sylvia Beach saw Pound at the Deux Maggots—a café that the poet referred to as "a low snail restaurant"—where he sometimes shared a table with Hemingway. American journalist Janet Flanner recalled the Deux Magots as Hemingway's favored spot "for serious talk, such as reading aloud in a rambling whisper the first poetry he had written after the war." Samuel Putman also recalled afternoons where "one might find Hemingway ... or Ezra Pound," and evenings when Ford Maddox Ford made an appearance."[17]

At the more spacious Dome, Pound—a former Penn State chess club member—occasionally played a game with friends. Pound later satirized this Montparnasse landmark as having "rather the air of a suburban strawberry festival in the America of my youth." He also observed that it had the air of New York's Eighth Avenue in the 1910s "except for the gaiety of paper lanterns, in place of that of the metal street lamps." Pound also attended the opening of the famed Le Boeuf sur le toit.

At dance parties like those held by Ford Maddox Ford, Pound displayed odd steps and movements. To British writer Sidney Huddleston, Pound's style of dance ignored "all the rules of tango and foxtrot, kicking up his fantastic heels in highly personal Charleston, closing his eyes as his toes nimbly scattered right and left." The American wife of poet Harry Crosby and a publisher in her own right, Caresse Crosby recalled a Parisian evening with Pound. "I took him to the Boule Blanche," she wrote, "where a remarkably beautiful and brilliant band of Martinique players were beating out hot music." Seated in front of the band, Pound shouted out that the dancers had no rhythm; he "shut his eyes," recalled Crosby, "thrust forward his red-bearded chin and began a sort of tattoo with his feet—and unable to sit still a minute longer he leapt to the floor and seized the tiny Martinique vendor of cigarettes in his arms, packets flying, then head back, eyes closed, chin out, he began a sort of voodoo prance, his tiny partner held glued against his piston-pumping knees." The other dancers cleared the floor to watch the "Anglo-savage ecstasy" until the number ended, and Pound "opened his eyes, flicked the cigarette girl aside like an extinguished match and collapsed into the chair beside me."[18]

But over time, Pound preferred the quiet of his apartment or Parisian high bohemia—fashionable salons, many presided over by women. Whereas Pound had little interest in alcohol or drugs—Baudelaire's "artificial paradises"—drinking was central to Hemingway's life. Son of religious non-drinking parents, Hemingway took up the habit as if it were a duty. Given to dark bouts of depression, a family trait that plagued his father, Ernest referred to alcohol as the "giant killer"—that it was essential in relieving the "black ass" and the stress of modern life. Beyond its pleasures and alleviation, alcohol was part of Hemingway's code of manliness. Though needing few excuses for his heavy drinking, Ernest informed his Russian friend Ivan Kashkin that he began at age fifteen, and in his adult life only refrained from it when writing or fighting. He went on to laud hard liquor's virtues, and how whisky made his mind "run on a different plane."[19]

Taste for hard liquor drew Hemingway into the company of nighttime revelers that sometimes ended evenings on the Right Bank nightclubs of Montmartre. As composer Virgil Thomson recalled, Hemingway belonged to "a Montparnasse hard liquor set which, though thoroughly fascinated by itself, was less interesting to people not also drinking hard liquor."[20]

Outside Hemingway's drinking friends, forming the characters of *The Sun Also Rises*, Pound and Stein encountered the writer in more temperate salon surroundings. When first visiting the Pounds' studio, Ernest and Hadley drank tea. On one occasion Hadley claimed to have been served seventeen cups. Wyndham Lewis recalled being served tea in London, when Dorothy, a beautiful woman of aristocratic manners and a talented painter, nodded in response to her husband with "a quick jerk of the head, unquestioning approval of Ezra's sallies, or hieratically rigid as she moved delicately to observe the Kensington teas ritual." Pound considered these time-honored London teas as a way to extend to new acquaintances hospitality without inviting them to a meal, and to observe the merits and talents of a possible new friend.[21]

Once an acquaintance interested him enough, he or she would be invited to dinner. In his letters at the time, Pound mentions frequently dining with the Hemingways. In one of the many letters written to Dorothy at this time, Pound tells of a place offering a down-home-style American menu: "Fed the Hems last night the restaurant with the corn-pone, and the black waiter. Cooks says he can make brown stew, but am not wholly convinced yet."[22]

At the Pounds' studio Ernest paid a great deal of attention to Dorothy. Hadley could not help but notice Ernest's attraction. "He thought she was wonderful and beautiful," recounted Hadley, "and was half in love with her." The Hemingways liked Dorothy's modernist-influenced paintings and later purchased some of her work—first influenced by cubism and the drawings of Pound's sculptor friend Gaudier-Brezska. When the Pounds' son, Omar, was born in 1926, it was Ernest, not Ezra, who accompanied Dorothy by taxi to the hospital in Neuilly.

Since first meeting Ezra, Dorothy had immersed herself in the poet's work and the literature that he read and admired. Decades later, writer Michael Reck noted that Dorothy seemed "to live only for her husband; she read the books he read and, to all appearances, her thoughts were his." As for their physical relationship, many believed the Pounds had an extremely close but sexless union. As Ezra once stated in middle age, "I fell in love with a beautiful picture that never came alive."[23]

As for Hadley's relating to Pound, she had differing opinions throughout the years. "Ezra and I sort of liked each other," she once claimed. On another occasion she stated that Pound "was quite cantankerous. Not loveable at all." Pound's outspoken views about male intellectual and creative superiority disturbed Hadley. In an essay written around the time of his meeting Hemingway, Pound described females as "the conservator, the inheritor of past gestures, clever, practical ... not inventive, always the best disciple of any inventor." When visiting Pound's studio, the little magazine editor Margaret Anderson observed her patriarchal host's habit of "kissing women on the forehead" or drawing "them upon his knee with perfect obliviousness to their distaste for these mannerisms." Yet other women like *Poetry* magazine editor Harriet Monroe had an entirely different impression. Older than Anderson and a member of Chicago's cultured society, Monroe described Pound in his studio during 1923, where she first encountered the supposed "fierce post-revolutionist," who proved "to be a mild-mannered man ... the very soul of courtesy and kindness."[24]

But this was not the impression Pound made upon Hadley, who countenanced his patriarchal behavior and misogynistic talk. She was shocked when Pound bluntly informed her that "we could never be friends; we were too much alike, both redheads, with redheaded feelings and skin." In support of her husband's career, Hadley tolerated Ezra's sexist behavior and personal flaws, greatly impressed that a poet of such renown had taken interest in Ernest's work.[25]

The topic of sex fascinated both Pound and Hemingway. A product of the Victorian era, Pound defied its stultifying values and was eventually fired from his teaching job at Wabash College for harboring a traveling female actress. But William Carlos Williams remembers the young Pound as bold in behavior, yet inhibited as far as young women were concerned. Over time, Pound was known as taking an occasional mistress.

"In Ernest Hemingway's ontology," observed writer Matthew Josephson, "fornication is ranked together with bullfighting, boxing, and elephant hunting as one of the competition sports in which the palm goes to the man of courage." But Hemingway, like Pound, came of age in a respectable family—non-drinking, churchgoers of the Chicago suburbs. Though Hemingway bragged of sexual conquests of a Native American girl in the Northern Michigan woods and a nurse in a Milan hospital, he was still in many ways the shy boy from Oak Park. Like many of his generation, including John Dos Passos and Edmund Wilson, Hemingway took much interest in the free love theories of the younger generation.[26]

In Pound, Hemingway found a companion drawn to the ideal of sexual power and the creation of art. For decades Pound divided his time between his wife, Dorothy, and his mistress, Olga Rudge. Despite initial rejection by Dorothy's English upper-class family, Pound finally married the daughter of the woman who, for a time, was the lover of Irish poet William Butler Yeats. In looks, manner, and upbringing, Dorothy had little in common with St. Louis–born Hadley. A sensitive upper-middle-class Hadley believed that the Pounds' marriage was passionless. This arrangement left Ezra free to take an occasional lover and, finally, a permanent mistress. Speaking about having an open marriage, Dorothy is said to have told Hadley, "But you must understand, it's not the same kind of relationship you and Ernest have."[27]

Pound ascribed to an absurd theory claiming that the male brain is surrounded by a residue of seminal fluid and that this residual sperm brought forth "original thought." This theory was influenced by Pound's 1922 translation of Rémy de Gourmont's *Physique de l'Amour; essia sur l'instinct sexuel*, retitled *Philosophy of Love*. Pound wrote, "The brain itself, is, in origin and development, only a sort of great clot of genital fluid held in suspense or reserve." In a strong-minded genius the brain's fluid was released in a high-pressure surplus. Thus, seminal fluid is the driving force in great thought and art. Pound's eccentric, non-scientific views may have also been inspired by the ancient Greek belief that the male brain was the producer of semen. Pound was fascinated with the Greek cult of Eleusis, believing it created a love cult that could be directly traced to the troubadours.[28]

CHAPTER 2

A Modernist Apprenticeship

Pound's vast, searching mind fascinated Hemingway, who came to consider him the greatest living poet next to William Butler Yeats. Like his contemporary William Faulkner, Hemingway tried his hand at writing poetry before turning exclusively to prose, and it was Hemingway's poetry and short prose sketches that first attracted Pound's interest. A one-time college instructor, Pound took Hemingway under his wing in a mentor/pupil relationship that the young writer accepted even when the poet blue-penciled his work or suggested major changes. T.S. Eliot, whose poetry also received Pound's blue-penciled emendations, knew the difficulty of being his understudy and thought Pound one of those "men so devoted to ideas ... that they cannot engage in profitable discussion with those whose ideas differ from their own."[1]

Compared to the learned Pound—who had earned a Master's degree from the University of Pennsylvania and was a student of several languages, including Greek—Hemingway had a respectable high-school education, which included three years of Latin. In Paris Hemingway was exposed to the vortex of modernism as it flourished in visual, letters, and on the stage. Since meeting Sherwood Anderson in Chicago, Hemingway began reading modernist literature.

Respect for Pound's opinions and insights about literature made Hemingway a willing listener and attentive understudy—one that Malcolm Cowley observed when visiting Pound's apartment in 1922. In the presence of Pound and Hemingway, Cowley recalled: "We spoke of Joyce, the Elizabethan drama, the danger of revolution in Austria, and the poems of Mr. Ezra Pound. Occasionally Hemingway let fall a sentence."[2]

In the role of elder teacher, Pound could be difficult company. When

William Carlos Williams first met the explosively energetic Pound, he believed the odd poet had the unfortunate habit of thinking himself as "an expert on everything." Yet at the same time Williams lauded Pound as "the liveliest, most intelligent and unexplainable thing [he'd] ever seen, and the most fun—except for his painful self-consciousness and his coughing laugh."[3]

Pound joked about nearly everything but his poetry, while Hemingway lauded him as the critic he most trusted. Hemingway's first publisher, Robert McAlmon, emphasized, "If Ezra Pound spoke of tradition and discipline it could be worth listening to, because Pound has interiorly disciplined his craft (when he is not scolding, but is being the poet he can be)." Late in life Hemingway reflected that Pound was "the man who believed in the *mot juste*—the one and only correct word to use—the man who had taught me to distrust adjectives as I would later learn to distrust certain people." He also remembered Pound's insistence that "prose is architecture, not interior decoration," and that "the Baroque is over."[4]

Pound the imagist no doubt stressed to Hemingway "the direct treatment of the 'thing," and to "use absolutely no word that did not contribute to the presentation." Pound's theories and approach to literature were eventually expressed in *The ABC of Reading*, in which he stressed that literature "is simply language charged with meaning to the utmost degree." In this influential work he insisted: "Good writers are those who keep the language efficient. That is to say, keep it accurate, keep it clear." Writers were to use a "word to throw a visual image on to the reader's imagination"—to charge words by sound or unique groupings. When reading Hemingway's prose, Pound no doubt saw qualities he demanded.[5]

Pound's much quoted "make it new" assertion was the hallmark of many early moderns. But Pound did not call for the destruction of all earlier traditions as did Marinetti and the Italian futurists. For Pound art was a seedbed from which new forms arose out of great ideas of the past.

Another young writer who sought out Pound at his studio, John Peale Bishop, noted how the elder poet immersed himself in the past and present: "The mind was his Mediterranean, whose shores are alive with antiquity, above whose islands the clouds seemed to rise in mythopoeic shapes of the past. There history accumulates and none can quite escape the presence of the past which strikes, like light on the wall, at passersby. Outside, as we talked, was Paris and that present which is now the past."[6]

Pound's demand to make it new was not reinvention, but uniqueness in expression through the combination of words, symbols, and abstract forms. Hemingway shared this belief. A great artist, he wrote, uses "everything that has been discovered or known about his art," and then absorbs aspects of it at such a rapid pace that it seems that the knowledge to have been "born with him," and he grasps "instantly what it takes the ordinary man a lifetime to know." He then transcends his influences and "makes something of his own."[7]

Applying vital lessons learned from Pound, Hemingway wrote small prose experiments. Hemingway biographer Kenneth Lynn attributes the influence of Pound's 1920 poem, the two-line classic "In a Station of the Metro," to his understudy's writing the finely crafted six-line panoramic work "Paris 1922." In July 1922, Pound wrote Dorothy concerning the progress of Hemingway's art: "Hem. has done a new two pages of condensed prose. O.K. I think he may get through by sheer force of cutting out slush, which he dislikes I think, rather more than anyone else I have met. Any excess, excessive aesthesia or intensity shd. be able to make itself the centre of a new thing in lit. He is thryro-centric, and must have a triple barrel thyroid."[8]

Pound also served as an aesthetic guide, bridging the world of the 1890s Aesthetic Movement—a period he came to reject—and that of early modernism. "The Romantics expressed their emotions, and the Symbolists poets dreamed," explains literary scholar Louis Simpson. "An age of science demanded the poet of facts." Whereas artists had been reoccupied by striving to attain "the beautiful," early moderns like Pound were primarily concerned with expressing the truth, a goal central to Hemingway's art as he sought to write "one true sentence." Literary scholar Frederick Karl, an astute historian of modernism, addressed this shift: "The connection of beauty to a moral and ethical dimension was passing into a new phase, in which beauty was identified, neutrally, with sensation and experience. Thus, beauty was longer a moral entity or the embodiment of a higher truth; it was associated with individual taste and individual striving."[9]

At the forefront of the early modernist avant-garde, Pound promoted an aesthetic elite. Unlike Whitman's longing to versify for America's "divine average," Pound surrounded himself with artists who sought communication with an informed audience to illuminate truth—enlighten the intelligent. Over time their influence would eventually reach the average citizen. Pound's 1907 poem "In Durance" expressed his longing for artistic kindred spirits, "I am homesick after my own kind," he wrote, those who "have some breath for beauty and the arts." As Hemingway wrote of his Paris companions—those described by Jake Barnes as being "one of us"—Pound also thought Hemingway a "kin of the spirit."[10]

Like he did for all his understudies, Pound offered Hemingway a required reading list and from his private book collection introduced him to works previously unknown to him. The poet likely urged Hemingway to read poets from Homer to Villon to John Donne. Pound considered poetry as the highest expression in words. "Prose is perhaps only half art," he contended.[11]

Pound had much to say about the finest aspects of prose. He stressed the importance to Hemingway of reading Gustave Flaubert's *Madame Bovary*. His list included Flaubert's *Three Tales* (1877), notably its short story *A Simple Heart* that had within it "all that anyone knows *about* writing." John Peale Bishop, introduced to Hemingway by Pound in 1922, noted Flaubert's influence on Hemingway, which he noted, had "many living proponents, but none more passionate than Ezra Pound."[12]

Pound's required reading list also included Stendhal's *The Red and the Black* and the first chapters of *Charterhouse of Parma*, about a romantic youth, Fabrice del Dongo, who, without any military training or experience, leaves his native Italy to fight at the battle of Waterloo. In Hemingway's introduction to *Men at War* (1942), he credited *Charterhouse* as "the best account of actual human beings" during a major battle, and described reading it as an unforgettable experience. Hemingway once told British poet Stephen Spender that he thought *The Charterhouse*'s opening description of a boy lost amid the action as "the best, though the most casual, description of war in literature." Hemingway stated in *Esquire* that Stendhal's *Charterhouse* and *The Red and the Black* were necessary to understand modern literature and in a 1958 interview listed his literary influences, first mentioning Mark Twain and then Flaubert and Stendhal.[13]

Pound also noted the vital importance of the Anglo-American writers Henry James and T.S. Eliot. Pound greatly admired James, who he had met twice in London in 1912. Throughout his years as an informal instructor to young writers, Pound often urged them at least to read the introductions to James' works. Though aware of James' genius, Hemingway at this time resisted being influenced by the American expatriate's European parlor world. Hadley's infatuation with James' novels only further irritated her husband. As he did with any artists he did not like at the time, Hemingway soon mean spiritedly lampooned James in a short story and in the expurgated section of *Sun Also Rises*, when he included fictional mention of James experiencing "an obscure hurt" during a bicycle accident that supposedly left him impotent.

Pound insisted Hemingway read poet T.S. Eliot. Hemingway rarely commented favorably about Eliot in print. To Hemingway, Pound was a major poet and Eliot a minor one. Later he lauded Eliot as an exceptional poet but one who would never "have existed except for dear old Ezra." To mock Eliot, he often conflated the poet's last name with the title of Pound's guru of Social Credit, C.H. Douglas, in calling him Major Eliot—a reference that remerged decades later in Hemingway's *A Moveable Feast*. But in regard to Hemingway's supposed resentment of Eliot, asserts biographer Kenneth Lynn, one "could argue that Hemingway adored Eliot, for he read and reread his poetry and paid close attention to discussions in literary journals of its intellectual origins."[14]

As for Joyce, Hemingway shared Pound's initial awe over *Ulysses* as its first chapters appeared in the *Little Review*. Writing Sherwood Anderson not long after arriving in Paris, Hemingway described Joyce's work as a "god-damn wonderful book." Over the years, Hemingway lost enthusiasm for Joyce to the point that by the late 1950s he expressed to interviewers that the Irishman's primary influence was in the liberation of various words, especially those considered indecent and prone to censorship. In that way, Hemingway stressed that Joyce opened the way for other writers to free themselves from such restrictions.

Outside of Pound's reading list of Anglo-American and French prose writers, Hemingway discovered the genius of Russian literature—Leo Tolstoy, Ivan Turgenev, Fyodor Dostoyevsky and Anton Chekov. In his reading French and Russian novelists, Hemingway was part of trend among young American writers of 1920s Paris. Van Wyck Brooks many of these writers rejected "English writers almost by instinct, as a matter of course,—the English who overawed their predecessors,—they read the Russian novelists and especially the French, and among these particularly, Flaubert. For Flaubert shared their contempt for the philistines and the businessmen of whom they had seen too much at home."[15]

Pound little respected Russian writers, and bluntly informed his young friend that he never had "read the Rhoosians." There may have been much truth in this statement. Robert McAlmon recalls during the mid-twenties Pound's low opinion of Dostoyevsky. When asked about which Dostoyevsky book to which he was referring, Pound did not answer, leading McAlmon to believe that he had only skimmed the Russian's works. In another instance when Pound was asked if he read Tolstoy, he dismissively answered, "Tolstoi, russian therefore a mess." When pressed further about the subject, he snapped, "Have I got to *read* the god damn thing, despite its being by the mess TolsthOIK? Balony!"[16]

In the previous decade Pound did occasionally allude to Turgenev's and Dostoyevsky's talent. In regard to Dostoyevsky, Pound stated, "Let us thank the gods he existed." But he also admitted that he did not read him for the fact that his work was mired in too much detail—"vast attention to detail, always detail uncorrelated with anything else." He also condemned Russian literature in a 1923 issue of the *Dial* as having "no didacticism on any points that can be of interest," with the exception of "some Dostoyevsky and Turgenev," who Hemingway was reading with great enthusiasm in Paris, especially the author's *Sportsmen's Sketches*, which Pound referred to when condemning Turgenev as a "vaporous, circumambient ideologue." Thus, it is understandable that Pound seeing Hemingway's reverence for Turgenev and Tolstoy had little to say about "the Rhoosians."[17]

At the heart of Pound's dislike may lie with his attitudes about Slavic people and culture. Émigrés from the 1917 Russian Revolution were a conspicuous presence in Paris. By 1924 it was estimated that one-fifth of the Parisian population was Russian. One observer at the time wrote that, with the exception of the American colony, this segment of the city's population "contributes more to the flavor of the city than any other alien group." The Parisian vogue for things Russian—the Ballet russes and Stravinsky—never interested Pound. Writing one of his "Imaginary Letters" in the *The Little Review* during the early twenties, Pound described "the Russian" as "the western European with his conning-tower, or his top-layer, or his upper-story, or his control-board removed." He, too, mocked the Russian as ethnic inebriate, a type so unlike the Frenchman and Englishman who can be understood by drinking hard liquor. "Civilized man, *any* civilized man who has a normal lining to his stomach," wrote Pound, "may become Russian for the price of a little mixed alcohol, or of, perhaps, a good deal of mixed alcohol, but it is a matter of shillings, not a matter of dynamic attainment."[18]

If measured by Pound's letters and his *Dial* "Paris Letter" column, one would get the impression there was never a vogue of Russia in Paris. Brushing off the composer's genius, Pound wrote: "Strawinsky arrived as a comfort, but one could not say definitely that his composition was the new music." Pound especially despised the aping of Russian culture and names as the act of the "Slobagob." When the Moscow Art Theater performed in Paris, along with a production of Chekov's *Cherry Orchard*, he wrote that it confirmed "one's deepest prejudices, and leave one wondering whether Lenin, or any possible series of revolutions and cataclysms, could possibly have *added* any further disorder to life of that unfortunate race." As years passed Pound became more virulent in his dislike for Russians, largely predicated upon his hatred of communism.[19]

CHAPTER 3

Among Pound's Constellation

Artistic friendships survive most often when those involved avoid heated topics and opposing points of view, while sharing humor and mutual dislike that takes the form of biting criticism and cruel satire. Pound's penchant for the mocking of American hicks and rubes entertained Hemingway. Their friend, Parisian bookstore owner and publisher Sylvia Beach, observed that in Pound there "was a touch of Whistler about him; his language, on the other hand, was Huckleberry Finn's." This same trait was seen by Wyndham Lewis, who wrote, "Tom Sawyer is somewhere in his gait, 'Leaves of Grass' survive as a manly candour in his broad bearded face; the 'tough guy' that has made Hemingway famous." Whenever wishing to shock a listener, Pound boasted that he had horse thieves among his ancestors (which is likely true); that he had been born in a cabin (actually, the first residence with plastered walls) in an Idaho mining town. Like Whistler in London, Pound often told tall tales about his American youth. Writer and expatriate Samuel Putman wrote, "Take away [Pound's] erudition and his poet's equipment, and he would not be out of place on the cracker-barrel in the Four Corners general store."[1]

Another keen observer in Paris noted that Pound was "quizzical in manner and complexly humorous and ... prone to answer one question by proposing another that seems simple but is actually a baffler, and has other mannerisms, in spite of which, however, the somewhat difficult Mr. Pound is a pleasant enough fellow." Pound also had a biting wit and gift for mimicry. Publisher James Laughlin marveled at Ezra's comic side—his "incredible ear" for dialect. Laughlin also recalled Pound as calling upon five

22

accents for mimicry—country rube, African American, cockney, "bistro French," and the 'Oirrish' of Uncle Willie Yeats. In his American bumpkin affectation, Pound often began his letters and utterances with a long drawn out, "Waal ..." and referred to Americans as "Murkins."[2]

While holding forth, Pound also listened to Hemingway's stories. If Paris was a moveable feast, northern Michigan was his moveable frontier, where his Indian friends and the locals once more came alive in fiction. For Ernest, northern Michigan was his imagined frontier that took hold on a brilliantly imaginative mind.

Pound listened attentively about Hemingway's wounding in wartime. Serving with the Red Cross on the Italian front in 1918, Hemingway, while in a forward position handing out cigarettes, was hit by enemy trench mortar fire. His legs shrapnel-ridden, Hemingway claimed to have gotten to his feet and hit once more in the legs by machine-gun fire (this did not appear on the Italian military citation awarded him). But Hemingway's shrapnel-ridden legs may have prevented him from getting on his feet— that machine-gun bullets did not wound him, and he did not, as he often claimed, carry on his back a wounded Italian soldier. Nonetheless, over time Hemingway's story of his wounding took on more mythical dimensions.

One version of Hemingway's wounding made its way into *The Cantos*. In 1922, poet John Peale Bishop and Pound visited Hemingway's apartment on the rue Cardinal Lemoine, where Bishop recalled encountering "a stalwart, smiling, good-looking young man," who limped when inviting them inside. Pound informed Bishop that this young writer "had been with the Italians during the war and, when his trench was blown up, wounded and, covered by falling dirt, left four days for dead."[3] Hemingway's fabricated tale of his wounding inspired mention in Pound's Canto XVI:

> And Ernie Hemingway went to it
> > too much in a hurry
> And they buried him for four days

Thus, Pound contributed to the Hemingway myth of the Red Cross volunteer who became transformed into a fierce member of the Italian Arditti, wounded by mortar and machine-gun fire. Many myths were made in Paris.[4]

Carnage of the Great War, however, was something neither writer could forget, and both shared contempt for false patriotic words and the flag-waving jingoism that led so many to their deaths. Pound referred to its artist victims as "war waste," among them his cherished French sculptor friend Gautier Brzeska. In reference to many writers lost during the conflict, Hemingway mean-spiritedly complained to Pound, while looking at a minor author's obituary, "I seen so many better guys bumped off!"[5]

The "war to end all wars" seemed, in retrospect, a conflict wrapped in patriotic words of courage and honor that sent millions to their deaths. American expatriate writer Harold Stearns—*The Sun Also Rises*' Harvey Stone—well understood Hemingway's "feeling of disgust" with "the safe-at home, civilian virtue-standards blindness of those who could still talk about correct and moral acts at the very moment the vilest and most immoral acts—the slaughter of the world's youth in a senseless war—were not merely being condoned but applauded."[6]

Hemingway's disillusionment surfaced in an early short story, "Soldier's Home." The story's disaffected veteran, Krebs, arrives home to Oklahoma in 1919, in the aftermath of the parades and celebrations, and hangs out in pool halls where talk of the Great War no longer arouses interest. Krebs "came home, home to a lie," a key phrase about the war in Pound's 1920 landmark poem "Hugh Selwyn Mauberley." Unable to adjust and desperately needing to share his overseas experience, Krebs seeks his audience by telling lies, and in doing so, falls into further despair.[7]

Sharing some of Krebs's disillusionment, Hemingway struggled to deal with his recent past in Paris while forming his art from a journalist's experience, the reading of literature and a great deal from the guidance of mentors like Pound and Stein. As Malcolm Cowley explained, "Since Hemingway could find no textbooks in many of his fields, or none that could be trusted, he went straight to the best teachers."[8]

When Hemingway met Pound, the poet was busied in creative endeavors, and he exposed his young friend to art and artists—past and present—which, he insisted, were essential in understanding "how to make it new." Ever since his twelve-year stay in London, Pound had a predilection for sculpture and the paintings of Wyndham Lewis. In Pound's studio, Hemingway took an immediate dislike to Lewis's paintings, and when he met the Englishman—wearing a wide-brim black hat in the bohemian manner of the famous Parisian singer and nightclub owner Aristide Bruant—he disliked him as well.

Despite the gravitational pull one experienced being Pound's friend, Hemingway had his own tastes in art. In Stein's studio he received a finer education in modern art, seeing on the walls what amounted to a small modern art museum, exhibiting works by Cézanne, Matisse, Picasso, and Braque. Though Gertrude and Alice had some respect for Pound, the poet, they thought his taste in visual art weak and uninformed. Alice later recalled Pound's obsession with Japanese prints, and believed he "didn't know Cézanne from Derain or the other way around." Later, Ernest would befriend André Masson and Joan Miró and buy their work. He also recalled his fondness for painter Jules Pascin, whom he often met at the Dome. Born Julius Mordecai Pincas in Bulgaria, Pascin, seen in the Left Bank wearing his signature bowler hat, he was dubbed "The Prince of Montparnasse." Remembered fondly by Hemingway in *A Moveable Feast*, Pascin enjoyed some marginal success before hanging himself in 1930.[9]

Pound, nonetheless, befriended many great artists. In Pound's studio Hemingway did admire Gaudier-Brzeska's imposing sculpture, *Hieratic Head of Ezra Pound* (1914), given as a gift before its French creator was killed in battle in 1915. As Richard Humphreys explains, this work is "indebted for its monumental, indeed phallic, form to the gigantic Easter Island figure, Hoa-Haka-Nana-la, which Gaudier had studied at the British Museum." Hemingway also liked the photographs of the sculptor's work showed him in Pound's book *Gaudier-Brzeska: A Memoir* (1916).[10]

Among the Japanese paintings Hemingway saw hanging on the walls were works by painter and actor Tamiguro Koumé. Son of a Japanese Noh actor, Koumé took up this art, painted, and later authored *The Art of Etherism of Spirtico-Esthetic Art* (1920). Pound met Koumé in London, fenced with him—"a fine chap," described Pound as looking "like a miniature" William Carlos Williams. At this time, Pound shared William Butler Yeats's interest in the Japanese art of the Noh play. At Pound's apartment Koumé danced this Japanese minimalist art for guests.[11]

In July 1922, Pound's studio hosted a Tamiguro painting exhibit. In August, Pound informed his father that Koumé's work was hanging on his apartment walls. When Koumé died the following year in the Tokyo earthquake, Hemingway wrote Pound in September, sympathetically inquiring about the fate of the Japanese painter. Despite Hemingway's later comments in *A Moveable Feast* that he disliked the paintings of Pound's Japanese visitors—he nonetheless expressed sympathy for Koumé, and included at least one of his works among his art collection.

Pound also showed Hemingway works by Francis Picabia. Though Hemingway thought Picabia's work to be worthless at the time, Pound—who had not liked Picabia's work while he was living in England—lauded this artist as the "man who ties the knots in Picasso's tail." In Pound's studio Hemingway may have seen Picabia's mechanistic cover design for Tristan Tzara's *Dadaphone*, to which Pound contributed. He would have no doubt seen the *Little Review*'s Picabia 1922 spring issue. Though Pound did not consider Picabia a master painter like Matisse and Picasso, he did consider him a supreme intellect, a cleanser of all that was superficial in modern life and art, of whom he wrote: "Take away the painting and there would still be nearly all of Picabia: Picabia the man who, in ten lines and an almost photographic drawing of a wheel or a valve will disassociate, or satirize, or at any rate expose all the formal thought or invention; that a salon painter or secondary cubist employs in a 'picture.'"[12]

Despite Pound's reverence for medieval and Renaissance poets, he shared Picabia's fascination of the machine. Artists could learn from machines. Pound argued that, although they were not "literary or poetic," machines "are musical." For Pound they were expressions of the moderns' "own desire for power and precision." "If America has given or is to give anything to general aesthetic," wrote Pound, "it is presumably an aesthetic of machinery, porcelain baths, of cubic rooms painted with Ripolin, hospital wards with patent dustproof corners and ventilating appliances. Only when these spaces become clean enough, large enough, sufficiently nickel-plated, can a sense of their proportion and arrangement breed a desire for order."[13]

Though Picabia temporarily disassociated himself from the Dada movement in 1922, Pound remained briefly interested in this irreverent movement that he considered as a direct outgrowth of Symbolism. In July 1923, Pound wrote Dorothy about visiting the Deux Magots with "Tzara and his new quartette." That same year, a group photograph taken during the opening of the Jockey in Montparnasse depicts Pound posing among the Dadaists—Man Ray and Tristan Tzara—in Whistlerian attire—floppy hat, open collar, and cane. In his memoir, Man Ray recalled the occasion as one of "affected poses": he "holding a useless little Kodak, Tristan Tzara and his monocle, Jean Cocteau and his black-and-white knitted gloves, Pound in his false bohemian get-up." Pound's short-lived interest in this circle prompted his composing several Dadaist-influenced poems, including "Kongo Roux."[14]

That same year one of the Dadaists proved dangerous to Pound. At a celebratory dinner honoring Pound at a small restaurant in the Place de l'Odèon, there gathered a circle—including Ford and McAlmon—connected with Samuel Putman's little magazine, *New Review*, for which Pound served as an editor. Dadaist Robert Desnos arrived with the intention of killing Jean Cocteau. Seeing that Cocteau was not there, Desnos drew a knife from his coat and was about to stab Pound in the back, when guests grabbed the assailant and escorted him into the street. "As a result," wrote Putman, "Ford's speech in Pound's honor and Ezra's reply was never made.

The American papers in Paris printed nothing about the affair, regarding it, for some reason or another, as too hot to handle."[15]

Pound enjoyed more sedate encounters with the genial Dadaist Marcel Duchamp, to whom he lost challenging games of chess. Pound informed Margaret Anderson that Duchamp "was intelligent and in touch with things," and that he deserved a special *Little Review* edition in his honor. By the time Andre Breton emerged the leader of the Dadaists and reformed them as the Surrealists in 1924, Pound had lost interest in this irritant band that abandoned much of its humorous irreverence and embraced French communism. Pound mockingly referred to the Surrealists as practitioners of "SUBrealism." Years later, Pound lashed out at Breton's coterie: "Nothing much against the Surrealists save that a lot of 'em are French, and therefore bone ignorant, like the English. I believe they write, but none of 'em has ever been known to read, and it is highly doubtful the alphabet is personally known to most of them."[16]

Unlike Pound, Hemingway stood by as American writers flirted, or became honorary members of the Dada circle. Later, as the literary sub-editor of the *Transatlantic Review*, Hemingway offered readers numerous attacks on the Parisian Dadaists—notably its Rumanian-born leader, the monocled Tristan Tzara. Hemingway had no interest in Dadaism's illogic and absurdism. He had nothing to learn from this experimental circle as he plumbed the bleak depths of human experience, while ultimately seeking success in the commercial publishing market.[17]

As with Pound's flirtation with Dadaism, anyone close to the poet at this time could not ignore his pastimes and creative side projects. Visiting Pound's studio, Hemingway put up with the poet's struggle to play the bassoon. Son of a talented vocalist and voice instructor, Hemingway, in his youth, had barely mastered the basics of the cello. In later years, Hemingway conveyed that he preferred irritable café chatter to Pound's bassoon playing.

As to Pound's musical ability, poet friends from his days in Philadelphia, William Carlos Williams and Hilda Doolittle (a.k.a. H.D.), later marveled at their friend's bold ventures into composition, since they recalled him as having little talent for music. "He seemed unintimidated by the fact that (to my mind) he had no ear for music," explained H.D., which she accounted for his clumsy dancing. Williams remembered Pound playing the piano without any instruction, confidently trying to entertain a small parlor audience. In Paris, when learning of Pound's taking up music, Williams offended Pound's sculptor friend, Romanian-born Constantine Brancusi, by stating, "Pound writing an opera, I said, 'Why, he doesn't know one note from another.'"[18]

Untrained in harmony and yet determined to create music, Pound sought to return it to sounds of the Middle Ages and the troubadours. Stressing the primacy of rhythm in poetry and music, Pound composed his first opera during 1920 and 1921, based upon François Villon's fifteenth-century poem, *Le Testament*. American avant-garde composer George Antheil then worked with Pound to revise the opera in 1923. Hemingway wrote to Gertrude Stein, "Pound has become a great composer"—a comment that is questionable in its sincerity, for it is not known what Hemingway truly thought of Pound, the composer.[19]

In his numerous letters to Pound, Hemingway made references to concerts of Pound's music. While in Spain in 1923, Hemingway sent Pound a letter asking about the poet's latest concert and relating that he prayed to St. Fermin for its success. During the following year, Hemingway wrote, complimenting Pound on his "very sound" music article in the *Transatlantic Review*. He also apologized for missing a concert and promised to attend Pound's forthcoming musical events.

It was in the *Transatlantic Review* that Hemingway insulted Pound's musical prodigy George Antheil. Son of a Trenton shoe-store owner, Antheil studied piano with a student of Liszt and, for a short time, with Ernest Bloch. From New York he traveled to Europe in 1922, and in November his *First Symphony* debuted in Berlin, where he met Stravinsky. After a series of concerts in Germany, Austria, and Hungary—for which he demanded being billed as "Futurist Terrible"—Antheil met Ezra Pound in Paris in 1923. Antheil described Pound as a "Mephistophelean red-bearded gent." Impressed by Antheil's avant-garde musical approach, the poet wrote a friend that the young American was "possibly the salvation of music." Pound believed that Antheil's music best captured the age, for as the poet commented, "Music is the art most fit to express the fine qualities of the machine." When Pound debuted his "Sonata for Drum and Piano" at a Montparnasse music hall, he played the bass drum with Antheil on piano. Though written out of reverence, Pound's *Antheil and the Treatise on Harmony* (Three Mountains Press, 1924) revealed his naïveté and lack of formal musical training, as it rarely dealt with Antheil's music.[20]

Hemingway initially dismissed Pound's young composer friend, writing in the *Transatlantic Review* that he preferred his "Stravinsky straight." This comment, implying that Antheil's machine music was simply imitative of Stravinsky, must have outraged Pound, who, against the tide of modern music critics, thought little of the Russian composer. The "Stravinsky straight" certainly upset Antheil, and Hemingway wrote that such impulsive opinions might lead to his being "dropped from the party." Hemingway later apologized to the composer and claimed to have learned a lesson from his hasty judgment: "Where one wrong opinion often proves fatal, one writes carefully ... I have been more careful since." For the hot-tempered and opinionated Hemingway this would be a difficult lesson—an impulse of judgment that would nearly cost him a friendship with Pound.[21]

On June 29, 1926, Hemingway, along with James Joyce and T.S. Eliot, attended a performance of Pound's opera *Le Testament* at the Salle Pleyel in the rue Rochechouart. Pound's opera, wrote American composer Virgil Thomson, featured "a *corne*, an animal's horn, five feet long, that could blow two notes only, a bass and the fifth above it, but with a raucous majesty evocative of faraway times. The music was not a musician's music, though it may well be the finest poet's music since Campion." Hemingway lauded *Les Testament* as a "splendid" and "first rate opera," but ultimately considered Pound's music an admirable part-time pursuit, just as he judged Constantin Brancusi a fine cook but, first and foremost, a brilliant sculptor.[22]

Later, in *Death in the Afternoon*, Hemingway viewed Brancusi's art as equaling that of sculpture and modern bullfighting. Brancusi's famed studio dinner parties were among several destinations to which Pound accompanied friends on his personal tours of Paris. At the time he met Hemingway, Pound was promoting Brancusi enthusiastically, as he had Gaudier-Brzeska, and planned on writing a book on the sculptor as well. Inspired by Brancusi, Pound briefly took up sculpture but found chiseling marble into odd eggshapes a much less rewarding effort than composing music. If Hemingway, like Pound, had indeed tasted Brancusi's cooking, he was among the many greatly entertained guests who lived in Paris in the twenties. In Brancusi's stone studio in the Impasse Ronstin, the cul-de-sac off the rue de Vaugirard, the much-loved, bearded sculptor entertained Pound and his visitors by a ritual meal that began with morning marketing. Brancusi's guests arrived to see their host laying out plates, silver, and napkins. Chicken soup simmered on a homemade clay stove, and chicken cooked over the coals. Potatoes and salad were served. All the while the host conversed, told stories, and refilled glasses. After dinner, guests drank Turkish coffee and danced to Brancusi playing Rumanian folk tunes on his violin.

As with all those who befriended Pound, Hemingway was occasionally called upon to participate in various causes. In early 1922, Pound talked Hemingway into participating in a philanthropic writer's fund, the Bel Esprit, which he established with May Sinclair and Richard Aldington, the fund's British treasurer. Witnessing the decline of aristocratic patronage, Pound thought it necessary to establish other means to support art. Since many serious writers and artists had to work mundane jobs or write or illustrate for popular magazines, Pound wanted private sponsorship to "release as many captives as possible." As to the program's economic sustenance, Pound confided to Kate Buss: "It is a risk. So is an oil well."[23]

Against the odds of failure, Pound called upon thirty writers to provide fifty dollars annually or semi-annually for the Bel Esprit to select artists who would be provided an allotted sum until they earned enough money to support their creative work. The first Bel Esprit candidate, T.S. Eliot, was to be freed from working at Lloyd's Bank in London. Pound first hinted at founding such a project—"a larger scheme" to get Eliot out of the bank—in the *New Age* on March 14, 1922. The Bel Esprit circular emphasized that the project would allow time for the making of "better literature, not more literature, better art, not more art." That same month Pound sent out carbon-copy outlines to possible contributors, including H.L. Mencken and William Carlos Williams. Pound's friend and art patron John Quinn contributed $300.[24]

In founding Bel Esprit, Pound angered Eliot. A story in the *Liverpool Daily Post and Echo* outraged Eliot when it claimed that Pound's Bel Esprit promised him an allotted amount of money to free him from working at Lloyd's Bank. This public announcement (along with alluding to his recent mental breakdown) threatened Eliot's livelihood in the name of a scheme that would pay even less than what he earned at the bank. Eliot wrote Pound, outraged that what was said in private, including the Bel Esprit circular, should never have been made public and demanded that any reprinting of the article should omit mention of the bank. Tired of Pound's clumsy efforts on his behalf, Eliot warned: "I didn't want a personal favor. I wanted it to be purely a question of production of verse, a small, very small, but still a public utility of work."[25]

Hemingway thought little of the scheme to free Eliot from the bank. Privately, he recognized Eliot's talents but often mockingly referred to him as Major Eliot—Pound's Social Credit finance guru, Major C.H. Douglas. In a 1922 letter to Pound, Hemingway alluded to Eliot's mentally ill wife, Viviene, and suggested that if Eliot "would strangle his sick wife, buggar the brain specialist and rob the bank he might write an even better poem." In *A Moveable Feast*, Hemingway claimed to have never contributed to Bel Esprit—that he squandered his earmarked sum at a Parisian horse race track. Although Pound tried to keep the Bel Esprit alive, the enterprise ended in 1923 when Eliot refused the stipend.[26]

The Bel Esprit was named by Pound's American friend Natalie Barney and took for its brochure motif the four-pillared Greek temple—TEMPLE

'A L'AMITÉ—that decorated her Parisian garden, where Sapphic rituals often disturbed the neighbors. Pound based his Bel Esprit venture upon one that Barney had conceived as a means to monetarily support poet Paul Valéry. "The American poet Ezra Pound," noted Barney, is "always generous to his often ungrateful colleagues." In reference to her influencing Pound's Bel Esprit, she wrote, "My Temple of Friendship was to be its sanctuary."[27]

Raised in upper-class comfort in Cincinnati and Washington, D.C., Barney inherited from her mother—a painter who had studied with Whistler—an interest in the arts, and from her father a substantial inheritance, allowing her to live comfortably in Paris. Barney moved to Paris in 1902 and, by 1909, rented a three-hundred-year-old residence (a detached house with a garden and pavilion) at 20 rue Jacob that a visitor described as coming from the time of Madame de Staël. William Carlos Williams thought it "something preserved in amber from the time of the Renaissance."[28]

Barney's friend Rémy Gourmont described her as "Les Amazon," not for her penchant for horseback riding but for her aristocratic lesbianism. He encouraged Barney to write poetry and lusted for her in letters. After Gourmont's death, Pound befriended Barney, who would also live in Italy and share Pound's enthusiasm for fascism. Pound enjoyed the exotic atmosphere of Barney's salon. At these Friday afternoon gatherings, women "could embrace, hold hands, be open about desire," while men "were admitted, but were not allowed to dominate the afternoons." Artists of both sexes would read their work, sing, and perform. This continued until 1927, when Barney excluded men from the salon's artistic events.[29]

At her salon, Barney introduced Pound to a French literary crowd, including Anatole France, Andre Gide, and Paul Valéry. It brought together Sorbonne professors, a stray count or countess, and innumerable American men and women—guests like Sherwood Anderson, Matthew Josephson, and Gertrude Stein, to whom she offered generous amounts of food. Tea was served, and drinkers enjoyed port, gin, or whiskey. In her book, *Wild Girls*, Diana Souhami describes the Barney's ground-floor salon with "its walls covered in red damask that faded down the years, its domed ceiling painted with nymphs." There was polar bear rug, "Spanish chairs, an Empire couch, a marble table, red curtains," and portrait paintings of her friends.[30]

In Barney's garden during the summer of 1922, Pound met his mistress, Olga Rudge, the twenty-six-year-old Ohio-born violinist. Among the guests Olga noticed was an animatedly conversing individual dressed in odd, brightly colored clothes. "She found him remarkably handsome," writes Pound biographer John Tytell. "They shared an immediate compatibility, and they continued to see each other for another half a century."[31]

Since Barney's salon was a must-see stop on Pound's tour of Paris, Hemingway must have visited Barney's salon. On Pound's trips around the city with friends, observed William Carlos Williams, Barney's "salon ranked high as a place of destination." Well aware of Barney's salon and garden temple, Hemingway, though he thought Parisian salons "excellent places ... to stay away from," may have attended her home with Pound.[32]

Mentioned in Hemingway's *A Moveable Feast*, Barney's salon aroused Hemingway's interest in female homosexuality. Though he disliked male same-sex behavior, Hemingway befriended lesbians like Gertrude Stein and Alice B. Toklas and Parisian-based American journalist Janet Flanner. Author of the famed "Letter from Paris" essays in *The New Yorker*, Flanner disliked Pound's poetry and thought him eccentric. In recalling the early American colony in Paris, Flanner wrote: "Ernest Hemingway was, of course, in and out constantly, often in the company of Ezra Pound, who seemed an odd friend for him to have, since Ernest was always the champion sportsman in every café he entered and Pound, with his little beard, looked and was conscientiously aesthetic."[33]

In his memoir, *Bad Boy of Music*, Antheil also noted the unique pairing of Pound and Hemingway. Apart from T.S. Eliot, Antheil recalled Hemingway as "the tallest" among the literary set of the time. "Ezra was not a short man, but he looked small alongside the other two." Antheil noted that while "Hemingway, exponent of the rough and ready, dressed like a lumberjack ... Ezra Pound wore a bizarre outfit of tweeds designed by himself and sewn with bright blue square buttons." Antheil also described Pound and Hemingway's diverse manners of speech, in that the former "spoke in a dialect only comparable to that of Lum and Abner of the radio," in contrast to Hemingway's "American midwestern accent, slightly higher than one would at first imagine to hear him."[34]

CHAPTER 4

Little Magazines

In February 1922, Pound served as Hemingway's agent, sending *The Dial*'s editor Scofield Thayer six of his poems. As *The Dial*'s former overseas editor and author of its "Paris Letter" column, Pound scored a triumphal success that year when overseeing the American magazine's publication of T.S. Eliot's landmark poem "The Wasteland," a work that, in its final form, had been shaped by his extensive excisions and editing. Expecting to be published in *The Dial*, Hemingway enthusiastically wrote Sherwood Anderson that Pound had sent a letter and six of his poems to Scofield Thayer. He enthusiastically assured Anderson that Pound thought him "a swell poet."[1]

Writing to Thayer about Hemingway's poems, Pound assured him that the author "seems to have his head screwed on straight" and that he had read "serious works and is allowing himself five years for first novel." He ended the letter by urging that "Dial Shd. occasionally take in a little new blood, and H. seems to me as sound a chance as is likely to offer." But Thayer informed Pound that he had considered the poems rough reading and that his publication already had enough "young blood."[2]

Hemingway's manuscripts were sent directly back to him. His pride wounded, Hemingway wrote to Pound, referring to *The Dial*'s editor as "Scofield Buggerin' Taylor" with a contempt for the man that never faded over the years.

Adding to Hemingway's anger towards *The Dial* was his belief that the editors were about to fire Pound as its "Paris Letter" contributor which had, along with T.S. Eliot's "London Letter," brought much attention to the magazine. Because of his increasing stays in Italy, Pound was well aware of his imminent termination at the magazine, and his disparaging remarks about Paris and its writers no doubt contributed to the editors' decision. When Pound left for another prolonged trip to Italy, Thayer and Sibley Watson thought it time to replace the poet. Out of his appreciation for the *The Dial*, Pound wrote *Little Review* editor Margaret Anderson: "My connection with the Dial ends on July 1st, after which I have no means of support visible or predictable. A tepid review, but it will be written on Thayer's tomb stone that he paid my rent for 15 months and there are few of whom such virtues will be recorded."[3]

When *Dial* editor Gilbert Seldes arrived in Paris, Pound had already left for Italy. Seldes explained that he was "commissioned to find a French correspondent but tried to keep EP on until he went to Italy." Seldes further explained, "The coincidence of my arrival and the supplanting of EP as *The Dial*'s Paris representative was unfortunate—Hemingway never forgave me." Around this same time, Thayer's rejection of Pound's "Malatesta Cantos" (9–12) once again confirmed Hemingway's conspiratorial view of *The Dial* as being dominated by a clique of Harvard elites.[4]

Meanwhile, Hemingway's first prose and poetry was published in the New Orleans little magazine, *The Double Dealer*. Hemingway was brought to the attention of the *Double Dealer* by Sherwood Anderson, who lived in the French Quarter at the time and contributed to the magazine. Hemingway's prose fable, "A Divine Gesture," was followed by the poem, "Ultimately," which appeared in the *Double Dealer*'s June 1922 issue alongside the poetic debut of William Faulkner. Hemingway's poem was accompanied by the description of their author "as a young American living in Paris who enjoys the favor of Ezra Pound." Hemingway wrote *Double Dealer* editor, named McClure, dropping Pound's name and boldly, if not arrogantly, mentioned his poet friend as having possibly lost his creative powers. McClure responded: "Your comment about Pound was interesting. I feel about him much as you do—worried as to whether he will ever write any more first rate stuff." While Hemingway questioned Pound's artistic ability behind his friend's back, the poet vigorously promoted him. Soon, their creative association proved vital in editing and promoting Hemingway's first two books in Paris.[5]

Hard work ahead of him, Hemingway, the ultra-competitive sportsman and overachiever, maintained a morning writing regimen. Unlike Pound, who, in the true spirit of the early moderns, never sought mass popularity that would result in serving a mainstream publisher's demand for creating what he considered second-rate work, Hemingway—an upper-middle-class American with an aggressive drive to achieve—would learn his art and seek fame through his own initiative.

Pound pursued art at an Old World pace, enjoying periods of idleness or expending his energy helping and promoting others. But one has to take into consideration that Pound had struggled for nearly thirteen years in London, launching the imagist and vorticist movements. If Pound appeared the bohemian artist, his occasional idleness was followed by furiously working his typewriter in eight-hour-long bursts of creative energy, while obsessively writing letters to his parents, friends, and editors.

Testament to Pound's influence, Hemingway wrote in 1922 the poem "The Age Demanded," that took its title from a line from the first section of Pound's "Hugh Selwyn Mauberley." Hemingway's eight-line satirical poem, punctuated by the refrain "the age demanded," appeared three years later in the German magazine *Der Querschnitt*. As Thayer had opined, this poem, like others Hemingway had written, was not great art and certainly did not equal his lean, innovative prose. In his discussion of Hemingway's poems, literary scholar Nicholas Gerogiannis observes: "From what we know now about his literary style, it seems only natural that as a young man he would have attempted poetic forms; the short lines, the concrete imagery, the potency of individual words, the rhythm, and the potential for achieving a condensed power in language must have appealed to him. But if his poetry was any kind of beginning, it was a false beginning."[6]

In the spring of 1922, Hemingway traveled to Genoa to cover the International Economic Conference for the *Toronto Star*. There he witnessed the joint Soviet and German delegations derail the economic negotiations of the British and French. During his stay in Genoa, Hemingway met leftwing journalist Max Eastman. Hemingway, along with Eastman and another journalist, made the dusty eighteen-mile drive to Rapallo. Famed journalist Lincoln Steffens, also attending the conference, described the route to Rapallo that "threads a string of towns and cities ... with intervals of vial and farm lands widening in between, until by it is all hills, vines, olives." In Rapallo, Hemingway and his two colleagues visited the home of famed Edwardian-era caricaturist and writer Max Beerbohm. An old fishing village of red-tiled mansard roofs buildings on the Ligurian Sea, Rapallo offered tourists inexpensive off-season rates. Since the eighteenth century it had been a destination for British travelers and became, by the 1920s, a frequent destination for the Pounds, who soon took up residence there.[7]

Beerbohm's seaside villa—the Villino Chiaro—was a twenty-minute walk south of Rapallo. Beerbohm and his wife lived simply and inexpensively on the Italian Riviera. Much respected by Pound, who had met Beerbohm in London, the famed caricaturist left London no longer interested in being a man around town and meeting the demands of making art and publishing. Given to "tranquility and contemplation," he relaxed on his terrace rooftop, savoring the scents of orange and lemon trees.[8]

During the summer of Hemingway's visit, Beerbohm worked little and saw few visitors. Occasionally he had tea or lunch with the famous and curious who passed through Rapallo. Aware of the Genoa conference, Beerbohm had no interest in the Russian delegation staying at the Imperial Hotel in neighboring San Margherita. Beerbohm's *Seven Men* was among the works on Hemingway's bookshelf in Paris. Arriving on Beerbohm's doorstep, Hemingway and his two fellow journalists entered a "little white cube of a building," its Whistler-inspired interior—pale gray and fawn walls and painted white woodwork. Beerbohm and his guests drank Marsala "and discussed the revolt of creative artists against the evils of commercial journalism."[9]

One of the most famous journalists attending the Genoa conference, Lincoln Steffens, whom Carlos Baker described "as a wrinkled old muckraker," was a writer much admired by Hemingway. He often spent the evening with Steffens and other journalists, drinking from a two-gallon container of Chianti. In a letter to Pound, Hemingway mentioned that, in his encounter with Steffens, he was forced to defend his journalistic skills. Hemingway informed Pound that he tried to avoid offending the older journalist by pointing out the weaknesses of his own work, which, as he wrote, "Steff admires because they are what he has always been shooting at. There is little gained to being snotty to sweet old men"—wisdom Hemingway would find difficult putting into practice as he turned against elder mentors like Sherwood Anderson.[10]

After the Genoa Conference, Ernest and Hadley vacationed in Switzerland and then hiked through the mountains to Italy. Several months before Mussolini's fascists made their 1922 march on Rome, Hemingway used his journalist credentials to interview Mussolini in Milan. Hemingway encountered Mussolini in his newspaper office, stroking his wolfhound pup, and considered his subject an impressive leader of a half a million, not an evil threat.

At the time of his Milan interview with Mussolini, Hemingway heard and read much about the black-shirted fascists' violent clashes with their leftwing opponents. To his Canadian readers he described the young fascists as "dragon's teeth," made up of World War I veterans and middle-class youth who, once tasting the thrill of bloodshed and arson, were no longer interested in working at their parent's shops or a desk job. Northern Italian communists were, according to the politically naïve Hemingway, fathers of well-meaning families, who forgoing Soviet influence "[were] Red as some Canadians are Liberal."[11]

An admirer of the Italian soldiers during the First World War, Hemingway was aware that Mussolini had also served on the Italian front against the Austrians and, like himself, wounded by shrapnel. But Mussolini, like Hemingway, added myth to his wartime experience, telling the young journalist that when Italy joined the war he immediately enlisted, when in fact he was drafted into the army. Mussolini did serve with a regiment of the Bersaglieri and was twice wounded: first, when suffering light shrapnel wounds on the Isonzo, and later in 1917 when an over-heated artillery gun exploded and severely wounded him, leading to his discharge.

While Hemingway quickly came to despise Mussolini, Pound envisioned Il Duce as a modern-day enlightened Italian despot. By the time Pound gained a private audience with Mussolini nearly a decade later, he came to believe that Il Duce would usher in a new age of art and Social Credit economics, and Italy the greatest hope against the spread of communism. Attracted to men of action in the arts and politics, Pound's move to the right was not hard for some to understand. Although Hemingway shared Pound's disdain for bureaucracies, he rejected Pound's championing of the modern demagogue.

An Italian that both Hemingway and Pound revered was Gabriele D'Annunzio—poet, novelist, playwright, and nationalist soldier of fortune. D'Annunzio had served in the Italian army and navy during World War I and, as an aviator—often making daring flights over the Alps—lost the sight in one eye during a plane crash. Hemingway read D'Annunzio's autobiographical novel *Il Fuoco—The Flame* (1900). Set in Venice, this work was based upon D'Annunzio's love affair with the famed actress Eleonora Duse. Hemingway also followed, as did Pound, the 1919 newspaper reports of D'Annunzio's taking control of Fuime, a former Italian city that had been ceded by the Versailles treaty to Yugoslavia (it had also been promised to Italy by a treaty with Britain). This controversial fifteen-month occupation ended when an Italian naval blockade and light bombardment drove D'Annuzio and his armed insurrectionists out of Fuime. Hemingway's interest in this fiery personage appeared in an early apprentice Nick Adams story—"The Passing of Pickles McCarthy"—and the poem "D'Annunzio" written in Chicago during 1920 and 1921.

In Pound's case, D'Annunzio's taking of Fuime represented the artist as a man of action. "Little troubled by D'Annuzio's resort to violence as a political instrument," explained literary scholar Leon Surrette, "Pound used him as an instance of a politically engaged intellectual." Just as Pound lauded the ruthless Renaissance soldier and art patron Sigismondo Malatesta, he saw in D'Annuzio a similar sprit in the modern age, much in the same way he would rationalize his later admiration for Mussolini.[12]

After interviewing Mussolini, Hemingway accompanied Hadley to Sirmione, where they unexpectedly encountered the Pounds. Formerly part of the Republic of Venice, Sirmione on Lake Garda was described by Pound as that "very large sapphire."[13] Sirmione first enchanted Pound when he visited in 1910 and made its lake the subject of several early poems. The Pounds and Hemingways spent several days in Sirmione, swimming and sunbathing. Pound most likely held forth about the sixth-century Roman poet Catullus, who had once lived in the city but never stayed in the second century AD villa bearing his name.

Meanwhile, Hemingway experienced another favorable prospect when American newsman Bill Bird offered to publish his work. Hemingway met Bird at the Anglo-American Press Club; they drank together while covering the 1922 Genoa Economic Conference, and hiked in Germany. Born in Buffalo, New York, Bird had attended Trinity College and the Sorbonne, served in the ambulance service during World War I, and from 1921 to 1922 worked for the *New York Herald Tribune*. In the summer of 1922, Bird purchased an old hand-printing press and established Three Mountains Press on the Ile Saint Louis. When Bird planned a limited series of prose works, Hemingway proposed that Pound become its general editor. Pound accepted and proclaimed the theme of these approximately fifty-page editions as "The Inquest into the state of contemporary English prose." As editor and an Inquest contributor, Pound recruited other talent, such as poet William Carlos Williams, to whom he wrote in August 1922: "I shall keep the series strictly modern. One can be more intimate. The private limited edtn. don't imply that one is talking to the public, but simply to one's friends."[14]

Among the six or seven writers originally selected for the Inquest series, Hemingway faced the problems of not having enough prose for such a publication as well as the daunting task of living up to Pound's literary expectations. This prompted Pound's listing Hemingway's contribution as a blank space in the advertisement prospectus. Known for his untimely schedule in producing his hand-press series, *in our time* appeared nearly a year after Robert McAlmon's Contact press published what became his first book, *Three Stories and Ten Poems*, in early August 1923. One advantage of Bird's slow hand-publishing process allowed Hemingway time to produce quality, if not innovative, prose for his edition.

The shop of Three Mountains Press became a gathering place for writers. *McCalls* European correspondent in Paris, Robert Forrest Wilson, dropped in and saw Bird and Pound working. "Now and then you can find the two of them in the little quay shop," wrote Wilson, "their sleeves rolled up over their elbows and their hands inky as they pull the pages of the ultra-limited edition of Mr. Pound's epic."[15]

Hemingway wrote Pound thanking him for including him—among "the sextette"—to be in the Three Mountains series. He then promised that he would "not crab the act, bust up the show." Hemingway also joked to Pound: "If it is no fucking good I'll know it and praise by Steffens ... Paul Rosenfeld, Bill Bird, Warren G. Harding, H.L. Mencken ... Eugene O'Neil ... Rudy Kipling ... will cut no bloody ice." He further confided to Pound that he intended to leave journalism for prose writing, and hoped to give him some samples within six months.[16]

In 1922, Pound sent the Hemingway family the Three Mountains Press prospectus for Ernest's unnamed book, priced at $2 each. In November, Grace Hemingway ordered five copies. Unaware that Grace had placed an order, Clarence also ordered five copies. In appreciation, Clarence proudly wrote to Pound, informing him that, as Ernest's father, he was thankful for the poet's encouragement of his son. But if Clarence had known Pound—the eccentric poet, the man behind his son's budding talent—he may not have been so appreciative, and probably regretted this statement when he and Grace received the copies, which they found shocking and abhorrent.[17]

On October 30, 1922, Pound wrote his father: "Hem. back from Constantinople, fed up with the Turks. Dirty job of selling munitions to irresponsible natives." That same month, Pound wrote his mother: "Hem. gone to Lausanne to look at thieves and liars."[18] Pound's "criminals" were the Russian, British, and Italian delegations attending the First Lausanne Peace Conference that met in Switzerland between late November 1922 and February 1923 to draft a settlement of territorial claims following the Greco-Turkish War. Letters between Hemingway and Pound kept each other informed about their activities.[19]

While covering the Lausanne Peace Conference in November 1922, Hemingway wrote Pound about having a second interview with Mussolini, in which the Italian leader, supposedly offended by the American journalist's critical comments in the *Toronto Star*, informed him that he could never live in Italy again. But James Mellow has substantiated that Hemingway never had a second interview with Mussolini. Pound, on the other hand, believed Hemingway and responded to his friend's portraying Mussolini as a demagogic thug by warning, "You musn't tease Benito."[20]

While in Lausanne, Hemingway experienced a serious setback when Hadley arrived there by train on December 3, 1922. For this trip Hadley took along his manuscripts so that Ernest could work over the holiday season. Upon leaving the Paris station, Hadley, to her horror, discovered that the valise holding the manuscripts had been stolen. Some sources plausibly claim that she had been instructed to bring her husband's work so that he could show it to Lincoln Steffens, who was also attending the conference. But what has never been determined by scholars and biographers is why Hadley brought along the typescripts and carbons.

Hemingway immediately left for Paris and found no trace of the valise or his manuscripts. Weeks later, Hemingway finally broke the news to Pound, who calmly informed him that his loss was an "act of Gawd." Pound's advice was insightful but not what Hemingway wanted to hear. On January 23, Hemingway wrote Pound about his loss: "You, naturally, would say 'Good' etc. But don't say it to me. I ain't yet reached that mood." A few days later Pound wrote back: "I never said the loss of your juvenilia was a blessing. It's possibly a calamity—certain damned annoying.... In the long run ... nobody is *known* to have lost anything by *suppression* of any work. But that ain't the same thing. The *point* is: how much of *it can you remember*. You are *out* of pocket is the *time* it will take ... to rewrite the parts you can remember.... If the middle, i.e., *FORM*, of a story is right one ought to be able to reassemble it from memory.... As has been remarked: memory is the best critic. If the thing wobbles and won't form then it has no proper construction, and never *wd*. Have been *right*. All of which is probably cold comfort."[21]

Calmed by wise words, Hemingway ended another letter by thanking Pound for his advice "on the occasion of the loss by stealing of his complete works. It is very sound. I thank you again. I repeat, I thank you. I will foller your advice." Despite Hemingway's claim of losing all his work, he still had three stories and a number of poems. Pound may have looked upon Hemingway's loss as a blessing. Earlier, when Stein looked over the war novel, she admonished Hemingway to "begin again and concentrate."[22]

Sure of his young friend's talent, Pound used his connections at Chicago-based little magazine, *Poetry: A Magazine of Verse* to promote several of his poems. Upon the eve of the magazine's founding in 1912, *Poetry*'s editor, Harriet Monroe, invited Pound to contribute, and as a result he became the magazine's self-appointed overseas editor. In January 1923, six of Hemingway's poems appeared in *Poetry* under the title "Wanderings"—

several of which were on war themes. The magazine informed its readers that these works were by Ernest Hemingway "a young Chicago poet now abroad, who will soon issue his first book of verse."[23]

Hemingway's poems in *Poetry* included "Mitrailliatrice," "Oily Weather," "Roosevelt," "Riparto d'Assalto," "Champs 'd Honneur," and "Chapter Headings." These works reflected the influence of Pound and Eliot, as well as Stephen Crane. Though none are exceptional, they served as exercises—words experiments for the development of a new, concise prose style. As literary scholar Nicholas Joost asserts, "What remained now was for Ernest Hemingway to drop the rhymes of poetry and the strongly emphasized musical rhythms of the new poetry of Imagism; he would carry over into prose the new freedom of choice in subject ... that the Imagists had fought for, and would insist, in prose, on the exact, not merely the decorative, word, in order to avoid cliché and the trite."[24]

Tired of the Paris scene, Pound looked to Italy as a possible home. While still living in Paris, he once informed *Poetry* editor Harriet Monroe: "Italy has civilized Europe twice and it may be that she has spiritual force enough in her to do it again. At any rate, she is very much alive just now to every manifestation of the modern movement that is going anywhere in the world." During early visits to Italy, Ezra and Dorothy stayed in Rapallo at the Albergo Rapallo, facing the sea. Pound had Gautier's hieratic head shipped from England, where it had been in Violet Hunt's Kensington garden. It was placed in the Albergo's café and then in its lobby. The Pounds typically took their meals at the Albergo. "I could eat there for three months," informed Pound, "without the proprietor presenting a bill or feeling uneasiness."[25]

In the early 1890s a book about Genoa provided a glimpse of Rapallo at the time. "Rapallo," its author wrote, "leans over the lip of wave of her own bay, with steeply crowding streets and houses, weaving her meshes of silken lace for the women of the land, and trafficking in olive oil." Later, a guide to Italy described Rapallo as "one of the most protected spots on the coast much frequented as a winter resort and for sea-bathing." Another book described Rapallo's tropical-like vegetation, and that "camellias and oleander bloom everywhere in the open air." Another writer observed, "Everyone who visits Rapallo climbs thought the rich olive-yards and under the shady ilex-oaks, right over the crumbling rock and scented heather."[26]

Intent to share Rapallo's quaint surroundings with friends, Pound sent several letters of invitation to Hemingway. From Chamby-sur-Montreux, on January 23, 1923, Hemingway answered Pound's gushing pleas to visit.

He considered making the trip but was disgusted by the fascists' burning of buildings and their humiliation of opponents when forcing them to drink castor oil. Hemingway bluntly asked Pound: "Can I ... preserve my incognito among your fascist pals? Or are they liable to give Hadley castor oil?"[27]

Six days later, Hemingway wrote to Pound stating he would rather go to Calabria, where it would be easy to travel to Sicily. This plan probably had more to do with the rumor of Pound's going to Calabria with Nancy Cunard, heir to the Cunard shipping line.[28] In earlier London years, Pound had known this young socialite and minor poet from whom he solicited money to support Joyce. While understanding that Pound may have had "a gutfull of Rapallo," Hemingway wondered if this was not a "conventional spring running down the road?" If so, Ernest was willing to visit Dorothy in Rapallo and play some tennis. Hemingway continued his correspondence, claiming that the altitude in the Swiss mountains had made him "practically sexless." After assuring Pound that he had not lost his male "sexual superiority," Hemingway then opined that high elevation reduced the human sex drive and proposed an annual study be made of "prostitutes above 2000 meters."[29]

Pound soon wrote back praising Rapallo's weather and hoped Hemingway would visit despite Mussolini's supposed threat that he could never return to Italy. In mid–February 1923, Ernest and Hadley took the train from Milan to Rapallo. Arriving from the sunny mountain weather of the north, Ernest found Rapallo a dull rainy backwater—its waves weakly lapping the shore—and summed up his impression by writing to Stein, "The place ain't much." But when the rain subsided, the seaside town seemed more pleasing. Hemingway's second-story room at the Hotel Riviera Splendide later inspired his short story "Cat in the Rain," dealing with a recently married couple's succumbing to domestic doldrums and divergent interests. The story's female character, based upon Hadley, longs for simple home-spun pleasures—among them a kitten—while her husband, as if not hearing a word, stoically looks out at the public garden's palm trees and green benches, rainwater dripping off its bronze war monument.[30]

Hemingway's time in Rapallo allowed for recreation and meeting new friends and contacts. His most pressing concern at the time was crafting several stories to be published in *The Little Review*. Again, Pound's connections made possible his being published in such a distinguished American publication, as he talked up Hemingway to Jane Heap—the review's co-editor and former companion of the magazine's beauteous founder, Margaret Anderson. As literary scholar Milton A. Cohen asserts, despite most Hemingway biographers' contentions that Heap solicited Hemingway's work for the *Little Review*, its appearance "clearly points to Pound."[31]

Three days after the Hemingways arrived in Rapallo, the Pounds left to research the Renaissance condottiere Sigismundo Malatesta—the most recent subject of *The Cantos*. Even if Ernest and Ezra's time together was brief, a few days spent with Pound, explains Hemingway's biographer Michael Reynolds, "went a long way." Fortunately, the poet did not have time to overburden Ernest with his non-literary obsessions.[32]

Ernest and Hadley played tennis with rackets loaned to them by the Pounds. One of their tennis opponents, Henry "Mike" Strater, was in Rapallo to do illustrations for Pound's *Cantos*. Hemingway met Strater at the Pounds' apartment in the fall of 1922. Starter recalled that when slowly sipping "a cup of weak tea," an imposing young man approached and offered a drink from a hip flask. The next day the writer and painter put on boxing gloves and "hammered one another" for hours. Kentucky-born Strater had attended Yale with F. Scott Fitzgerald and served as the inspiration for Burne Holiday in Fitzgerald's *This Side of Paradise*. Strater studied under French painter Édouard Vuillard, and praise for his *Nude with Dog*, shown at the 1922 Paris Salon d'automne, attracted the notice of Pound, who recruited him to illustrate a section of *The Cantos*.[33]

Like Pound, Hemingway found Strater a good-game guy, a spirited tennis partner, and good company. Despite a sprained ankle, Strater joined Hemingway—an aggressive companion whom he discovered "liked to win everything"—for a game of tennis and long "no-call out rounds" of boxing.[34] The writer and painter also discussed their artistic callings. More memorable of their time together are Strater's Hemingway portraits—a profile and a second, known as "The Boxer Portrait"—painted in the Hemingways' Rapallo hotel room.[35]

That February, Rapallo attracted others taking a respite from the Parisian scene, including writer Robert McAlmon. A heavy drinker, attractive to both men and women, and independently wealthy from a marriage of convenience to Winifred Ellerman, McAlmon impressed Hemingway. Hemingway later wrote to Pound that he had read a number of McAlmon's stories and a novel, and informed him that his new friend had written nine new stories in Rapallo. Although Hemingway would later consider McAlmon a mediocre talent, he gushed to Pound that he had better make a quick investment in this promising young man before the market took notice. A friend of both writers, Pound tried to dampen Hemingway's heated enthusiasm by stating that McAlmon's "price was still too long." Pound warned that rushing to write a score of stories in a week was "a little *too* much," that Hemingway not be impressed by greater output but work crafted carefully and skillfully. Nonetheless, Hemingway had good reason to befriend McAlmon. The founder of an independent Paris-based press, Contact Editions, McAlmon had published a book of poetry, two short-story collections, and was working on a novel. In Rapallo, McAlmon read a sampling of Hemingway's work and, upon a handshake, agreed to publish it.

On his return to Rapallo, Pound again urged the Hemingways to join him on a walking tour tracing the historical battle sites of the Renaissance ruler of Rimini and condottiere, Sigismundo Pandolfo Malatesta (1417–68). One of Pound's early introductions to Malatesta was reading the Swiss scholar Jacob Burckhardt's classic study *The Civilization of the Renaissance in Italy* (1860). Pound spoke of Burckhardt's writing as having "the verve of the best French heavy prose." In his study Burchhardt describes the fifteenth-century soldier/statesmen Malatesta as "the tyrant of Rimini" for his brutal treatment of enemies, and writes how "unscrupulousness, impiety, military skill, and high culture have seldom been combined in one individual as in Sigismundo Malatesta." A soldier of fortune who had fought for numerous provinces, Malatesta—conversant in philosophy and history—became a patron of the arts and assembled numerous scholars in Rimini. In the arts, Malatesta is most remembered in Rimini for his patronage of Leon Battista Alberti's Christian "temple of flame," the Tempio Malatestiano, dedicated to his beloved Isotta. When first seeing the Tempio in 1922, Pound experienced what became a lifelong fascination for this renowned structure.[36] One of Pound's men of action, Malatesta was lauded by him as Mussolini's political descendent. Mussolini "will end with Sigismondo and the men of order," Pound later wrote, "not with the pus-sacs and destroyers."[37]

Pound's walking was to research what would become known as the Malatesta Cantos. Though Hemingway had little knowledge of Malatesta and did not want to eat tasteless food in expensive inns, he finally agreed to the trip. The rucksack-carrying couples went by foot along the northern Italian coast. Hiking southward, they lunched "al fresco on fresh figs, cheese, and olives and drinking the local wines." As Hadley recalled, "Ezra's knowledge of Italian and Italian people and Italian history shone brightly against those gorgeous old ruins." While Pound rhapsodized about Malatesta's history, Ernest could not help but draw upon his military experience to speculate about the condottiere's tactics in fighting neighboring city states. Afterwards, Hemingway believed that he might have misled Pound by his comments. The tour ended nearly two-hundred miles south of Rapallo at

Ortibello, a city of fifth-century Etruscan walls, which Hemingway told Pound he "was just crazy about."[38]

His legs strained from the walking tour, Hemingway briefly stayed in Ortibello, and then relaxed for a few days in a Milan hotel. He jokingly wrote Pound that he was bedridden, suffering from angina. Robert McAlmon's mockery and gossip provided Hemingway with the idea for a poem that he sent along in his letter to Pound. This biting satire of female poets, "The Lady Poets with Footnotes," took as its subjects Edna St. Vincent Millay, Alice Kilmer, Sarah Teasdale, Zoe Atkins, Lola Ridge, and Pound's nemesis, cigar-smoking Amy Lowell. Some scholars claim that Hemingway's reference to footnotes could not have been a stab at Eliot, since the early magazine versions of "The Waste Land" did not carry footnotes. Literary scholar Milton A. Cohen notes that "during his first visit to Pound's apartment in February 1922, Hemingway could have seen on Pound's desk a draft of Eliot's long poem, soon to be entitled ["The Waste Land"] which Eliot (en route from Lausanne to London) had left for Pound to mark up."[39]

By mid–March 1923, Hemingway submitted several prose sketches to the *The Little Review*. Edited by Pound and Margaret Anderson, *The Little Review* spring issue's theme, "Exiles," conceived by Pound, proved a crucial showcase for Hemingway's work. When the issue finally appeared in October that year, it placed Hemingway's six contributions first—before those of Gertrude Stein, E.E. Cummings and Mina Loy, as well as Jean Cocteau, Joan Miro and Ferdinand Léger. Collected under the title *in our time*, "the paragraphs appeared ... as six unnumbered pieces, separated by three spaced periods." Apart from Hemingway's prose work there also appeared his satirical poem "They All Made Peace—What Is Peace?" that captured the author's impression of the Lausanne Conference in which he mocked Mussolini and satirized others in attendance.[40]

In between fulfilling journalistic obligations, writing poetry and experimental prose, Hemingway found time to enjoy the pastimes of horse racing and boxing. On June 21, 1923, Pound wrote Dorothy about his attending boxing matches with Hemingway. "Hem has got another ticket for the boxe on Saturday. Seems determined I shall see a GOOD one. I must stop the outlay somehow. Shall I have to demonstrate its inferiority to fencing." Around this time, Englishmen Sisley Huddleston accompanied Hemingway to Parisian boxing matches and observed how his novelist friend excitedly "cheered on the bespattered pugilists," losing himself "in primitive physical sensations that he meant to turn into literature." Three days later,

Pound again reported. "Hem had got me a much too expensive seat at the BOXE last night." At this fight of "two collosi" Pound joined Hemingway's other guests, Robert MacAlmon and *Little Review* editor Jane Heap. Pound did not share Hemingway's enthusiasm for boxing and informed Dorothy that it was "much more interesting to do than see."[41]

Several months later, in June, Pound and Hemingway met writer Glenway Westcott. In a letter about this meeting, poet Marianne Moore related: "Glenway has been in Paris and saw Robert McAlmon whom he says everybody loves for his simplicity and good nature; he saw Ezra who he says wears a pointed beard and side whiskers, which makes him look as he hadn't shaved." Pound wrote to Dorothy that he thought Wescott "at least has all the proper ideas," and added that "Hem approves; McAlmon inclined to consider him a bore." Hemingway, in fact, did not care for Westcott and later wrote that he thought him a "literary fake." In complete opposition to Pound's initial judgment of Wescott, Hemingway dismissed Wescott's literary approach and mocked him as "Weskit," author of "pineapple of the eye," in reference to the author's modestly successful *The Apple of the Eye.* Hemingway went on to satirize Wescott in *The Sun Also Rises* as Roger Prentiss, who appeared in the novel's first bar scene.[42]

In the summer and fall of 1923, Hemingway still had to write the remaining vignettes for *in our time.* These short works, most of them paragraph length, were inspired by Pound's insistence that the Inquest series constitute short prose books or booklets, numbering around fifty pages. One vignette, or what Hemingway referred to as chapters, written in June, troubled Pound, who stressed that the matador Maera's bedside death scene needed a new, more poignant conclusion. He lectured Hemingway that as creator he could kill his character in any way he chose, twice if he so wished. By August, Hemingway collaborated with Pound in determining the sequence of the vignettes—dealing with war, American crime, an assassination in Greece, and recent events in Spain.

Pound stressed a well-thought-out strategy and settled into a daily routine with Hemingway, playing tennis then retiring to his studio where they discussed what order the sketches should be so they would "all hook up." Hemingway wrote Pound in August, informing him that he "fixed" some of the works, and, in regard to the matador vignette, assured that the "New Death is good." Hemingway's revision kept the action in the bullring—a horn thrust passes through Maera and into the sand. This was not, as Michael Reynolds asserts, a great story, but a valuable experiment in shifting between narrator and the matador's last-moment point of view. In regard to the order of the vignettes, Hemingway explained to Pound that each would be titled as a separate chapter. Having placed the vignettes in what he determined as a satisfactory order, Hemingway submitted them to Bird.[43]

Though Bird frustrated Hemingway in his slow publishing approach, the publisher wanted to make it a stand-out edition by interspersing in the page margins collages of newsprint from American and Greek newspapers. This design was intended to enhance *in our time*'s modernist content—its snapshot-like reportage. Bird introduced the lower-case title and had designed for the frontispiece a woodcut Hemingway portrait, one of the two painted by Mike Strater in Rapallo. The newsprint was to be placed in the page margins but was eventually abandoned and instead utilized in the cover design.

More concerned about the prose and the vignette's arrangement, Pound left the design decisions to Bird and Hemingway. Pound wrote Hemingway in September: "Bill has noble plan for doing yr. book with MODERN typography. I wrote him he shd submit ideas to you. I can not undertake the so delicate responsibility of this so delicate matter." In October, Hemingway informed Pound: "I cabled Bill to commence firing on the newsprint borders. It all depends on how it is done. It's a good hunch. If not well done it will sour quick as hell. That's up to Bill. Christnose he rates a little excitement out of the Press. I tell him to shoot. He is the man to do it."[44]

By this time Robert McAlmon's Contact imprint had published Hemingway's *Three Stories and Ten Poems*. This slim volume was rushed into print, appearing on August 13, 1923, and came out before *in our time*. It included the stories "Up in Michigan," "My Old Man," and "Out of Season," and poems—"Along With Youth," "Montparnasse," "Roosevelt," "Oily Weather," "Mitrailliatrice," "Chapter Heading," "Captives," "Riparto d' Assalto," "Champs d' Honneur," and "Oklahoma."

In November, the *Paris Tribune* featured Gertrude Stein's review of *Three Stories and Ten Poems*. Contrary to many contemporary critics and reviewers, Stein thought Hemingway's poetry superior to his prose: "Three stories and ten poems is very pleasantly said. So far so good, further than that, and as far as that, I may say that of Ernest Hemingway that as he sticks to poetry and intelligence it is both poetry and intelligent.... I should say that Hemingway should stick to poetry and intelligence and eschew the hotter emotions and the more turgid vision. Intelligence and a great deal of it is a good thing to use when you have it, it's all for the best." Stein's strong reaction to the volume's prose was no doubt based upon her utter distaste for "Up in Michigan"—the story of forced seduction of a waitress in the northern woods that Stein once condemned as "unaccrochable," an artwork that could not be displayed.[45]

As Hemingway's first book appeared (and with another about to be published), he dealt with becoming a father. Hadley had entered the advanced stage of pregnancy. A product of a troubled family and fearing the responsibility of fatherhood and its economic responsibilities, Hemingway was torn between family life and the prospect of becoming a writer of literature. From his recent reading he may have been thinking of a line from Stendhal's *The Red and the Black*—"The tedium of matrimonial life inevitably kills off love, even when love has preceded marriage."[46]

Pound eventually had two children—Omar with Dorothy, and Mary with Olga Rudge. Mary was raised by surrogate parents in the Italian Tyrol, and Omar in England among the Shakespear family. This Old World arrangement, typical of the upper class, would not be an option for Hemingway.

Although the recently built American Hospital in the suburb of Neuilly had a repetition for "the latest American ideas of arrangement and equipment," Ernest and Hadley decided to have their child in Toronto. There, Ernest would again work at the offices of the *Toronto Star*, as he had during the winter of 1919–1920. Before leaving Paris for Canada, the couple visited friends. At the Pounds' apartment, Ezra took Hadley aside and cautioned, "Well, I might as well as say good-bye to you here and now because [the baby] is going to change you completely." As Hadley's biographer points out: "Pound thought that motherhood damaged women in a fundamental way, rendering them unfit for anything else. In his view, artists and their wives should not have children—lesser mortals should be the world's parents." Before his guests departed, Pound, in an odd gesture, gave Hadley his old brown velvet smoking jacket as a present."[47]

The Hemingways also visited Sylvia Beach's bookstore and lending library, Shakespeare and Company, at rue de Odeon. Popular among the American literary crowd, most referred to it as simply "Silvia Beach's Bookshop." When first arriving in Paris, Hemingway, according to one account, saw no need to present Anderson's letter of introduction when first encountering her. Ms. Beach instantly took to Hemingway and allowed him to check out books from her lending library, without charge. Composer Virgil Thomson described congenial Ms. Beach in "her boxlike suits," as "Alice in Wonderland at forty," and her female partner "buxom Adrienne Monnier, bodiced, with peplum, and a long full skirt as an eighteenth century milkmaid." Another writer at the time took note of Beach's "businesslike bobbed head, and ... frequent cigarette."[48]

On his goodbye visit to Shakespeare and Company, Hemingway most likely gave Ms. Beach a photograph of himself taken by Man Ray, inscribed, "For Sylvia Beach/Ernest Hemingway August 1923." One of the honorary American Dadaists, Man Ray—a brilliant visual artist—recalled Hemingway as "a tall young man of athletic build, with his hair low on his forehead, a clear complexion, and a small moustache." This photograph, Ray believed, gave Hemingway "a poetic look, making him very handsome besides."[49]

Beach hung this brilliant portrait of a contemplative Hemingway among her bookshop photographs of Pound, James Joyce, Sherwood Anderson, and T.S. Eliot. Given that Hemingway was relatively unknown outside Paris literary circles, his image among such famed writers must have seemed an auspicious portent.

Whereas Man Ray befriended Hemingway and attended a boxing match with him, he had an entirely different impression of Pound. When the poet entered Man Ray's studio to be photographed, he "flopped into an armchair with his legs stretched out, his arms hanging loosely, his black tie flowing, and his pointed red beard raised aggressively, as if to take possession of the place." Aware of Pound's "kindhearted" reputation in helping artists, Man Ray still thought him "dominatingly arrogant where literature was concerned. It worked very well in English-speaking community, but I never heard him mentioned in European circles." Man Ray believed that Pound's erudite verse did not translate well or was easily understood by non–English-speaking readers. "Pound had never looked or commented upon my work," complained Man Ray, "so I classed him at once among the many other egotists who came to me."[50]

Among their belongings to be taken to Canada, the Hemingways packed their paintings by Andre Masson, Koumé, and Dorothy Pound. After a nine-day delay in Paris, they sailed on August 26. Hemingway later reported to Pound that during the ten-day Atlantic crossing passengers were subjected to a relentless gale. The Hemingways checked into Toronto's Hotel Shelby. Morley Callahan—known among Hemingway enthusiasts as the Canadian reporter who knocked Ernest down in boxing match in Paris—recalled encountering the fellow reporter at the *Star* office, and how this "tall, broad-shouldered, brown-eyed" man with a "heavy black moustache" and "wearing a peak cap," politely smiled at him. Hemingway told Callahan that he was in Toronto to see that his baby would receive first-rate care, but that he wanted to go back to Paris.[51]

At this time, Toronto was undergoing development, as old housing and buildings were being replaced by taller, more modern structures. But for Hemingway it could never compete with Paris, where, although bathtubs and electric fixtures were a rarity, one could find, as he wrote his older sister, some of the best food, drink and company in the world. As one Ontario-born writer observed, the Toronto of 1923 was "a cultured city of 560,000 but lacked the glamor and excitement of Paris and the friendly cosmopolitan traditions of Rapallo and Vienna and Nice." Another factor in Hemingway's dislike of the city was the scarcity of alcohol. Though reputable hotels and restaurants could be found, Toronto had no cafes, and liquor was outlawed by a provincial prohibition from 1916 to 1927. During his four-month stay, Hemingway did not go without a drink. He bought a bootleg bottle or found a taste in the "speakeasies along Queen Street."[52]

Away from Paris, Ernest and Hadley played up their Left Bank experience in bohemian attire. Beret-wearing Ernest went about without a tie, in sports shirts and boots; while Hadley, boyishly shorthaired, dressed simply, without jewelry or makeup. Ernest's defiantly dressed-down look would have turned many heads at the *Star* office. But aside from cub reporter Callahan and a few others among the younger staff, most of the experienced, older newsroom reporters dismissed, or at least greatly questioned, the idea of Hemingway the artist.[53]

Before starting work at the *Star*, Ernest already had an intuitive feeling about his future, informing Pound that he should have followed the impulse to take up residence in Quebec and live there simply until they ran out of funds. Though Hemingway admitted to Pound that Toronto's medical reputation made it the right place to have a child, he complained about living in a boom-and-bust country of failing banks, businesses, and newspapers. Hemingway arrived in Toronto when Canada was still in a post–World War I recession that lasted until 1923. Away from the company of artists and writers, Hemingway experienced creative isolation. Compared to Paris, Ernest found Toronto a sober-minded Protestant city, and he poured out his frustrations to Pound, who agreed that the Canadian venture had been a mistake. In a letter to Hemingway, Pound addressed his friend as "Col. Hemingway Tomato Star, Tomato Can," and then admonished, "I hope you won't do it again, there was an old troubadour who said that if he 'ever went to Syria again, he prayed God wd keep him there, fer bein sech a damn fool."[54]

Overworked and claiming to be exceedingly underpaid, Hemingway went to the Toronto horse races, reporting to Pound that he took more money home from the track than he made in two weeks at the *Star*. This money went to support his son, John Hadley Nicanor, to whom he referred (in a tribute to Pound) as "John Nicanor Ezra Malatesta Hemingway." Ironically, it would be Gertrude and Alice who became the godparents.

The Hemingways stayed three weeks at the Shelby Hotel, then signed a one-year lease for a small apartment at the Cedarville Mansions. Located in the northern section of the city, their cramped room in the four-story apartment building had a balcony that looked out upon a wooded ravine and to open land beyond. Mention of the Hemingways' adopted cat reached Pound, as Ernest wrote about tracking down its "shitting place" and wiping it up "with a copy of the *Toronto Star*."[55]

Though Hemingway's stay in Toronto is typically portrayed as a miserable interlude, notably captured in his letters to Pound, there were instances when he thought otherwise. He informed Stein, for instance, that he liked his apartment, which looked out upon "a ravine where the town leaves off into country sunny, a stretch of fine country" with a hill that one might possibly ski down with the coming of winter. Ernest also wrote his sister Marcelline an enthusiastic letter about this stretch of land near a prestigious equestrian and golf club.[56]

On November 24, 1923, there appeared in *The Toronto Star Weekly* Hemingway's anonymous article for "Nobleman Yeats" that observed the Irishman's winning of the Nobel Prize. "William Butler Yeats has written, with the exception of a few poems by Ezra Pound," noted Hemingway in the article, "the very finest poetry of our time." This opinion would change little in the coming years, as Hemingway distanced himself from Stein.[57]

Upon John's birth on October 10, his father boasted to Pound that though the baby bore a resemblance to the King of Spain, he had not yet contemplated divorce proceedings. After this good news, Hemingway slipped into a bleaker mood. He compared his Toronto experience to his 1918 war service and complained that he lived in "the fistulaed asshole of the father of seven nations." Then Hemingway related the news of his learning that novelist/publisher Ford Maddox Ford "had laid hold of Magazine," whom Pound kept in mind for one of its contributors. Hemingway was composing a possible contribution, "Oh Canada," inspired by his miserable Toronto experience. Foul in mood and feeling worthless as a writer, Hemingway concluded his correspondence with a pithy, off-color comment: "Still the diseased oyster shits the finest pearl the palmist says. For Gawd sake keep on writing me. Yr. letters are life preservers."[58]

Source of artistic support and comic relief, Pound received Hemingway's humorous letters. When learning that Pound's upstairs neighbors did not appreciate hearing the poet's collaborative musical compositions with

Antheil, Hemingway suggested that Pound abandon the bassoon for an English horn that would guarantee to nauseate the offended listeners. After this bit of humor, Hemingway then vented his disgust about the artsy and the pretenders of art. As "a man who likes to drink and fuck and eat and talk and read the papers and write something," he vowed to "keep clear of the shits." Hemingway's mocking shit list included everything from literary and artsy types to writers and the entire city of New York. "<u>Shit on them all</u>," he concluded."[59]

Fellow journalist Morely Callaghan had yet to see the angry side of Hemingway, someone he greatly admired for writing *Three Stories and Ten Poems*. Hemingway talked enthusiastically to Callaghan about Twain's *The Adventures of Huckleberry Finn*, Stendhal, Flaubert, and proclaimed Joyce the greatest of his age. When Callaghan asked Hemingway what writers in Paris thought of his work, he answered, "Ezra Pound says it is the best prose he has read in forty years." To a serious student of literature like Callaghan, this bold claim was quite impressive. As Callahan explained: "At that time the poet Ezra Pound was not a big name in Toronto, but to young writers in English, whether they lived in New York, Paris or London, he was prophetic, the grand discoverer, the man of impeccable taste. I think I saw why Hemingway wanted to get out of Toronto like a bat out of hell."[60]

On December 3, Hemingway received a letter from Pound addressed to "Ernest Hemingway, Tomato Can." It stated that Ford Madox Ford was starting a new Paris-based magazine, the *Transatlantic Review*, and suggested the possible submission of "Oh Canada." "WHHHHHHHHere's your copy? Wot's the use of your pore old grandpa Ford sittin in a dammap cottage sweating 'is neck off to perduce a revoo where the Young can exPRESS 'emselves IF you aren't goin ter com across wif de PUNCH? I think, meself, you'd better come bak here and direk the policy of the damn thing." But under strain of his newspaper job, and being miserable away from Paris, Hemingway could not bring himself to write creatively."[61]

Later that month, Ernest took the train alone from Toronto to spend Christmas in Oak Park. Ernest stayed at his parents' house only a few hours. During the gathering, he secretly gave his oldest sister, Marcelline, a copy of *Three Stories and Ten Poems* and told her to read it later. Marcelline put the book in her suitcase and did not open it until on the train back to her home in Detroit. Shocked by the book's contents, Marcelline was especially disturbed by "Up in Michigan," in which she recognized the real individuals behind its characters. Marcelline was certain her parents never saw the book as it surely would have outraged them as well.

Ernest's short visit would be the last time he saw his father before

Clarence took his life, nearly five years later, in an upstairs room. Once close to his father, Ernest had come to see him as weak and dominated by Grace. In earlier years, Clarence's increasing time away from the family created a cold distance between them. But unknown to Ernest, these periodic absences were needed to settle his father's nerves during severe bouts of depression. Unaware of his father's mental illness, Ernest perceived this behavior as a weakness in character, resulting from Grace's domineering personality.

Not one to tolerate defiance when dealing with children, Grace demanded respect from her insolent son, who came home from the war and refused to attend college and lived for extended periods off the family, while spending time in Northern Michigan, drinking and fishing with friends. While Ernest worked as a reporter for the *Kansas City Star* and the *Toronto Star*, Clarence and Grace did not take him seriously as a writer, but came to accept his vocation.

Back in Toronto, Hemingway could not tolerate working under his *Star* editor. Out-of-town assignments only made his job more unbearable, especially when he longed for Paris. On Hemingway's last day at the *Star*, on January 1, 1924, he spent time with his older co-workers, and spoke of creating a new style of prose. Before Hemingway left the office building some of the senior reporters, aware of Pound's satiric reference, gave him a gift of a tomato can.

While Hemingway was still in Toronto, Pound entered the American hospital in Paris for treatment of his appendix. Glad to know that Pound did not need surgery, Hemingway humorously wrote his friend that once an ignorant veterinarian had nearly removed his Adam's apple by mistaking it for a cyst. To cheer up his friend, Hemingway informed him that he was "rushing two hundred pound California bathing beauty" to his "bedside."[62]

CHAPTER 5

Transatlantic Paris

In January 1924, Pound wrote his father: "Hem. is expected back shortly. His opinion of Canada not likely to be printed anywhere save in Africa." Not long after the Hemingways arrived in Paris with their infant son, John Nicanor, nicknamed "Bumby." While in Italy the Pounds invited the Hemingways to stay at their apartment. Ernest may well have accepted, but Hadley—no real friend of Ezra and dreading the memory of the Pounds' salon teas—refused to live in the cold, dimly lit apartment.[1]

In early February the Hemingways moved to a second-story apartment at 113 rue Notre Dame des Champs, not far from the Pounds. Other prominent American artists, like John Singer Sargent, had lived and worked on this tree-lined street in the sixth Arrondissment. In 1892, James McNeil Whistler rented a spacious studio at no. 86. At that time, the Notre Dame des Champs is said to have had more studios than any other street in Paris.

The Hemingways' semi-furnished apartment was rented on a three-to five-month basis. A short walk took them to the Luxembourg Gardens, Montparnasse hotspots, and Ernest's favorite intimate café, the Closerie de Lilas. Nearby, the rue Vivian shops sold quality meat, desserts, and bread. If their new neighborhood bettered the Cardinal Lemione, their apartment had some drawbacks—no electricity or running water, and the gasoline engine of their landlord's next-door sawmill was a noisy inconvenience. In the building's cellar underneath a bakery Hadley played her piano; in winter, she took to wearing several sweaters to keep warm. Hemingway cheerily wrote that he had good whiskey and a comfortable home full of books with an open fireplace, where "a guy can read or sit around and go out when he feels like it."[2]

Around this time, Pound took his Irish friend Brigit Patmore and her son to 113 rue Notre Dames des Champs. There, he promised they would meet "a nice young American couple." Pound led them through a "narrow street and into a small square." In front of one the apartments, Pound tilted back his head and shouted up to a second floor-window—"Hem! ... Hem!" From the balcony a dark-haired figure appeared, shouting—"Oh, it's you, Ezra! Come on up!" Following the energetic poet up the stairs, the Patmores beheld a handsome Hemingway "clean-shaven and fit," wearing "grey flannel trousers and a white pullover." Invited into a small living room, Ernest's guests were joined by Hadley, nursing their son, Bumby. To calm the infant, Patmore recalled, Ernest "took it and tossed it in the air and tried to amuse it in the most endearing way." Years later, Patmore never forgot the bond between Pound and Hemingway, writing that the latter was "the kindest and most loyal of men and was ever grateful to Ezra for his early encouragement."[3]

Meanwhile, as Pound spent more time in Italy researching his cantos, Ernest missed his tennis partner and literary mentor. In a letter announcing his becoming Pound's neighbor, Hemingway—addressing his friend as "Prometheus"—confided: "It's no fun living on your street in your absence. Would come down to Rapallo to see you but can't face any more traveling.... The town is no good without you all." After announcing that he was about to write seven stories, Ernest went on to complain: "The town seems, when you can distinguish the faces through the rain and snow, to be full of an enormous number of shits. I however am quite happy eating oysters and drinking the wine of the country."[4]

Hemingway enjoyed Pound's company and that of other university-educated friends, steeped in the classics and foreign languages. But what Hemingway lacked in higher education, he made up in adventurous life experience. As for Pound, he understood the poet's need to immerse himself in history and myth to write his epic cantos. Though never an outstanding student, Pound held a bachelor's degree from Hamilton College and a masters in fine arts from the University of Pennsylvania—with distinction in Anglo-Saxon, Bible study, advanced French—where he enrolled in every course offered in Romance languages: Latin, Old French, Provençal, and Italian. Despite Pound's dismissing a university education as stultifying, it nonetheless introduced him to Browning's *Sordello*, Flaubert, and the art of the troubadours, inspiring his ideal of the lone and "aggressive wandering minstrel, an outcast who nevertheless commanded the attention of a cultured audience."[5]

As for his own art, Hemingway confessed to Pound that, while he lacked a university classical education, he would come "to know everything about fucking and fighting and eating and drinking and begging and stealing and living and dying." Pound called this experiential approach to life and to art as Hemingway's "self-hardening process." Robert McAlmon remembered how Hemingway once lectured him, when seeing a dead dog in Spain, on the necessity of learning from reality: "It seemed that he had seen in the war the stacked corpses of men, maggot-eaten in a similar way.... He tenderly explained that we of our generation must inure ourselves to the sight of grim reality." In *Death in the Afternoon*, Hemingway explained his astute study of Spanish bullfighting. "I was trying to learn to write, commencing with the simplest things," he asserted, "and one of the simplest things of all and the most fundamental is violent death."[6]

Like Pound, James Joyce admired Hemingway's full embrace of life that made for powerful prose. "He writes as he is," Joyce once commented. "And ready to live the life he writes about. He would never have written it if his body had not allowed him to live it. But giants of his sort are truly modest; there is much more behind Hemingway's form than people know." According to Hemingway, when once drinking with Joyce, the Irishman spoke about his prose possibly becoming "suburban" and suggested seeing a bit more of the world. Joyce's wife, Nora, recommended lion hunting. Joyce responded by saying that he "couldn't see the lion." Having the last word, Nora simply explained, "Hemingway'd describe him to you and afterwards you could go up and touch him and smell of him."[7]

Hemingway, the agnostic, saw the world through a realist's eyes. Though he did write short stories based upon his friends' experiences—like Chink Dorman Smith's account of fighting at Mons in World War I—he could not have written so effectively on the subject without having seen death firsthand, or having a sportsman's finger-on-the-trigger instinct.

Though Stein urged Hemingway to quit journalism, Pound's outspoken hatred of popular magazines also played an important role. Pound's crudity in vilifying what he detested found its source in popular magazines, "the smear sheets" as he often called them. Pound had long ascribed America's lack of letters to "dry-rot, magazitis," which produced "mental sewage" for the masses. *Vanity Fair* Pound referred to as "Vanity Puke," and *The Ladies Home Journal*, "The Ladies Home Urinal." He once wrote that "art and popular magazines are eternally incompatible, for it is the business of the artist to tell the truth whoever dislikes it, and it is the business of the magazine editor to maintain his circulation." Pound warned popular magazine writers that by succeeding "in the periodicals or in some other branch of popular publication, he is nearly always dated" and "ceases from making revelations."[8]

Hemingway left journalism to be an artist, a title he refused, and instead insisted that he was a writer no longer enslaved to mundane reporting and commercial publishing demands. But Hemingway also faced the challenge of supporting a family, especially when the embezzlement of Hadley's railroad bonds by her St. Louis broker greatly reduced the family's income. In a letter dated October 15, 1924, Pound, learning of his friend's hardship, informed his parent: "Hem's lawyer in St. Louis has been trying, apparently, to swipe all Hem's hard-earned."[9]

A few days before receiving this letter, Hemingway dined at the Pounds' apartment at the invitation of Hans von Wedderkop, the German editor of the Berlin-based *Der Querschnitt* magazine that published nude drawings alongside experimental prose and poetry. "Although it made fun of Hitler," comments Michael Reynolds, "the magazine also fostered the spirit that would become the Nazi Youth Corps and encouraged the anti–Semitism that led to the holocaust." Free spirited and open to sex and art, the magazine interested Hemingway, who submitted for publication: "The Soul of Spain with McAlmon and Bird and the Publishers," "The Lady Poets with Footnotes," "An Ernest Liberal's Lament," "Part Six, A Serious and Vivid Account of a Dramatic Moment in the Cruel Spot," and, finally, the Pound-influenced "The Age Demanded."[10]

Two of Hemingway's *Der Querchnitt* poems drew the attention of Eugene Jolas of the *Paris Tribune*. In the magazine's October 1924 "Open Letter to Ernest Hemingway," Jolas praised Hemingway's prose but found fault with his poems. "You are the most genuinely epic talents of any youngster writing English today," lauded Jolas. The poems in *Der Querschnitt* also perplexed the *Tribune* staff and their American writer friends who thought that Hemingway was "on the wrong track," writing inferior poems which would only alarm the censors. Jolas concluded by stating, "Please give us another 'My Old Man' and let it go at that."[11]

In August and September 1924, Hemingway sent several stories to H.L. Mencken, editor of the *American Mercury*, or what Pound called "Murkn Mercury." This Baltimore-based magazine was one of the most widely read of the 1920s literary and arts magazines. Pound and Mencken had been corresponding by letter since 1914. Mencken's previous magazine, *The Smart Set*, had published some of Pound's work. But when Mencken and theater critic George Jean Nathan founded *The American Mercury* in 1924, the magazine never published Pound or Hemingway. Whereas Mencken liked some of Pound's early poems, Nathan refused to accept any for publication. Pound's exclusion from the *Mercury* was also due to the poet's eventually sending prose and essays of what Mencken called "wild propaganda." Though he would become abusive in his letters about not being published in the *Mercury*, Pound remained Mencken's friend and shared, as the latter noted, many of the same ideas and prejudices, especially their "violent dissent from the orthodox credo and from the moral order of the world of which it was so innocently based."[12]

Whatever role Pound played, if any at all, in the submission of Hemingway's work, Mencken recognized aspects of Hemingway's talent while disliking the writer. In his memoir Mencken recorded his impression:

> I never met Hemingway, and my view of his work never altered. He had a great hand for dialogue and he knew how to shock the women's clubs with dirty words, but his longer stories always struck me as melodramatic and obvious. He was best in the short story. Some of his most effective tricks, though his admirers never noted it, were borrowed from Rabelias. He was an excessively vain fellow—challenging bellicose and not infrequently absurd. Anyone who refused to hail him as a towering genius was an evil doer, and probably in receipt of foreign money.

As in the case of Scofield Thayer and the *Dial*, Hemingway never forgot Mencken's rejection—typically sent by Jean Nathan—and once threatened coming to Baltimore for revenge.[13]

His ego bruised, Hemingway found comfort and confidence in having Pound and Stein's encouragement. He played tennis with Pound several times a week, and the latter soon played promoter again by helping Hemingway land a sub-editor position at Ford Maddox Ford's Parisian-based *The Transatlantic Review*. While Hemingway was still in Toronto, Pound wrote him about the new independent magazine and prodded him for a contribution. Hemingway promised a piece, "Oh Canada," that he never wrote.

First conceived by Ford Maddox Ford's brother Oliver, the magazine was to be called the *Paris Review*. *The Transatlantic Review*'s name reflected a bi-continental spirit, and its lowercase cover title resulted from a typographical error during layout and printing. The first issue, December 1923, inaugurated its one-year run as important magazine of the arts. The magazine's English-language contributions were to be equally represented by British and American writers, balanced by works printed in French. Brought on board, Pound offered his promotional talents, once again teaming up with his old friend Ford, whom he met in London not long after arriving there in 1908.

To reach a broad bi-continental readership, the *Review* fostered young talent while cultivating older established writers. From its inception, the *Review* would have none of the angry vigor of Pound's London-based *Blast* or the absurdist experimentation of Dada publications. The *Review*'s backers initially banned Joyce from their publication, well aware that the serialization of Joyce's *Ulysses* nearly ruined the *Little Review* when its editors were taken to court in New York and found guilty of breaking obscenity laws.

Ford's promoting new American talent attracted a dominant number of writers from the Midwest, including Hemingway. In early 1924, Ford visited Pound's studio and saw a young man shadowboxing "in front of a Chinese silk portrait." Pound supposedly told Ford: "He's an experienced journalist. He writes very good verse and he's the finest prose stylist in the world.... He's disciplined too." This was not received well by Ford who, just days before, heard Pound call him the world's greatest prose writer. "You!" exclaimed Pound to Ford, "You're like all the English swine." This, again, may have been more legend than fact, as were much of Ford's later accounts.[14]

In February 1924, Hemingway became a *Transatlantic Review* sub-editor and worked in its office on the Ile St. Louis, housing Bill Bird's Three Mountain Press. Ford recalled Hemingway as having a Herculean disciplined look of a "Harrow-Cambridge General Staff young Englishmen who make such admirable secretaries until they let you down."

First impressions aside, Hemingway emerged as one of Ford's cruelest critics. When writing to Pound, he referred to Ford's magazine as the "Transportation Review." In *The Sun Also Rises*, Hemingway parodied Ford as the novel's Braddocks, leader of a group of dancehall revelers. In this invented guise, Hemingway reduced Ford from a famed novelist/editor to a dance-party host. These Thursday evenings, called "Ford Nights," were well known among Quarterites who came to dance to an accordion and a pounding drum—their wild dancing urged on by a jubilant Ford, who one attendant described as a "behemoth in tweeds."

Decades later, in *A Moveable Feast*, Hemingway described Ford as a wheezing, overweight duffer. As Ford's biographer Alan Judd explains: "Ford was not a hero in the Hemingway mould: he was vulnerable, untidy, sentimental, funny in a way that Hemingway could sense but not see, and genuinely heroic, he was superior in age, status, experience, knowledge of his craft, sensitivity and ability; he was unaggressive, fat and wheezing, had fought in the trenches and was unaccountably popular with women." But another *Transatlantic Review* sub-editor—also brought to the publication by Pound—poet Basil Bunting, thought Hemingway's treatment of Ford in *A Moveable Feast* "another sort of lie" told by a writer whom he admired. Bunting, who knew Ford and Hemingway, reacted to Hemingway's unflattering portrait by stating that he "would never have guessed the unlaughable caricature was meant for Ford if Hemingway had not named it."[15]

Ford was a talented storyteller with the habit of out-storytelling others. As Robert McAlmon recounted, "It was quite impossible to talk of a place or a person without Ford topping your story." Given to elaboration and fabrication, Ford may have publicly overshadowed the young Hemingway, who, known to stretch the truth for bettering one of his own stories, could not tolerate it in Ford. In a conversation with Pound, Hemingway complained about the accuracy of Ford's stories and his penchant for anecdotes that grew more detailed when a listener did not respond favorably. Pound defended his friend: "Well, he has a prodigious memory—he can quote from all the books he's read. Of course, he can not help it always if the memory is embroidered a bit."[16]

Ford's telling of his wartime service unnerved Hemingway. Ford attributed his weak lungs to being gassed near the front lines in 1916 at Nieppe when serving in an infantry supply battalion. It is possible that Ford may have gotten a whiff of gas as it lingered on the battlefield, but his lungs could have been affected just as easily by heavy cigarette smoking and damp quarters. Most important is that Ford believed he had been gassed. Following this incident in 1917, Ford was injured by German artillery and suffered shellshock. A man who had already suffered a near-mental breakdown years earlier, Ford's short-lived wartime experience left a haunting shadow.

Hemingway—who claimed to have served with the fierce Italian Ardittiti and was buried alive for several days—listened unsympathetically to his editor's experiences. In March 1924, Hemingway wrote to Pound complaining that he could not stand Ford's playing the English country gentleman and resented his inability to come to grips with the war as a writer. He then praised Pound as the only one who knew anything about writing. Though Hemingway believed he had written some fine new stories, he regretted not having his poet friend on hand to reassure him that they had the makings of greatness.[17]

As much as Pound could be spirited company, he often proved troublesome to his old friend Ford at the *Transatlantic Review* when his vociferous and critical comments about the magazine appeared in its poets' supplement section. As Ford biographer Bernard Poli noted: "As editor of the review Ford had good reasons to fear the wild ideas that Pound was likely to favor." But Ford put up with Pound and informed his readers that his contributor had shown "contempt" in a way that "we have not been able to see what else to do."[18]

Despite Hemingway's dislike of his head editor, Ford commented in the *Literary Review* of the *New York Evening Post*: "The best writer in America at this moment (thought for the moment he happens to be in Paris), the most consummate, is my young friend Ernest Hemingway.... Hemingway, with immense labor and excruciating thought and knowledge, turns out a short paragraph.... That would damn Mr. Hemingway if it were not for his youthful bloodlust which is admirably derivative.... Mr. Hemingway writes like an Angel; like an Archangel; but his talk—his manner—is that of a bayonet instructor."[19]

Such praise did nothing to endear Ford to his young sub-editor. As with Anderson and Stein, Hemingway was unforgiving to writers he thought past their prime and no longer useful in the advancement of his career. Hemingway later complained that his duty as a *Review* sub-editor was hard work without little or no compensation and that it prevented him from writing his literary work.[20] But as Nicholas Joost asserts, Hemingway's association with the *Review* furthered his career by printing Nick Adams stories, editorials, and newsletters. It enabled him to work under Ford, a gifted editor and novelist. It also provided the opportunity to Gertrude Stein's novel *Making of Americans*, serialized in the magazine as a result of Hemingway's prodding and clever promotion. Unknown to Ford, Hemingway had promised Stein that her entire work would be serialized in the *Review* (*Making of Americans* was later published in unabridged book form, numbering 925 pages). Instead, some 111 pages of Stein's work appeared in nine installments.

It is generally acknowledged that Ford was aware of Hemingway's promise to Stein that *Making of Americans* would be an ongoing serialization, though, by its very length, one would be hard put to think any magazine would publish it in its entirety. But such a possibility ended with the magazine's collapse. Like so many other little magazines, *The Transatlantic Review* died a quick death. Ford's business ineptitude resulted in his magazine lasting only a year, and Pound—one of the magazine's stock holders—could do nothing to save it.

Freed from responsibilities of magazine work, Hemingway unrelentingly pursued writing as an art. In March of 1924, Hemingway complained to Pound that Bill Bird had still not published *in our time*. It tested Hemingway's nerves that the book had yet to be sent to the bindery and lacked a reliable publication date. On March 17, a day following John "Bumby"

Hemingway's christening, Hemingway voiced his frustration to Pound, writing, "Fuck Literature."[21]

In April 1924, Three Mountains Press finally published *in our time*. Because of a printing error, the initial run of 300 copies was reduced to 170. A review by Roscoe Gordon made its way into the pages of the *New York Herald Tribune*. After reading the review, Hemingway vented his rage to Pound, decrying that Roscoe had attributed *in our time* to Ring Lardner's and Sherwood Anderson's influence. This pattern of critics linking Anderson with Hemingway aroused extreme resentment in the young writer. A myth maker about his own life, Hemingway soon attacked in words the first mentor largely responsible for his coming to Paris and meeting many of its leading literary lights, including Pound.

In May, Ernest and Hadley, their books and furniture having arrived from Canada, worked hard at fixing up their home. Ernest enjoyed the Parisian spring weather—the blooming horse chestnut tree outside his apartment window. In a letter to the family, Hemingway calmly wrote that his publisher had mentioned that someone by the name of Hemingway from Oak Park had returned five copies of *in our time*. To get back at his disapproving parents, Ernest stated that the publisher was pleased with the books' return because these first editions had already increased in price. In later years, Ernest's boast proved true when these hand-press limited editions did indeed become collectors' items.

Clarence Hemingway, who once thanked Pound for helping his son, obviously did not approve of the book promoted by him. Masking disappointment over his parents' disapproval of the book, Hemingway also privately voiced his frustration over Pound's supposed delaying the publication of *in our time*. Hemingway later wrote his family doctor that *in our time* had been delayed because of Pound's decision to place it sixth in the series. Hemingway also thought he deserved better placement because he had introduced Bird to Pound. This was unappreciative, since Pound and Bill Bird included an unknown writer like Hemingway in a series with Ford Maddox Ford, William Carlos Williams, Wyndam Lewis, and himself.

In October, one of America's eminent literary critics, Edmund Wilson, wrote a dual review of *Three Stories and Ten Poems*, nearly a year after its publication, and *in our time*. Wilson's review in the *Dial* marked Hemingway's first mention in a major publication. At the outset of his review, Wilson dismissed, as did most critics, the poems. Then, after recognizing the author's debts to Anderson and Stein, he lauded the author's creating a series of "dry-point" miniature portraits that seemed as if he had "almost invented a form of his own."[22]

At this time, Pound still played a behind-the-scenes role in shaping Hemingway's prose. In August 1924, Hemingway finished "Big Two-Hearted River," a two-part short story that he informed Stein was composed in the painterly style of Cézanne. "Big Two Hearted" was inspired by a 1919 fishing trip when Ernest and two high-school friends traveled to the Fox and Little Fox Rivers in Michigan's Upper Peninsula. In a search for a striking title, Hemingway poetically substituted for the Fox, the Big Two-Hearted, which lies in the Upper Peninsula beyond Tauqaumenon Falls and flows into Lake Superior.

A masterpiece of short fiction, "The Big Two Hearted" drew upon first-hand experience—an acute realism—expressed through the formalistic approach of modernism. Though "The Big Two-Hearted" bore the influence of Stein, it was Pound who received mention in the first draft. In an expurgated section—featured as "On Writing" in *The Nick Adams Stories*—Nick Adams reflects upon his friends Bill Bird and Pound. In this early draft, Nick quotes Pound as considering fishing "a joke." Nick's, or rather Hemingway's, passion for fishing needs no apology, and, after confessing his love of the sport, he repeats two more times in the narrative, "Ezra thought fishing a joke." Hemingway's mention of Pound in the first drafts of "Big Two-Hearted" reveals the author's response to his friend's opinion of his cherished sport. Ironically, he took Pound's advice about literary concision and exactitude and removed mention of the poet from the story.

Tennis and fencing were sports that Pound thought suitable for a writer and warned that Hemingway's fishing obsession, and, later, big-game hunting, might take valuable time from the writer's art. In reference to his friend's newest pastime of bullfighting, Pound once jokingly wrote William Bird: "Hemingway has been killed by a bull in Sargossa."[23]

Whereas Hemingway considered bullfighting a life-and-death ritual, Pound believed that Hemingway's obsession with bullfighting tapped into ancient Persian Mithraic worship of the bull. Pound's suggesting a link between Spanish bullfighting and Eastern ancient ritual irritated Hemingway. In a 1926 letter, Hemingway replied caustically, if not rudely, to Pound: "Leave us get bulls straight. I have never regarded bulls as anything but animals. I have never been a lover of animals. I have never heard of Mithra—lacking a classical education." This sarcastic response was not entirely honest when one takes into account Hemingway's affection for cats. In many ways, Pound was the more lacking in affection for animals, showing interest only in feeding stray cats in Italy and later birds and squirrels during his confinement at St. Elizabeths. Several years later, Pound once more noted a possible link between Mithraism and bullfighting, explaining, "So far as one can make out," it had "nothing to do with civilization ... the bullfight is an arguable exception but no one has proved that the features of bull-fighting which Mr. Hemingway admires can be traced to Mithra. The killing is Mithraic but the pageantry is debatable property."[24]

While Pound criticized other writer's non-literary pastimes, some expressed negative opinions about his extra-literary activities. Joyce considered Pound's making of homemade furniture as unnecessary, given that one could buy such things; the poet nevertheless took pleasure in constructing chairs, tables, and fixing objects.

Tolerant of Pound's many eccentricities and habit of speaking frankly, Hemingway also detected occasional lapses in Pound's aesthetic judgment. Later, he commented that Pound's loyalty to his friend's art was "beautiful as loyalty but ... very dangerous as judgment." Yet the youthfully confident Hemingway did not consider himself among those unworthy of Pound's support, unlike the poet's friend Wyndham Lewis, whom Hemingway despised along with his art.[25]

Even more perplexing to Hemingway was Pound's loyalty to the opium-addicted American poet Ralph Cheever Dunning. Detroit-born and a resident of Paris since 1905, Dunning had attended Harvard and had written neo–Victorian verse that Pound found refreshing and "a marvel of precision," he wrote in 1925. Few were in agreement. Joyce described Dunning's poetry as "drivel." Poet Archibald McLeish thought helping Dunning was a waste of time—proof that Pound had gone "cuku" and acting as "an ass."[26]

Pound called Dunning the "melancholy man of the courtyard" of the Notre Dame des Champs; others endearingly called him "Cheeve." Living on the same street as Hemingway, Dunning survived as a near-starving artist, primarily on a milk diet. Known around Montparnasse as the "Buddha," Dunning resided in small studio called "The Bird Cage." In the *Paris Tribune*, Wambly Bald described Dunning's living space as "a shelf-like single room that overlooks a garden," in which Dunning would sit at the foot of a large chestnut tree "wrapped in contemplation indifferent to the usual exigencies of existence," where "the poet composed lyrics and sonnets." In 1925, Pound contributed an essay on Dunning for *Poetry* magazine, which also published thirteen of Dunning's poems under the title "Four Winds."[27]

Dunning received Pound's financial assistance. Upon his moving to Italy, Pound requested Hemingway to deliver Dunning a jar of opium— its contents supposedly purchased from a Cherokee chief. Hemingway kept Pound informed about Dunning, who claimed that Pound pretended to be his friend and then stole all his money. Hemingway reported that one evening Dunning slept on the apartment roof until being called down by the concierge. On another occasion the concierge, attempting to calm a noisy Dunning, called upon Hemingway, who brought the little jar, but was chased away when the skeletally wasted Dunning threw milk bottles at him. Hemingway, unable to hold back his disgust, expressed to Pound his frank opinion: "Dunning, Cheever, is Shit!"[28]

CHAPTER 6

Ascendant Star, Poet Outlier

T.S. Eliot once referred to Pound as a "temporary squatter," having the "kind of resistance against growing into any environment." Not long before Pound left Paris, poet and publisher Alfred Kreymborg had the same impression. Kreymborg recalled that Pound "seemed ill at ease, even in Paris" and "that possibly Italy or Spain would call to him next." In the end, Kreymborg perceptively added, Pound was "a victim of the illusion of places, he turned on each town as the illusion wore away and betrayed the many spotted faults of a commonplace surface."[1]

After four years in Paris, Pound became a fixture of the Left Bank—his presence parodied in the *American Mercury* article "Aesthete: Model 1924." This contribution, by writer and translator Ernest Boyd, portrayed the typical dilettante of the arts—the young American in Paris who stayed on "a little longer ... to participate in the joys of the La Rotonde and Les Deux Magots. There for a brief spell he breathed the same air as the Dadaists, met Picasso and Phillip Soupault, and allowed Ezra Pound to convince him that the French nation was aware of the existence of Jean Cocteau, Paul Morand, Jean Giraudoux, and Louis Aragon."[2]

By this time, Pound had turned against Paris and its modern French writers much as he had turned on English society and art. The Pounds' domestic life in Paris was being disrupted as well; their apartment became a must-see for many aspiring writers and those wanting a cultural tour of Montparnasse. In July 1923, Ezra wrote to Dorothy, who was out of town at the time, complaining: "Flood of humanity sweeping over this place. Must stop it somehow." The increasing flood of Americans in Paris made for more interruptions that disturbed the couple's "privacy-loving tempera-ment," noted Ford Maddox Ford's mistress, Stella Bowen. "Being on the ground floor they were at the mercy of anyone who chose to stroll in or knock." Dorothy disliked Paris, notably its winter weather. Supposedly ill at the time of their move, Pound may have evaded packing up his belong-ings. In October, Hemingway wrote to Gertrude Stein, joking that Ezra had a "small nervous breakdown necessitating him spending two days at the Am. Hospital during the height of packing."[3]

In regard to his now-empty Parisian apartment, Pound wrote pub-lisher William Bird from Rapallo in November 1924: "If Hem don't want it, can yr. friends find 2000 fr. recompense for beds, cookstoves, electric wiring?" Pound also asked if he could leave his large Koumé painting there for the time being. "If they dislike it, they can put it face to the wall on gallery."[4]

After three months in Sicily, the Pounds moved permanently to Rapallo in 1925. Pound had visited Italy as a child in 1898, accompanied by his mother and Aunt Frank (Frances) Weston, touring Genoa, Como, Florence, Rome, Naples, and Venice. In Venice, he had published his first volume of poetry before taking up residence in London in 1908.

The Pounds had first visited Rapallo in 1922 and, during the next year, spent several weeks there. Rapallo landmarks included the Castle on the Sea, built in 1551, to ward off Ottoman attackers and Barbary pirates; the fifteenth-century Tower of the Fieschi; several churches; and the ruins of the thirteenth-century Monastery of Valle Chrisiti.

Rapallo had once been a wealthy tourist destination and a widely rec-ognized health resort. But the building of new railroad lines offered easy access to more fashionable resorts (all the main tramlines came through Rapallo). A late–1920s travel book described Rapallo and the Rivera coast as appealing to "moderate folk" and "people of small manners" as "emi-nently suitable for leisurely and unexciting, unexacting holidays or pro-longed residence." The author lauded the small town as having "all the resources of civilization and all seasons of the year maintains an air of well-brushed beauty" of nature—gardens and the sea, complemented by "beau-tiful houses" and several first-class hotels. "In a fairly quiet way," explained the author, "it is one of the most popular resorts in Europe, and in the win-ter and spring months all the nationalities are represented there."[5]

A frequent visitor to Rapallo who later took up residence there, William Butler Yeats described it as quiet place on "a motionless sea"—of "no great harbor full of yachts, no great yellow strand, no great ballroom, no great casino." Far from modern urban culture, Pound made his home, as Hugh Kenner informed, "in a salubrious overgrown village ... with mountains and sea and olive trees." To serve tourists and its British residents, Rapallo had an English church, a doctor, and a library.[6]

The Pounds eventually took a top-floor apartment in a five-story building. Guests were entertained at their building's ground-floor café, the Albergo Rapallo—what Pound referred to as the Albuggero. When the elevator failed not long after their moving in, the couple climbed one hundred steps to their new living quarters, comprising two sitting rooms, a dressing room, kitchen, and a bedroom facing the mountains. In his apartment, Pound constructed an elaborate filing system. "He had it well organized," remembered publisher James Laughlin, "he hung his glasses and extra glasses, his pencils, his pens, his scissors, and his stapler on strings from the ceiling over his desk." On his top-floor terrace Pound strode back and forth, ship- and bird-watching. "From the terrace, while Pound worked, he looked south over the sea," noted literary scholar Louis Simpson. "On the twenty-third of March the swallows would fly directly over on their way to two streams in the vicinity."[7]

Pound appeared on the street as a professor/poet, feeding Rapallo's stray cats by reaching into his pocket and throwing them food scraps and bones. As in London and Paris, Pound still had the proud stride of a dandy poet—his white sport shirt worn loosely and a floppy linen hat sheltered him from the sun. Known to locals as "Ill Poeta" or "Signor Poeta," he played at the nearby tennis club or swam out into the bay. Pound told Laughlin that he moved there for the swimming. He also spent time watching poorly produced Italian films, laughing with his feet up on the movie-house balcony. Pound's English friend Brigit Patmore recalled seeing him "sitting in a quiet café during the un-busy hours, playing chess with the waiters and in deep concentration."[8]

Having spent a decade in English salons and drawing rooms and subsequent years among Paris circles, Pound brought with him to Italy visions of the past, illusions of peace which became more delusional and seditious as he lashed out at world bankers and America's role in defeating fascism. Pound foresaw great things coming from his new home by the sea, noting that many a Renaissance city-state produced great art. While noting that great culture typically arises from major urban centers, Pound believed it could sprout in small communities like Rimini or in Mantua, if led by a determined individual effort. In expressing his admiration for Malatesta as Rimini's patron of the arts, Pound looked to Malatesta as a cultured man who wanted civilization in a small town. But as historian Jacob Burkhardt notes, "In general it may be said of the despotisms of fifteenth century, that the greatest crimes were most frequent in the smallest States."[9]

Italian Quattrocento literature, painting and sculpture inspired Pound's quest to make new art from history. From his earliest influences, especially Walter Pater and John Ruskin, Pound had been exposed to the Romanesque and early Renaissance art. In Italy, he lost himself in past epochs, often seeing the modern age through fifteenth-century eyes that naïvely elevated Mussolini to an exalted patron of the arts and economic reformer. As literary scholar Louis Simpson asserts, Pound tried to create in Italy "the audience that was denied him" and from his base in Rapallo attempted to "change the world so that people would read his poetry." But his isolation "made him ignorant of what was happening in the world, so that he backed Mussolini."[10]

Pound's Rapallo neighbors included other writers, like Thomas Mann and Nobel Prize recipient and playwright Gerhart Hauptmann, to whom Pound introduced the work of Yeats and Joyce. Another famed resident, English set designer, producer and actor Gordon Craig, Pound had met in London, and made such a favorable impression that he wrote of this brilliant Englishmen as "a great artist and very pleasant person."[11]

Pound sometimes lunched with his neighbor Max Beerbohm, mentioned in "Hugh Selwyn Mauberley" as "Brennbaum 'The Impeccable.'" But the famed caricaturist and writer thought him an odd specimen— something out the American wilderness. Beerbohm wrote a friend, observing that Pound seemed "out of place" in Rapallo, that he should return to "the primeval native forests of his native land." Beerbohm's biographer, Cecil, summed up his subject's view of Pound: "Max thought him crazy— fancy believing in Fascism!—and too obstreperous to be a comfortable companion." Pound's view of his neighbor did not reveal fondness either. Once while lunching with Beerbohm, Pound remembered a conversation as being dominated by his host's recalling members of his pre-war English circle. Still drawn to the romantic poets and to Swinburne and A.E. Housman and little interested in current literary innovations, Beerbohm did not share Pound's enthusiasm for Eliot, whose talents the elder writer looked upon with suspicion. As for Hemingway, Beerbohm later praised his work of his one-time guest, notably *Old Man and the Sea.*[12]

Away from Parisian crowds and circles, Pound sustained his Italian isolation by obsessive letter writing—personal greetings and stinging missives that praised Social Credit economics and Confucianism. Pound came to Social Credit in 1918 when he participated in discussions about monetary reform in the London offices of the *New Age*. There, *New Age* editor A.R. Orage introduced Pound to Charles H. Douglas, who espoused the tenets of underconsumptionist economics that would soon form his theory of Social Credit. Untrained in economics, Douglas, an industrial engineer, formulated the basis of Social Credit while working for the Royal Aircraft Works and examining the factory's accounting and financial reports. Douglas's Social Credit theory principally stated that "aggregate payments to individuals in wages, salaries, and dividends, (A) plus aggregate costs of materials, bank charges, royalties, and taxes (B) produce aggregate price (P). Obviously P will always be larger than A, since it must include B. The theorem shows that in the income of all citizens (the A figure) will be insufficiently large to buy the produce of a nation—a classic underconsumptionist argument."[13]

With all its faults, notably recognized by such eminent economists as John Maynard Keynes, Social Credit was enthusiastically embraced by Pound with a fervor that seemed to equal his interest in art. Based upon Social Credit and stamp-script theory, Pound conceived of economics and the state largely by simplistic argument and intuitive search, while thinking he was spreading the light of truth. He came to economics as a poet and mystic interested in science, seeing possibilities in reforming monarchies, democracies, even fascist Italy. As Pound scholar Leon Surette explains: "The political appeal of Social Credit was that it promised a resolution of the endemic problems of capitalism—notably the business cycle and maldistribution of wealth—without any significant alteration of prevailing social and political structures." Thus, Social Credit was an adaptable economic solution that could be embraced by fascist Italy as well as a democratic capitalist country like the United States.[14]

But Pound's literary genius did not aid him in the understanding of economics. Yet in its simplicity—over-simplification—he thought Social Credit would be easily understood and practicable in implementation. Pound believed that his writings would bring whole nations and entire economies to embrace the cure-all of Social Credit. While Lenin interested Pound as a dynamic leader for a time, Pound opposed violent revolution because the ills of the state could be corrected by the distribution of currency.

For Pound, Social Credit would free artists from mundane work and allow them to pursue full-time creative work. Pound wrote in the *Criterion*: "C.H. Douglas is the first economist to include creative art and writing in an economic scheme, and the first to give the painter or sculptor or poet a definite reason for being interested in economics; namely, that a better economic system would release more energy for invention and design." Richard Humphreys observes that the poet "used Douglas's ideas to criticize contemporary Western culture, to place the artist and economic context, and to develop a means by which to judge the comparative 'health' of any art's epoch. For example, he saw the art of the Quattrocento in Italy, which he characterised as linear and 'clean,' as the product of a relatively non-usurious period: whereas the Seicento, with its baroque *sfmato* and 'fleshiness,' was the typical expression of a corrupt and commlercialised culture."[15]

Pound encountered ideas and figures out of the past that aroused his passion and suited his temperament. Intuition, myth, and symbol, crucial to poetry—were not sound principles for the understanding of economics. As Wendy Stallord Flory observes in *The American Pound*, "The very ideogramic approach which had allowed him in his poetry to set up complex interrelations of echoes and resonances in a way that deepened and amplified the significance of the whole was now being used with the opposite effect."[16]

Pound struggled to spread his own variation of Social Credit. When encountering those unsympathetic or dismissive of it, he resorted to verbal viciousness that condemned both friends and supposedly blind politicians, leaders of the mindless herd. If Jacob Burckhardt spoke the Renaissance conception of "the state as a work of art," Pound was an artist determined to shape the economics and politics of the state.

But as a result, notes Leon Surette: Ezra "only sunk further and further into contradiction, confusion, and incoherence. Unable to admit his own confusion, which others made manifest to him, he grew more and more shrill. At the same time, international tensions rose, making it necessary to chose sides." Unfortunately, as Pound crusaded for Social Credit and promoted younger writers, he largely neglected his art.[17]

Meanwhile, Hemingway saw Pound slip into obscurity as literary prizes were being awarded to T.S. Eliot and others. But Pound cared little for literary prizes and asserted in *Poetry* magazine his "contempt for such enterprises"—that the "whole system of prize-giving," he thought "smacks of high school, is better than nothing." Recognition was one thing. What mattered most was being accepted by the vanguard literary community.[18]

Hemingway, nonetheless, wanted his friend to be justly rewarded. In his poem "Soul of Spain with McAlmon and Bird the Publishers," Hemingway came to the poet's defense. "The Soul of Spain" appeared in the German little magazine *Der Querschnitt* through the connections of Pound's composer friend, George Antheil. In this poem, published in 1924, Hemingway voiced his contempt for Scofield Thayer's "Monument to Proust" that appeared in the *Dial*. In "Soul of Spain," Hemingway wrote: "They say Ezra is the shit/But Ezra is nice/Come let us build a monument to Ezra."[19]

Thayer's urging monuments for Proust fueled Hemingway's contempt. It was not until the efforts of *Dial* editor Marianne Moore that Pound received the magazine's annual ward until 1927. But as long as Thayer was editor, no such award or praise of his work could be expected. Thayer thought Pound an artsy eccentric, and the poet dismissed the former as a dilettante of the *Dial*'s Harvard clique. Thayer referred to Pound's ongoing translation in the *Dial* of Remy de Gourmont's *Dust for Sparrows* as "shit for sparrows"—a slight that most likely got back to Pound.

If Pound's literary stock appeared to be dwindling, Hemingway's was on the rise. In October 1925, Boni and Liveright published *In Our Time* (now changed to upper case). The book's fourteen stories included material from Bill Bird's Three Mountain edition, along with several new short works. Boni and Liveright's 1925 fall catalogue listed Hemingway's *In Our Time* on page twenty-five. After praising the young writer as "a man who has become an authentic and important figure on the literary horizon," the catalogue listed Pound among other literary lights who recognized his shining talent.

In Our Time received largely favorable reviews in prominent and popular publications, such as *Time*. Hemingway was outraged at critics who praised the book while crediting his literary achievement to Anderson and Stein's influence. To distance himself from these two former mentors, Hemingway wrote *The Torrents of Spring* in an inspirational rush between November 23 and December 2, 1925. This 28,000-word satire—inspired by Henry Fielding's *Joseph Andrews* and taking its title from Turgenev's 1871 romance novel (1871)—principally targeted Anderson and Gertrude Stein, while mocking the awkward use of the narrative flashback. Set in Northern Michigan's Little Traverse Bay region, *Torrents* interweaves the tale of two men, World War I veteran Yogi Johnson and Scripps O'Neal, and two Petoskey waitresses. Johnson, a war veteran who had briefly visited Paris, sarcastically talks of Gertrude Stein and quips that "Scofield Thayer was my best man.... I'm a Harvard man." In this brief reference, Hemingway once more took a crack at *The Dial*'s editor and his circle. As for another magazine editor who had rejected his work, Hemingway mentioned H.L. Mencken of the *American Mercury* as courting O'Neal to publish in his magazine. But O'Neal thought it "not a pretty prospect to face."[20]

What may have also intensified Hemingway's contempt for Mencken is that, in August, just a few months before he wrote *Torrents*, the *American Mercury* had belatedly published a negative blurb about his Parisian-published *in our time* (1924). In a voice sounding much like Mencken, the *Mercury* observed: "The short brave, bold stuff that all atheistic young newspaper reporters write. Jesus Christ in lower case. A hanging, a carnal love, and two disembowelings. Here is set forth solemnly on Rives hand-made paper ... with the imprimatur of Ezra Pound."[21]

Hemingway's turning to satire also provided a means to break his publishing contract with Boni and Liveright. Astute in his business and legal dealings with Boni and Liveright, Hemingway brought up his three-book option. According to the contract, if the firm rejected his second book after sixty days following the manuscript submission, the contract would lapse. Because Boni and Liveright had expected the second book to be Hemingway's anticipated novel—not a satire—it put them in a difficult situation, as *Torrents* primarily targeted *Dark Laughter* by Sherwood Anderson, one of Boni and Liveright's most lauded authors. Hemingway also complained that the publishing house had not adequately promoted *In Our Time*; thus, he demanded a $500 advance to assure that his second book would find wider recognition.

Boni & Liveright's refusal to publish *Torrents* ended its contract with Hemingway. Promoted by Scribner's new star, F. Scott Fitzgerald, Hemingway ignored the expressed interest of Knopf and Harcourt to sign with Scribner's Sons, which, under its editor Max Perkins, remained his perennial publisher. Fitzgerald's role in helping Hemingway sign with Scribner's is well known. It is important to point out that when Fitzgerald initially talked up Hemingway to Perkins, he mentioned Pound's association with this relatively unknown writer. Writing to Perkins in October 1924, Fitzgerald stated: "This is to tell you about a young man Ernest Hemingway, who lives in Paris, [an American] writes for the transatlantic Review + has a brilliant future. Ezra Pount [sic] published a collection of short stories in Paris, some place like the Egoist Press. I haven't it hear now but its remarkable + I'd look him up right away. He's the real thing." Though this letter contains factual errors, it emphasized the role of Pound in Hemingway's rise among writers in Paris.[22]

In November 1925, Hemingway wrote Pound that *Torrents* was a "funny little book," most likely "unprintable," yet intended to "destroy Anderson and various others." He informed Pound that his book would show up all the "fakes" in current literature and that he would send along a typed carbon copy. In a moment of misjudgment, Pound thought the book better than Hemingway's short stories, including "My Old Man" or "The Undefeated." Not among those Hemingway mocked, Pound could have a laugh at the Northern Michigan rubes and the literary figures and styles parodied in the book. A few years later, when writing a program to be distributed in independent magazines, Pound urged more satiric works like it. "We need several more novels in the vein of Hemingway's *Torrents of Spring*," wrote Pound, "dealing not with helpless rural morons but with 'our rulers' and 'the representatives of the people.'"[23]

Many of Hemingway's friends considered his satire mean-spirited. Hemingway's Canadian friend Morley Callaghan certainly thought so. "It was a painful experience," he wrote. "How torn I was in loyalties.... Anderson's style, God knows, had become affected. Certainly he was vulnerable to mockery and satire, but the mockery shouldn't have come from Hemingway." In the end, Callaghan asked: "Didn't friendship count?" Aware of Hemingway and Pound's friendship, Callaghan posed a vital question, one that revealed the many broken bonds and betrayals in the literary world.[24]

Hemingway insisted that *Torrents* was parody, therefore supposedly not hurtful to those it targeted. This was lost on Anderson, whose recent praise on the dust jacket of *In Our Time* stated: "Mr. Hemingway is young, strong, full of laughter, and he can write. His people flash suddenly up into those odd and elusive moments of glowing reality, the clear putting down of which has always made good writing so good." Anderson found his friend now having a laugh at his expense. In answer to Hemingway's letter that contained a weak apology for *Torrents* while explaining the need to make its author aware of his recent literary decline, Anderson spoke out: "Damn it, man, you are so final—so patronizing. You always speak to me like a master to a pupil. It must be Paris—the literary life. You didn't seem like that when I knew you." Anderson hinted at one of the sources of this Parisian conversion. "You speak so regretfully, tenderly, of giving a punch. You sound like Uncle Ezra [Pound]. Come out of it, man. I pack a little wallop myself. I've been middleweight champion. You seem to forget that."[25]

Around this time, Hemingway, incensed at Stein's not offering to review *In Our Time*, angrily informed Pound, by letter, that he believed she would not promote him in print until he published a novel. Pound had earlier turned down Hemingway's suggestion that he review the book with the excuse that he had stopped writing prose at the time. In his letter to Pound, Hemingway excoriated the "safe-playing kikes" who failed to promote him as well, then poured his venom on Stein, whom he believed had little or no confidence in his writing a novel—that she would regret writing a favorable review of *In Our Time* if his novel indeed turned out to be a failure. This angry response is typical of Hemingway, who seemingly (or conveniently) forgot that Stein had reviewed *Three Stories and Ten Poems*. Over time, what he said about Stein in private would become more public and vicious.[26]

Hemingway's growing animus towards Stein only seemed to strengthen his loyalty to Pound. When Ernest Walsh and Ethel Moorhead founded *This Quarter* in 1925, they dedicated an issue to Pound that featured Hemingway's "Homage to Ezra." A man who hated critics—"the eunuchs of literature," at least those who did not like his work—Hemingway avoided a critical analysis of Pound's art and instead approached his essay as "an appreciation" of a great living poet—ignored, underappreciated, and, in some cases, hated. Playing upon the "a good poet is a dead poet" theme, Hemingway reminded his readers that Pound was no martyr; that he pursued his art in relative poverty, nobly, and with pride. Avoiding a mention of many of Pound's negative attributes, Hemingway also assured his readers that his subject "takes no interest in Italian politics."[27]

If judged by Hemingway's tribute it would appear that Pound had nothing to do with right-wing Italian politics. Privately, Hemingway considered his friend's support of fascism as the unfortunate leanings of a politically naïve poet who thought Italy best suited for a simple lifestyle and artistic inspiration. Hemingway, on the other hand, had conflicting feelings about a country that he once considered living in after World War I. Hemingway, tired of Pound's laudatory letters about Mussolini's Italy, finally stated in a 1926 letter: "[W]hat makes you think that a gent can't be au courant abt. the state of affairs in that unforchnit country when everyone who knows or cares anything abt. same is expelled into France where they arrive fresh all the time with the DOPE. Not to mention the agents of the govt., itself—Chief of Police of Rome—Ricciotti and Co.... . Only don't you ever call me on Dago politics. Yes, I know the lire is stabilized and all about the improvements in the TRAIN SERVICE."[28]

Pound's praise of fascist Italy emerged when he became convinced that American democracy was becoming outmoded. It did not bother Pound that, after 1924, Mussolini placed the press under censorship, ended universal suffrage, decimated labor unions, and abolished all but the Fascist party. Hemingway's reference to the chief of police in Rome had to do with Mussolini establishing a secret police and tribunals to deal with opponents.

With the tightening of Mussolini's dictatorship, Hemingway despised him even more. A fierce individualist, Hemingway compared a good writer to a Gypsy who "owes no allegiance to the state" and "never likes the government he lives under." As early as 1922 he asserted in *The Toronto Star* that he was not "anti-any nationality" of any sort and not "pro–Bolshevik, pro–Irish, pro–Italian." As much as Pound and Hemingway tried to avoid politics in their friendship, world events pulled them into causes that influenced or, in Pound's case, radically transformed their life and art.[29]

CHAPTER 7

Fame and World Crisis

After nearly two years of living on the Notre Dame de Champs, Hemingway left behind the street where he had met Pound, his former neighbor. In early August 1926, he and Hadley returned to Paris from Antibes, knowing their marriage was over. Hadley came to the realization that Ernest had a new lover, Pauline Pfeiffer, soon to be his second wife. Hadley stayed with Bumby in a hotel, while Ernest moved into the studio of his friend Gerald Murphy. Ernest emptied their apartment and, by wheelbarrow, made several trips carrying away their belongings, including Miró's *The Farm*.

If briefly humbled or penanced by this labor, Hemingway knew well what awaited him—a new lover and the publication of his novel *The Sun Also Rises*. When the book debuted in 1926 it made him a literary celebrity and transformed the Parisian Left Bank into an American tourist destination. An American writer among the Parisian Dadaists, Matthew Josephson later noted that *The Sun Also Rises* brought floods of Americans "from the East, the West, and the Main Streets of the midlands—all evidently filled with the resolve to become full-fledged members of the Lost Generation that the novel so provocatively invoked."[1]

In anticipation of Hemingway's forthcoming novel, Pound wrote his father from Italy in November 1926, "Mr. Hemingway said to have bagged large contract with Scribner, and his friends all gloomily praying for his soul and the remains of his wits." Though Pound would be mentioned in several of Hemingway's later books, he is spared mention in *The Sun Also Rises*. Others of the Montparnasse community are represented in the book's first eighty-five pages as thinly veiled characters, often in unflattering portraits as in the case of Ford Maddox Ford, Harold Loeb, and Harold

Strearns. Never one to forget a slight or rejection, Hemingway also found opportunity to take a stab at H.L. Mencken. In the novel Jake Barnes comments how Mencken influenced the "likes and dislikes" of scores of young Americans.[2]

Though Pound had little or no direct influence on the writing or editing of *The Sun Also Rises*—that job went to Fitzgerald, who suggested toning down some of Jake Barnes's wise-guy talk and omitting the first sixteen pages—he remained a valuable literary advisor, but one with whom Hemingway did not always agree. Upon finishing *The Sun Also Rises*, Hemingway informed Pound that he would follow it up with a short-story collection. Pound responded firmly: "Now, mong cher ami. You will do no such GOD DAMD thing. You will publish ANOTHER NOVEL next, and *after* that, and NOT UNTIL AFTER THAT you will make them pub. The sht. stories. Wotter yer think yer are, a bloomink DILLY-tanty?????"[3]

Hemingway ignored this advice and pursued the writing of shorter works that would be collected in his next book, *Men Without Women* (1927). One of the book's short stories, "An Alpine Idyll," he had sent in manuscript form to Pound, who, with his discerning eye, suggested cutting the beginning. In December 1926, he informed Hemingway that he thought the story good, but "a leetle too litterary and Tennysonian." Pound lectured: "[K]eep your "eye on the objek MORE during the introductory pages.... ANYTHING put on top of the subject is BAD. Licherchure is mostly blanketing up a subject. Too much MAKINGS. The subject is always interesting enough without the blankets." But when "An Alpine Idyll" was published, it appeared without Pound's suggested emendations.[4]

Before *Men Without Women* appeared, Hemingway vented to Pound in January 1927 that if Scribner's did not publish his short story "Up in Michigan" with "the fucking in it ... I won't publish book at all." Despite this private demand, the book did not include "Up in Michigan"; once again, as Stein had warned, this particular story never seemed destined for a mainstream publishing house. That same month, Pound asserted, in boxing-ring vernacular, the importance of short, emphatic sentences: "I think you are more intelligent than this mss.," and added, "HELL, I want stuufffff that'll END discussion. I want to say: me frien Hem, kin knock yew over the ropes; and then I want to see the punch delivered. I don't want t gentle embraces in the middle of the ring."[5]

Published in October 1927, *Men Without Women* included the story "Che Ti Dice La Patria?" Originally a *New Republic* travel article, this fictional version was intended as a reply to Mussolini's bold claim of restoring order and efficiency in Italy. The article (and its subsequent short-story version) were based upon an eleven-day trip to Italy that Hemingway made with his friend Guy Hickok. Responding to a letter in which Hemingway suggested his visiting Rapallo, Pound expressed his delight "to receive you and Le Sieur Hickok on you[r] prox. visit to the Kingdom of Italy." In Hickok's old Ford coupe they traveled from Ventimiglia, south to Genoa. On March 18, they dined with Ezra and Dorothy in Rapallo. During their time together, Hemingway brought up—as he had when visiting Pound with Hadley several years earlier—the possibility of the fascists forcing them to drink castor oil. Pound assured him that tourists were exempt from such treatment. On the road once more, Hemingway sent his old friend a postcard from Rimini: "Gave your card to Sigismundo [Malatesta] and the Elephant," a humorous reference to their 1923 walking tour.[6]

Hemingway's taunts and side remarks about Mussolini seemed not to bother Pound, who stood firm in his admiration for the Italian leader. "I personally think extremely well of Mussolini," Pound wrote Harriet Monroe. "If one compares him to American presidents (the last three) or British premiers, etc., in fact one can NOT without insulting him. If the intelligentsia don't think well of him, it is because they know nothing about the "state" and government, and have no particularly large sense of values." Pound pointed his friends toward the virtues of Mussolini as a sage trying to instill wisdom in a resistant youth. In time, perhaps Hemingway would come to see Il Duce's greatness.[7]

By 1927, Pound took up with fervor the teachings of Confucius and melded its teachings with his admiration for strong leaders, men of action and patrons of the arts. That year he translated the Confucian classic, *Ta Hio*, from a French-language edition. Pound's embracing Confucius has puzzled many scholars, in that, as Pound biographer Humphrey Carpenter points out, Confucius "teaches that a man can only master others when he has mastered himself, and that he must aim for moderation in all things, learning to consider his motives before taking action." Pound's underlying conflicts and contradictions—an aversion to Christianity and communism, hatred of banks and bureaucracies—found justification in Confucianism.[8]

Pound's growing role of poet/economist distanced him from friends. Hemingway longed for him to compose new verse instead of spending most of his time writing didactic letters, manifestos, Social Credit questionnaires—all preaching a deluded vision of world events. During the late 1920s, William Butler Yeats warned Pound about the futility of a poet venturing into economics and politics: "Neither you nor I, nor any of our excited profession, can match those old lawyers, old bankers, old bankers, old business men, who, because all habit and memory, have begun to govern the world." Poets involved in such matters, added Yeats, would find themselves "as much out of place as would be the first composers of sea-shanties in an age of steam."[9]

Visited in Rapallo by Pound's friend Brigit Patmore, Yeats expressed his despair over his poet neighbor's pro-fascist leanings. At a hotel dinner with Patmore, Yeats hung his head and then proceeded to ask, "'How do you account for Ezra?'" Silence pervaded until Yeats confided, "'Here we have in him one of the finest poets of our time, some erudition and high intelligence and yet he is so—amazingly clumsy—so tactless and does what one might call outrageous things.'"[10]

An admirer of Yeats's poetry, Hemingway had come to the same conclusions about Pound. In February 1927, Poet Archibald McLeish wrote to Hemingway that he was a "bit fed up with the Ezriac assumption that he is a Great Man." Hemingway agreed and later responded to McLeish that Pound, acting the "ass," "makes a bloody fool of himself 99 times out of 100 when he writes anything but poetry."[11]

Hemingway looked on as Pound campaigned against the breach of copyright laws. For decades Pound had decried the loose enforcement of copyright laws. A self-proclaimed man of action, Pound urged James Joyce to battle against the piracy of *Ulysses* in the United States. When an American magazine publisher, Samuel Roth, pirated nearly half of *Ulysses*, Pound refused to sign a mass petition on Joyce's behalf, and instead urged the Irishman take up the cause himself in a general campaign against breach of copyright. Hemingway advised Joyce against this tactic and dismissed Pound's project as "moonshine."[12]

Hemingway did agree to contribute to Pound's new magazine, *Exile*, a forum for economics and art which he edited and Dorothy financially managed. *Exile* lasted four issues, ending with a fall installment that included McAlmon's cutting piece on Gertrude Stein. In the magazine's first issue (spring 1927) Pound announced: "Exile will appear three times per annum until I get bored with producing it. It will contain matters of interest to me personally, and is unlikely to appeal to any save those disgusted with the state of letters in England, and ironically amused by a standard of criticism designed chiefly to protect vested interest in electroplates."

Taking note of *Exile*'s first issue, the *Paris Tribune* announced: "The first number contains several selections the quality of which may be taken for granted by the prospective publisher who is acquainted with Mr. Pound's judgment. The editor himself, Ernest Hemingway, John Rodker and Guy Hickok are among those represented. The magazine is for sale at the Titus bookshop, just back of the Dome, for ten cents a copy." *Exile* "featured articles on politics and commerce, with a strongly anti–American bias, and supplementary pieces on Prohibition and sex."[13]

To attract contributors, Pound had sent letters to possible contributors. He wrote Hemingway in 1926: "If you feel like writing the life of Calidge Colvin or doing some other IMPRACTIcable or unpractical half sheet of verse, like the Peace Conference; don't sqush the impulse jess cause there aint no where to go." Hemingway's contribution to *Exile*'s first number was "Neo-Thomist Poem," misprinted as "Nothoemist Poem." This two-stanza work simply read: "The Lord is my Shepard/I shall not want him for long." "Mr. Hemingway's POEM," asserted Pound in his editorial, "refers to events in what remains of the French world of letters," a country that he had turned against just as he had England. Other misprints in *Exile*'s first issue, included Hemingway being listed as "E.W. Hemingway." Before his magazine's publication, Pound alerted Ernest about the poem's title: "The error does NOT occur in proofs. I suppose some G.D. NEOcroyant in the print shop had been abaht his MASTER'z bizniz. Holding proofs here to prove it teh yuh, w'en youse kums."[14]

If Hemingway's "Neo-Thomist Poem" in *Exile* seems blasphemous, the author's private beliefs were much more complex. Hemingway, the non-joiner distrustful of bureaucracies and big government, came to religion as a doubting soul in need of solace. Raised in his mother's Congregational Church and fondly remembering the prayers of his Episcopalian grandfather, Hemingway ultimately rebelled against his mother and non-drinking and non-dancing Baptist father. In search of a non–Protestant faith, Hemingway, unlike Pound—who embraced ancient myth, medieval love cults, and Confucianism-became a reluctant monotheist.

Like many artists of the modern age, Hemingway was never able to bring himself to embrace a belief requiring strict ritual observances. Yet Hemingway often saw himself having a priest-like calling. As he told Canadian journalist Morley Callaghan: "A writer is like a priest. He has to have the same feeling about his work." Often considered a nihilist or a naturalist, Hemingway—neither entirely godless or rejecting all traditional values or objective truths—was a defiant modernist in search of truth beneath the façades, the empty slogans, and hypocrisy that paraded as moral and righteous.[15]

Seeing himself in the no-man's land between religious belief and passion for art, Hemingway inherited the early modernist sensibility of what Frederick Karl terms "the spiritual autobiography." For most of the nineteenth century, explains Karl, the novel "was based on individual and society, with the assumption that a mature individual will be a social asset, finds its focus shifting, from individual and social well-being to matters of spirit, soul, self." Hemingway, embracing this, created protagonists that Karl describes as the author's "shadow figures" existing as his un-redemptive literary creations not having to answer to any social unit. Hemingway's portrayal of characters as they existed—or might exist—on streets, battlefronts, and bullrings shocked his parents, who saw no virtue in their son's stories and books.[16]

In the end, Hemingway's parents' religion could not be his religion, any more than Pound was to remain a follower of his parents' Presbyterianism or his grandfather Thaddeus's Quakerism. If Hemingway would have religion at all, it would be the Catholicism of his adopted Spain and Italy.

A fleeting interest in the Roman Catholic Church became more serious when Hemingway married his second wife, Pauline Pfeiffer, in a Catholic ceremony on May 27, 1927. After his divorce from Pauline in 1940, he remained a closet Catholic, sometimes visiting cathedrals or privately confiding that he was a "non-practicing Catholic." In *The Sun Also Rises* Jake Barnes mirrors Hemingway's own ambivalence towards Catholicism. In Pamplona for the bullfights, Jake takes time out to enter a cathedral, where he kneels and prays for friends and bull fighters, while his mind wanders with thoughts of making money and his longing for Brett Ashley. Suddenly aware that he is praying, Jake admonishes himself, ashamed that he is "such a rotten Catholic," and hoping he would ultimately experience the grace of such "a grand religion."[17]

In March 1928, Hemingway began *A Farewell to Arms*, his second novel rife with religious imagery. Its main character, Frederick Henry, has deep respect for his friend, the priest, while he spends wartime leave in bars and brothels. When the priest asks about Henry's belief in God, he responds of his being "afraid of him at night sometimes." When the priest asserts that Henry "should love him," his American friend confesses, "I don't love much."[18]

Conversely, Pound, the polytheist, was the enemy of Abrahamic monotheism. Pound insisted: "The principle of evil consists in messing into other people's lives. Against this principle of evil no adequate precaution is taken by Christianity, Moslemism, Judaism, so far as I know, by monotheistic religion." For Pound each branch of Christianity equally sought to control its followers. In 1910, Pound wrote his mother that "most of the so-called 'Christian sects" ought to be sued for breach of copy-right." In *Jefferson/and or Mussolini*, he recalled telling a nun about his preference for paganism: "I wasn't a Protestant, but wasn't a Catholic either, I wasn't a Jew, I believed in a more ancient and classical system with a place for Zeus and Apollo."[19]

Pound's interest in Catholicism was his belief that it arose directly from pagan sources, that it had no roots in Judaism. Thus, he could appreciate many of its artistic achievements, notably Renaissance cathedral architecture, through a historical lens that saw a linkage of its supposed pagan rites rooted in Greek Eleusinian myth and leading up to the troubadour love cults. Prone to pick and choose elements to fit his aesthetic and spiritual beliefs, Pound had no problem bringing together disparate elements to form his own religio-world. At the time of his meeting Hemingway in 1922, Pound expressed that his gods were Ovid and Confucius.

CHAPTER 8

Friends on Different Shores

Writers who tired of major cities and their distractions, Hemingway and Pound lived during the 1930s in places where they could work, relax, and mix with the locals and receive visitors as they saw fit. Neither was attracted to New York City, where they stayed briefly, visiting friends and conducting business. Their 1920s experience began in Paris and ended in their retreating to out-of-the-way seaside towns where a modest income allowed them to live simply.

Many Americans shared Pound's reverence for Mussolini as they visited Italy during the mid–1920s. Novelist Louis Bromfield, writing about expatriates in 1927, reported, "Rome is almost clean and if Mussolini succeeds in evading bullets long enough he will, in his energetic American way, perhaps make certain quarters smell less like a garbage can from which the lid had just been lifted." This positive response was shared by another novelist and journalist, who stated, "Italy drew more Americans last year [in 1926] than it has for many years, and one reason is Mussolini. This compelling personality has aroused a great deal of interest in America and last year many Americans went to Italy as much to see how the Mussolini government was working as to see the Coliseum at moonlight."[1]

But in what appeared to be Italy's rise in prosperity did not help Pound, who wrote Hemingway in 1928 alluding to his near-poverty in Rapallo, humorously asking if it might be lucrative for him to write American political-campaign songs.

Riding high on newfound fame in 1928, Hemingway received shocking news that his father, Clarence, had committed suicide by a pistol shot at the family home in Oak Park. Long at odds with his father for his lengthy absences during his teenage years and the perception that Clarence had become weak in standing up to a domineering wife, Ernest nevertheless felt the loss of the man he admired in his early youth. His mother, on the other hand, a high-strung neurotic personality expecting her children to fulfill upper-middle-class expectations, saw Ernest come of age as a rebellious youth, unwilling to attend college and venturing into journalism, then into a literary art that shocked her Victorian sensibilities. So heated was Ernest's attitude toward his mother he often referred to her as "that bitch."

Unlike Hemingway, Pound enjoyed a relatively amiable relationship with his parents, to whom he wrote almost daily. Presbyterians without rigid religious observances, the Pounds, especially Homer, read, took interest in, and tried to understand their son's art. After Homer retired from the Philadelphia Mint, he and his wife came to live in Rapallo in 1929. It had been fourteen years since they had seen their son. Unlike Hemingway's parents, who thought his work full of unseemly, if not immoral, people and crude dialogue, Homer Pound proudly followed Ezra's career and even became—under his son's influence—a faithful follower of Social Credit. Pound's mother maintained a more distant relationship, hoping that Ezra would have taken a path into Ivy League academia and finding respectability like his distant relative Henry Wadsworth Longfellow, a poet Ezra never liked or mentioned.

Before the Pounds took up residence in Rapallo, Ezra wrote his father, "Hemingway has a faculty for doing all sorts of stuff." This faith in Hemingway's talent came at a time when Pound's own place in the literary world seemed to be dimming, as many writers considered him a fading figure still fighting the good fight, drawing upon European and Chinese verse of past epochs. As Daniel Aaron asserts, "Expatriates and former expatriates no longer sympathized quite so unqualifiedly with Pound's obstinate clinging 'to an obsolete political idealism' or felt the same nostalgia for the 'romantic-looking backwards to medievalism' that informed" *The Cantos*. Hemingway's friend John Dos Passos had praised Pound's earlier poetry, but considered his later work as "full of romance and ingrown literature."[2]

While living in Paris during the 1920s, Matthew Josephson avoided contact with Pound because it seemed that the poet was living "in a world of his own illusions, formed by books he was reading in Provençal, Italian, or Chinese; *The Cantos* themselves were in part a pastiche of his bookish borrowings, and divorced from the realities of this world." In his 1928 "Open Letter to Ezra Pound" in *transition*, Josephson recognized Pound's importance as a poet and mentor but complained that "his idea of poetic function was still that of the 1890 decadents." More important to Josephson is that Pound seemed to have become lost under a regime that was trying to resurrect the Roman Empire in the age of tanks and machine guns. "He was striking attitudes," continued Josephson, "making words play with each other. Yet time was passing, and it seemed vain for the exiles to linger in a Europe still ruled by old doctrines and national hatreds that had brought her to disaster many times before."[3]

Edmund Wilson, in his seminal work, *Axle's Castle* (1931), also recognized Pound's marginalization as resulting from his work being "particularly sunk by a cargo of erudition." But Wilson also observed: "[A]t the present time that Eliot is being praised too extravagantly and Pound, though he has deeply influenced a few, on the whole unfairly neglected."[4]

Surveying the American expatriate scene in 1931, writer Samuel Putman noted that Pound still had a following among American college students. Yet he reported that "his interest shows signs of abating and there is evidence of an anti–Pound reaction." From "the sun-drenched terraces" of Pound's adopted Rapallo, Putman noted that the poet wrote constantly to friends and American politicians. Though Pound had cut himself off from the centers of culture, Putman did credit him with "moving away from the vague aestheticisms and the vaguer revolts of the after–War era.... One thing he has learned from all the groupings, the strivings and questings of the past ten years, and that is the infinite superiority of life to literature, of life to art. On the side of art, which henceforth is to be life's servant, he is coming into a new subjectivity."[5]

But many of Pound's new paths were leading him to crackpot economics, enthusiasm for Italian fascism, and virulent anti–Semitism. Testament to Pound's allegiance to Mussolini, he began in 1931 to address letters by the fascist calendar—ANNO 9, marking the years since the 1922 Fascist March on Rome. Upon receiving letters with this date, Hemingway must have fumed, considering it as evidence that his friend had blindly embraced the government led by a man he considered the "Biggest Bluff" in Europe.

As Pound fell into obscurity, magazines thrived on covering Hemingway's pastimes and personal misfortunes. When Hemingway stumbled into his Paris apartment bathroom late at night and pulled what he thought was a flush chain to his apartment's toilet, he instead yanked the dangling cord attached to a dilapidated skylight that crashed down upon him, causing a deep gash on his forehead. Reading of this incident, Pound wrote Hemingway, on March 11, 1928, in American hick vernacular: "How the hellsufferin tomcats did you git drunk enough to fall upwards thru the blithering skylight?"[6]

While Hemingway enjoyed fame, he sought to live a relatively secluded life and in out-of-the way places, where he could invite friends. In April 1928, the Hemingways first visited Key West, Florida. Nine miles square, this slow-paced backwater had a population 10,000, made up of white locals, or conchs, black Bahamians and Cubans. The tallest building, the seven-story Colonial Hotel, towered over the island's tile-roofed buildings. From the cafes came the aroma of Cuban coffee, and midday shops closed for siesta.

In 1931, Pauline's money, provided by her uncle Gus, went to purchase the Hemingways' Key West home on Whitehead Street. Built by a naval officer in 1851, the two-story Spanish-style colonial house had fallen into disrepair, and Pauline set out to oversee the remodeling. Flat-roofed and surrounded on three sides by double iron-grilled porches, the Hemingway house had arched windows fitted with yellow shutters. This residence, one of the island's oldest, contrasted Key West's typical one-and-a-half-story structures, few of them painted.

No matter how remote his place of residence or choice for recreation, Hemingway could not escape making headlines. He made news in November 1930, when, during a Montana hunting trip, he drove his Ford roadster to Billings, accompanied by John Dos Passos and another friend. Blinded by oncoming headlights, Hemingway lost control of the car, which veered off the road and flipped over, resulting in his being hospitalized. Returning to Key West in January 1931, he wrote Pound, detailing his injuries: a broken right arm and three fingers. Hemingway mentioned the possibility of visiting Pound but said it would not be in Italy, because he could not countenance the fascist regime. In an attached note, Hemingway offered kind words to Dorothy and went on to assure Pound: "If there were any justice in this world you'd a got the Nobel Prize. You'll get it yet." Over the next decades Hemingway repeatedly stated this position, until symbolically offering Pound his own Nobel Prize in 1954.[7]

As Pound's admiration for Mussolini grew, Hemingway's disdain for fascist Italy intensified, especially when the regime banned his books. During 1932, Samuel Putman (editor of *The New Review*), with an interest in modern Italian writing, assembled an international jury to select the three best American and Italian books of the year. His jury included William Faulkner and Hemingway. With the announcement of Hemingway on the jury, the *Giornale di Genova* printed a column with examples of Hemingway's writing believed to be anti–Italian. Reaction to Hemingway among

Italians was so bitter and controversial that Putman removed him from the jury. In reviewing this event in the *Paris Tribune*, Waverly Lewis Root wrote, "Italy intolerantly rises in wrath against Hemingway, missing the basic understanding and of friendliness for the Italian character."[8]

In January 1933, Pound had a brief private meeting in Rome with Mussolini. Handed a book of Pound's poems, Mussolini commented "*divertente*"—entertaining. Pound came away convinced the Italian leader had recognized the greatness of his poetry. Pound's biographer Noel Stock observed of this meeting: "Pound seems to have taken this as a serious comment indicating that in a flash the statesman had seen through to the heart of the matter—the liveliness and strong flavour of the work—which was at once a proof of Mussolini's brilliance and of the fact that the cantos were meat for strong men and men of affairs." This would the first and last time Pound had a private audience with Ill Duce.[9]

Whenever the opportunity arose, Hemingway saw himself in the reverse role of a younger writer helping an old poet patron. Several weeks before Pound met Mussolini, Hemingway wrote to his poet friend in Rapallo, inquiring if he needed any monetary assistance. Pound turned down the offer and explained that he was getting by sparingly, but not going without meals. Early in 1933, Pound emphasized that Mussolini was "getting on with his job," and that Italy was now a much better place to visit. Pound's near-poverty still concerned Hemingway, and not long after he sent a check for the purchase of several of Dorothy's sketches. In April 1933, Dorothy expressed in a letter to Hemingway that her sketches were intended to be a gift, and thanked him by stating that the money would be set aside as a long-term loan for the Pounds' "Literature and Arts Fund."

In 1933, Ford Maddox Ford produced a pamphlet, *Cantos of Ezra Pound: Some Testimonials: by Ernest Hemingway, Ford Madox Ford, T.S. Eliot, Hugh Walpole, Archibald McLeish, James Joyce, and Others*. This was to coincide with the publication of Pound's *A Draft of XXX Cantos*. Invited to contribute to Ford's pamphlet, Hemingway wrote back: "Any poet born in this century or in the last ten years of the preceding century who can honestly say that he has not been influenced by or learned greatly from the work of Ezra Pound deserves to be pitied rather than rebuked. It is as if a prose writer born in that time should not have learned from or have been influenced by James Joyce.... The best of Pound's writing—and it is in *The Cantos*—will last as long as there is any literature." Hemingway agreed to help Ford "cow the reviewers" to take notice of the work. That same year some of Hemingway's poems were reprinted in Pound's publication *Profile*.[10]

The year 1933 also saw the publication of Pound's *ABC of Economics*. At this time, Pound took an interest in the Swiss-born naturalist Louis Aggasiz. Pound applied Agassiz's attention to "nature's minute realities" to writing—what Pound referred to as "the luminous detail." In the opening chapter of Pound's *ABC of Reading*, he cited Aggasiz's example of teaching a post-graduate student the value of acute observation by demanding he study a decaying sunfish. "The student," explained Pound, "produced a four-page essay. Agassiz then told him to look at the fish. At the end of three weeks the fish was in an advanced state of decomposition, but the student knew something about it."[11]

A close observer of man and nature, Hemingway had long been aware of Agassiz's scientific contributions, notably in paleontology. Five-year-old Ernest joined the local Aggasiz Club founded by his father, who took members on nature walks. The extremely religious Clarence would have no qualms about being a follower of Agassiz, who, as one of Charles Darwin's most outspoken opponents, dismissed the idea of evolutionary change through natural selection in favor of what he termed "special creationism" that saw each organism as a separate product of the "Divine Mind."[12]

Clarence instilled in his son a reverence for the outdoors, teaching him hunting and fishing and sparking his interest in collecting fossils and Native-American artifacts. At ten, Ernest was elected assistant curator, and on summer Sundays Ernest and his friends gathered "specimens in Thatcher's Woods and identifying birds in the thickets along the banks of the Des Plaines River." Over the next several years he collected various specimens for the club.[13]

But it was artistic formalism that brought together two such diverse individuals as Hemingway and Pound, as it was politics that would nearly drive them apart. When writing *Jefferson and/or Mussolini* in 1933, Pound rightly concluded that his friend would not find it to his liking and informed Hemingway that he did not "'advocate' boy scouts for America," that as Noel Stock explains, "he did not recommend for his own country the Fascist system as such, with its uniforms and other trappings." In *Jefferson and/or Mussolini* (1935), Pound states that he did not "'advocate' fascism in and for America." He did think it "possible in America" to have a new order "without a Mussolini." For America to produce such a dictator was a false expectation as that of an "enlightened bolshevik" thinking "communism is possible in America without Lenin."[14]

Jefferson and/or Mussolini emerged out of Pound's 1933 lectures in Milan, entitled "An Historical Background for Economics." These nine lectures delivered daily, in English, were featured at Milan's Luigi Bocconi

University. Lectures discussed topics from the temple at Delphi to modern economics, including the economic ideas of Jefferson, John Quincy Adams, and Martin Van Buren.

Pound thought it imperative that a strong Italy shield Western Europe from Soviet communism and create a needed balance of power with Germany, something he believed only Mussolini could achieve. *Jefferson and/or Mussolini* expressed Pound's Jeffersonian Confucianist view that saw in Italy a spirit of political innovation resembling the America of John Adams, Thomas Jefferson, Andrew Jackson, and Martin Van Buren. In drawing parallels between Jefferson and Mussolini, Pound argued that both ruled in the public's best interest as pragmatists adapting their governance to their country's unique conditions.

Pound wrongly claimed that Jefferson ruled America until his death in 1826. This was one instance, among many, in which Pound manipulated the facts to fit his own ends. T.S. Eliot once stated that Pound claimed to know history, but that it was his history. Archibald MacLeish noted this also, writing to Hemingway that he doubted Pound's "conviction that he has read American history—which the facts don't seem to support."[15]

For Pound the Russian Revolution was the end of the "Marxian cycle." Where Lenin foresaw a bold new beginning, Pound predicted the waning of a labor-driven struggle. Pound wrote, *"The fascist revolution is infinitely more INTERESTING than the Russian revolution because it is not a revolution according to preconceived type."* Pound saw modern Italy exemplifying Burckhardt's "the state as a work of art." Mussolini, according to Pound, was a creator, an artist, a man of the people rather than a figure ruling over an impersonal and self-serving bureaucracy.[16]

At the heart of Pound's *Jefferson and/or Mussolini* was the Confucian assertion that both his subjects were genius statesmen—driven not by a will to power but by "the will toward order." In his refutation of Nietzsche, Pound wrote: "The 'will to power' (admired and touted by the generation before my own) was literatureifyed by an ill-balanced hysterical teutopollack." He assured his readers by concluding that Mussolini did not thirst for power and that Il Duce, like Jefferson, would not "stand with despots and the lovers of power but with the lovers of ORDER."[17]

Rife with ideas and theories, including obscure names and references—also typical of *The Cantos* at this time—Pound's book suffered because his prose had become increasingly disjointed. He had never aspired to be an essayist and, at most, considered it a means of economic survival. Erudition in obscure and non–Western literature and ideas taxed his readers. As far back as his early lecture days in London, Pound had the habit of assuming his audience knew the subjects he was addressing and used quotes, some unknown even to well-read listeners. This, coupled with the inability to conjoin his topics of discussion in coherent prose, made even short works like *Jefferson and/or Mussolini* nearly incomprehensible. What worked for modern poetry—the coloration of words and unique rhythm—largely failed in Pound's writing of politics and economics.

Twice mentioned in *Jefferson and/or Mussolini*, Hemingway had little (if anything) good to say about the book. Pound first brought up Hemingway in reference to journalism and the mainstream media: "The journalist has often no greater motive than a desire to make the front page or any page, and, at one remove, the lesser literary journalist may merely want to stir up a shindy, as has been the case recently *re* Mr. Hemingway." This reference described Hemingway's role in the popular media in 1933—possibly his *Esquire* magazine articles or his much-publicized African hunting trip that he considered detestable. In reference to Gabrielle d'Annunzio, Pound again dropped Hemingway's name about a man they both admired. Pound warned critics in their assessing d' Annunzio's writing and life: "I do not believe I am any more impressed by rhetoric than is Mr. Hemingway, I may have a greater capacity for, or sympathy with, general ideas (provided they have a bearing on what I consider good action) but Gabrielle as aviator has shown just as much nerve as any of dear Hem's pet bull bashers."[18]

Pound's affection for Hemingway was revealed to visitors to Rapallo. When poet Robert Fitzgerald called upon Pound he was shown "a letter in which there was a snapshot of a tanned Hemingway grinning beside a shark he had caught in the waters off Cuba."[19]

No matter how much that Pound considered Hemingway's deep-sea fishing a diversion for a serious writer, he was more concerned about big-game hunting. Before embarking for Africa, the Hemingways visited Paris. In July 1933, Hemingway informed Pound that he and Pauline would be in Europe from August until leaving for the safari in October. In August and September, Hemingway wrote Pound to arrange their meeting in Paris, but, as Michael Reynolds notes: Pound's "replies were disoriented and ragged. He might come as far as Toulon, because Ezra was worried about" Hemingway's first African hunting trip.[20]

On August 7, 1933, Hemingway, Pauline, and a Key West friend, Charles Thompson, sailed from Marseilles to Africa for a three-month safari. For Pound sportsmanship should never get in the way of writing, and several years later Pound commented about Hemingway's wanting to kill "pussy cats, however titanic, that ain't got no guns to shoot back with, you god damn lionhunter." He asked, "What was the poor brute don' to you?" In the exchange of letters over this topic, Hemingway informed Pound that "I may have become a naturalist." Pound shot back, "An if you are going to be a nacherlist//thass O/K/ but ef you air goin to Afric fer to annoy a tranquil family of man eatin lions etc /// I reprobate you." Pound wrote E.E. Cummings, addressing Hemingway as Oinis: "[S]o let him catch tunny fish/ all drore the line iz lions/ I can't have him shootin lions. the lion izza sympathetic animal up to a cetain age/ or with a bit of grill work between us."[21]

Pound later wrote magazine publisher Arnold Gingrich, criticizing Hemingway's aversion to politics and economics, stating: "Hem. may shoot lions; but he don't play with 'em, in the domestic cage. I like my photo of M. [Mussolini] with a live one, better than Hem's with a dead one." This comment referred to a photograph of Mussolini playing with a young lion. As biographer Hugh Carpenter points out, the "comparison with Hemingway is striking; as with 'Hem,' Ezra seems to have been attracted to Mussolini largely as an image of tough masculinity." But at this time, before Mussolini's brutal conquest of Ethiopia, Pound may also had inferred that the Italian leader was more humane in making a pet of a wild animal than stalking and killing one.[22]

After visiting Spain, the Hemingways spent three weeks in Paris between October and their sailing from Marseilles on November 22. It was at this time that Hemingway may have last seen his poet friend. In several letters, written nearly ten years later, Hemingway explained that James Joyce came to be frightened at Pound's odd state of mind. Accepting an invitation to dine with Pound, Joyce asked Hemingway to come along.[23] Most of Pound's leading biographers place this meeting in 1934—based upon a letter cited in Charles Norman's work *Ezra Pound*. This date was also given during the 1940s in a letter to Pound's lawyer, Julien Cornell. But as Pound biographer J.J. Wilhelm points out, "This date is very suspect." In a 1945 letter to Archibald McLeish and Allen Tate, Hemingway claimed the event occurred in 1933. A Hemingway letter to McLeish also places the dinner in 1933 at Joyce's place of residence, after the Irishman had just returned to Paris during early September and had taken a furnished flat on the rue Galilée.[24]

At this dinner, Pound, whose recent books expressed the virtues of Social Credit and fascist politics, no doubt ranted to Hemingway and Joyce with crackpot sermons, praising Mussolini and theories straight out of the *Protocols of Zion*. In his writings, Pound feared the "Huns" living east of Germany—Bolsheviks, who were working with the Jews to undermine

Western Europe. Even if he claimed this echoing of Nazi ideology as the product of his own vision, Pound espoused a Judaic-Bolshevik conspiracy theory, and an equal hatred of Slavic people and the Soviet Union. Years later, Hemingway wrote Allen Tate about his 1933 dinner with Pound, in which his old friend ranted "utter rot, nonsense and balls as he had made sense in 1923." Hemingway fictionally recounted this evening in his posthumously published novel *Islands in the Stream* (1970). In the novel, Thomas Hudson and Young Tom, his son, tell of their meeting Joyce and Pound in Paris. Young Tom—modeled after Ernest's eldest son, John—recalls hearing Joyce tell his father, "Ezra's mad, Hudson."[25]

This dinner was the last meeting between Hemingway and Pound. Both Hemingway and Joyce had clearly agreed that Pound was not the same man he had been in 1923. Pound thought himself a righteous Confucian with a duty to reform and reinvigorate civilization. There were moments of doubt. In *Jefferson and/or Mussolini*, Pound claimed that he lived more freely in Italy than anywhere in Europe, yet openly admitted to his "capacity for illusion"—"right or wrong," and concluded "that is my feeling." It was Pound's belief in the power of the intuitive and the need to express his ideas that prompted him to test dangerously the limits of free speech during wartime.[26]

CHAPTER 9

Two Voices, Two Men

The year 1933 saw a cultural triumph with the removal of the ban of Joyce's *Ulysses* in America. That same year Pound and Hemingway found themselves mocked in Gertrude Stein's best-selling memoir, *The Autobiography of Alice B. Toklas*. Written through the voice of Alice, the more reliable of the two when recounting events, *The Autobiography* was serialized in *The Atlantic Monthly*, reaching a mass American audience, and was followed up by a nationwide book tour. The *Autobiography* recalls Toklas and Stein's first meeting Pound, when he talked about Japanese prints and spoke incessantly of T.S. Eliot. Gertrude liked Pound but found him a boring, talkative man. Stein's oft-quoted phrase in *The Autobiography* describes Pound as "a village explainer, excellent if you were a village, but if you were not, not." Pound's banishment from Stein's 27 rue de Fleurus occurred when he fell out of a chair and broke the back leg. Hemingway rightly explained that Pound's visits to Stein's ended when he broke a piece of furniture, but added myth to the incident in *A Moveable Feast* when he claimed that Pound was possibly set up for such an outcome by being offered an inferior chair. Unlike Hemingway, Pound brushed off Stein's comments. After Stein turned down his suggestion of meeting once more after the chair incident, Pound permanently kept his distance and came to refer to her as an "old tub of guts."

But competitiveness—and even viciousness—was typical among this generation of writers, some of whom, like Hemingway, became more vindictive—fomenting feuds and settling old scores—as years passed. In *The Autobiography*, Hemingway received a verbal drubbing far more severe than Toklas and Stein had meted out to Pound.

In many ways, Hemingway had it coming. He voiced his growing dislike for Stein in private correspondences and ridiculed her in *The Torrents of Spring*. In 1927, Pound had encouraged him to write an article attacking Stein. Pound later wrote, "Somewhat contented to see from yr. hand script, that Gertie Stein is losing her hold on what we used a few years ago to call the 'younger generation.' Does this come under the caption: Personality tells." But Hemingway responded to Pound that he would gladly insult Stein but preferred "to do it through a more widely circulated medium."[1]

This effort to hold back criticism of Stein proved difficult for a hot-tempered Hemingway as he read *The Autobiography*. In her book, Stein repeatedly pressed Hemingway to reveal his true self—the accident-ridden, frail artist hidden behind the image of the virile man and his characters that killed bulls and tempted fate. The real man she asserted was "yellow" and hinted that Hemingway was a closet homosexual. Issuing *The Autobiography* shortly after the appearance of Hemingway's bullfighting book *Death in the Afternoon* (1932), Stein could take credit in sparking Hemingway's interest in bullfighting, when she showed him pictures of herself and Alice in the front row of a bullfight in Valencia. Seeing his interest, she urged him to attend the bullfights in Pamplona.

The Autobiography further criticized Hemingway when it brought up Sherwood Anderson. Stein claimed that "Hemingway had been formed by the two of them and they were both a little ashamed of the work of their minds." Hemingway's rejection of Anderson's talent, the thrust of *Torrents of the Spring*, now was met by Stein's defense of Anderson, her longtime literary friend who had provided Hemingway with a letter of introduction to Stein. To add insult to injury, Stein condemned Hemingway as a conventional storyteller hiding behind a modernist façade. In a much-quoted clever barb, she wrote, Hemingway "looks like a modern and he smells of the museums." This was not the first time a female writer had questioned Hemingway as a literary modern. Virginia Woolf, in her 1927 review of *Men Without Women*, wrote that Hemingway "is a modern in manner but not in vision."[2]

Now that Hemingway had been called weak-bellied, possibly homosexual, and a creative cast-off of Stein and Anderson, he and Pound—the so-called "village explainer"—responded. In July 1933, Hemingway wrote to Pound admitting he did learn from Stein through intelligent conversation, but he resented her claiming that she and "mother hubbard Anderson" had "made me up in their spare time." He then attacked Stein: "I stuck by that old bitch until she threw me out of the house when she lost her judgment with menopause but it seems that I'm just a fickle, brittle brain bastard. Read the damned piece. She disposes of you too." Hemingway then vowed that he would get even one day when writing his own memoir that would call upon his "rat trap" memory of a man who, supposedly, as he claimed, was not "jealous" and had "nothing to prove." Never one to forget a slight, Hemingway later parodied Stein's "Rose is a rose is a rose" by inscribing a copy of *Death in the Afternoon*: "To Gertrude Stein, A Bitch is a Bitch is a Bitch."[3]

Prompted largely by Stein's stinging words of condemnation, Hemingway took up publisher Arnold Gingrich's offer to write for his new magazine, *Esquire*. He needed an outlet to answer what he considered as baseless, foul-mouthed gossip. Hemingway wrote Gingrich about a scathing article he wrote about Stein but did not want to see it published during her 1933 American book tour. In April 1933, Hemingway informed Gingrich that Stein had been exceptional until "old menopause" led her to lose her professional judgment."[4]

In the fall of 1933, Hemingway wrote Pound, joking that he typed six pages titled, "The Autobiography of Alice B. Hemingway" subtitled "Or Who Taught the Fifth Grade—Then?" Hemingway assured Pound that he would like this satire suitable for the *New Yorker*. Pound wrote back: "The Stein piece sounds superb. Can't wait to see it. Hope it is funny."[5]

It would be decades before Hemingway carried out his promise. Meanwhile, Stein continued her "tough guy" assessment of Hemingway. In an August 1935 issue of the *Atlantic Monthly*, Stein commented that Hemingway had "not sold himself" or "settled into any literary mold." However, she noticed a significant change in his shy persona and the emotion of his early short stories. She asserted that Hemingway had lost his initial sensitivity by shielding himself in "a big Kansas City–boy brutality" while falling into an obsession of "sex and death."[6]

With the publication of *Green Hills of Africa* in October 1935, Hemingway expressed some more thoughts about Stein. Based upon his 1933 African safari hunting trip, Hemingway often digressed in his book to comment about writers and American literature. In *Green Hills*, Hemingway takes a stab at Anderson and Stein: "At a certain age," explains the narrator, "the men writers change into Old Mother Hubbard. The women writers become Joan of Arc without the fighting." Among Hemingway's three most important early mentors, Pound survived as a respected poet and a likable friend. In *Green Hills*, the author boasts of knowing many literary anecdotes, especially "some good ones about Pound."[7]

By 1933, Pound started to address his letters to Hemingway as "Yr fexunate unkl." At this stage of life, Pound took on the avuncular role of the poet sage who, from his base in Rapallo, headed what he pridefully called the "Ezuversity." He would remain an uncle to his followers until taking on the role of "grandpaw" when institutionalized in America after the war.

Concerned that Pound was struggling financially, Hemingway wrote him offering money. On January 15, 1933, Pound wrote back assuring him: "Thanks fer kind offer. Me earnin capacity still remarkably low, but credit still good at eat-house.... Thanks all the same." Pound ended the letter by informing Hemingway that Mussolini was taking care of business in Italy, a country Ernest would now find more to his liking.[8]

Meeting on art's high ground, Hemingway tried to remain silent about Pound's support of fascism. Like many of Pound's friends, he was tired of the poet's obsession with economics that found its way into *The Cantos* and numerous essays. In a 1933 letter to Pound, Hemingway dismissed Mussolini and Social Credit. Pound responded that he was "all wet on the subject." Pound went on to urge Hemingway to get all his money "out of America" and reinvest it in Italy, where new homes flourished, smokeless trains ran on time, and grain grew in abundance. No longer able to hold back his anger, Hemingway shot back: "Since when are you an economist, pal? The last I knew you you were a fuckin' bassoon player."[9]

Hemingway wrote Pound, in July 1933, about his fifty-four-foot marlin catch and the one that leapt forty-four times. He then went on to warn that a writer had more important matters to attend to than wasting time on theorizing about economics. But Hemingway reiterated in this letter that he "learned more about how to write and how not to write from Pound than from any other son of a bitch alive."[10]

Never knowing when to let up on a subject, Pound continued his quixotic mission. If he could not sway friends like Hemingway directly by letter, he would hound and pester them by mailing circulars and broadsides, revealing the light of Social Credit that would save world economies through the fascist example. In August 1934, Pound wrote Robert McAlmon: "My usual role of butting into something that is not strictly my business. But I think both you *and* Hem. have limited yr. work by not recognizing the economic factor." That same year Pound sent out a one-page circular, outlining the main tenets of Volitionist Economics. In "spaces to reply," the circular asked readers to explain if they agreed or disagreed with the circular's eight statements about basic economics. Varied replies came from bankers, politicians, and writers—Hemingway is not known to be one of them.[11]

His life riddled with contradictions, Pound sought to reconcile his obsessions with Social Credit, Italian fascism and Confucian. Assessing Pound's life at this time, literary scholar John Tytell writes: "Rather than becoming a literary kingpin, he became seduced by the Confucian notion of the writer as political advisor to a ruler. But it was an illusory notion. Confucius had been regarded as a quirky, rambling talker in his time; he was not taken seriously by those in power." This was true of Pound as well, as he took on the role of poet/advisor to fellow artists and powerful leaders.[12]

Though Pound was deluded in thinking he could influence world leaders, he was not without some credibility in hoping Mussolini might take some interest in Social Credit as the regime had no official economic policy. At this time, explained Hugh Carpenter, "Its only influence on the economy so far had been to oppress industry with a hierarchy of civil servants, who were intended to police the so-called 'Corporate State,' in which management and workers theoretically shared power but which was really run by the bureaucrats."[13]

Pound also preached his Social Credit gospel to James Joyce whose "work in progress," he believed, suffered artistically from avoiding economics. This "work in progress"—the future *Finnegan's Wake*—evoked little enthusiasm from Pound and Hemingway. Once early champions of *Ulysses*, they now thought Joyce was lost in abstruse and invented language. Conversely, Joyce never paid much attention to Pound's work and thought little of him as a critic—an individual who "makes brilliant discoveries and howling blunders." Each a literary universe unto themselves, Pound, Joyce, and Hemingway had their own preoccupations and artistic interests.[14]

In 1934, Hemingway suggested Pound contact *Esquire* editor Arnold Gingrich about writing an article on Mussolini. This came at a time when Gingrich opened his magazine to literature and the arts. Issues featured such names as D.H. Lawrence, Theodore Dreiser, F. Scott Fitzgerald, Dos Passos, Ben Hecht, and Rockwell Kent.

Though Pound did not write a Mussolini article for *Esquire*, he utilized his opportunity to write economically oriented articles. Pound also sent Gingrich articles about artists Henri Gaudier and Francis Picabia. For *Esquire*'s January 1934 issue he wrote on Social Credit and the stamp script theories of Sylvio Gessel. In the second *Esquire* article, "A Mugs Game?," Leon Surette writes that Pound "compares banking to banditry and drug trafficking." In 1936, Pound contributed his third and last *Esquire* article, "How to Save Business," which Surette describes as an "eccentric survey of the economic reform movements of the day."[15]

Hemingway's extreme dislike for Il Duce only increased with Italy's military aggression in Africa and Europe. When Italy invaded Ethiopia in October 1935, Pound defended his host nation's brutal action and claimed that Italy would bring civilization to east Africa. Additionally, he thumbed his nose at the League of Nation's opposition to the aggression. Pound wrote pro–Mussolini articles for various publications, including the *British-Italian Bulletin*, in which opposed what he believed to be the British "Judo-cratic" media. Pound's longtime friend Nancy Cunard, daughter of the wealthy shipping magnate and also a friend of Hemingway, was disturbed by a letter she received from Pound. The same man who had spoken out in defense of the Scottsboro Boys—nine African American young men falsely accused of raping two white women in Alabama—wrote her claiming that "the Abyssians were Black Jews." This comment shocked Cunard since it revealed an anti–Semitism she had never known Pound to express before. For a woman who had been the lover of African American pianist and composer Henry Crowder, this disparaging of Ethiopia's Jews seemed like the ranting of a stranger who looked upon them as the rationale for Italian occupation.[16]

In Hemingway's friendship with Pound, Mussolini continued to be a contentious subject. Hemingway's 1935 *Esquire* article, "Malady of Power," criticized former French Premier Georges Clemenceau, whom he had once admired. Pleased with Hemingway's assessment of Clemenceau, Pound wrote: "Waal, me deah Hombo / Glad to see you doin man's woik and spillin dirt on Georges, etc. / wich dont lower me respekk for Benito but raises wot I have fer E.M.H." A year later, Hemingway voiced his outrage over Mussolini's invasion of Ethiopia. In a January 1936 *Esquire* article, Hemingway did, however, sympathize with the Italian infantryman—"poor simps"—sent to battle the unprepared Ethiopians who had no air force.[17]

Pound's admiration for Mussolini equaled his obsession for Social Credit. In his effort to attract American policy makers to Social Credit, Pound wrote to Hemingway suggesting, "Might be easy for you to put me over in Washington, as to push me into the front page of *Esquire*." Without any formal training in economics, Pound—never having done the numbers—promoted an economic system that he believed most laymen could understand. In a January 1935 letter to T.S. Eliot's *Criterion*, Pound asserted that "economics are about as complicated as a gasoline engine and igno-rance of them is not excusable even in prime ministers and other irrespon-sible relics of a disreputable era."[18]

Pound's contact with rightwing public intellectuals and amateur econ-omists in 1910s London exposed him to many virulent Anglo anti–Semites.

Like these Englishmen, Pound subscribed to a supposed Jewish conspiracy. Social Credit founder C.H. Douglas was an outspoken anti–Semite, and Pound's patron New York lawyer, John Quinn, revealed his anti–Jewish prejudice in letters to friends and associates. According to Leon Surette, Pound did not embrace the Nazi obsession with biological determinism. Rather, he viewed Jews in historical and sociological terms as a migrant, herding people from which no great art could evolve. As a rootless tribe, they came to control world finance. In one of his many disjointed utterances, Pound echoed in *Guide to Kulchur* (1938) the Nazi belief that communism was a "Judeo-Bolshevik" conspiracy. "Communism," he wrote, "with its dictatorship of the proletariat is merely barbarous and Hebrew, and it is on a level with the primitive theocracies."[19]

Though Pound did not openly advocate violence towards Jews, he still had much to answer for in the aftermath of world war. In his defense, he often pointed out that he argued for a pogrom at the top—that the bankers were the root of the problem, not an entire people. Fascism did not always coincide with anti–Semitism. Pound's hero, Mussolini, did not decree racial laws until 1938, and then to appease his ally Adolf Hitler. But what is inexcusable about Pound is that he did not speak out against such policy. In these cases, silence can be a form of complicity.

Pound's life was not entirely taken up with politics. His Ezuversity in Rapallo attracted a number of young writers looking for direct instruction and guidance. In 1934, Harvard student James Laughlin came to Rapallo in search of the famed poet. This tuition-free tutorial placed Laughlin under Pound's instruction. Pound thought Laughlin lacked the talent to write first-rate verse and warned that prose writing was a waste of time since no one could better Flaubert, Stendhal, and Joyce. Instead, he urged Laughlin, heir of a steel fortune, to go into publishing. Following this advice, Laughlin founded New Directions Books, later a major publisher of Pound and William Carlos Williams.

Laughlin encountered Pound at a time when the poet was obsessed with early American history and fascism. Aware of his mentor's seeing the past largely through his own perspective, Laughlin either steered the conversation to literature or discussed history and economics in "the way he wanted to revise it, because, of course, as he insisted, all history had been miswritten since Gibbon." Pound's outspoken anti–Semitism disturbed Laughlin, a prejudice he believed was rooted in off-color jokes and cruel mockery.[20]

Like Hemingway's time with Pound in Paris, Laughlin enjoyed the poet's wit and recreational pastimes. He lunched with the Pounds at the Albergo and went back to their apartment, where Ezra relaxed upon his bed, a Chinese dictionary resting on his stomach, while a cowboy hat shielded the light coming in from the window. Afterward, Ezra rented a pontoon craft and rowed out into the bay to swim. In the distance were the cliffs of Zoagli and the Portofino peninsula. Laughlin remembered Pound as a strong swimmer who would dive "and come up like Proteus," his red beard glistening. He also thought Pound an able tennis player with a "forehand drive, executed with a 90-degree body pivot, which none of us could return." Back at the apartment, Laughlin listened to Dorothy read from Henry James, while Ezra worked away on one of his two typewriters—one was always being sent out for repair due to the poet's forceful pounding of the keys.[21]

On a return trip to Rapallo, Laughlin discovered Pound's heightened interest in Italian fascism and an increased anti–Semitism. Although Laughlin considered Pound's move to the far right as an unfortunate trait of an otherwise brilliant visionary, he claimed to have learned more about Greek, Latin, and Provencal than through any of his courses at Harvard.

Thousands of miles from Mussolini's Italy, Hemingway lived in relative isolation in the Florida Keys. A 1930s WPA Florida guide book described Key West in the afternoon heat, the shuttered houses and "dogs sleeping on the sidewalks" undisturbed by "pedestrians, none of whom is ever in a hurry." The island offered a variety of Cuban-owned restaurants and coffee shops. Its "isolation ... and the proximity to West Indies" gave Key West "characteristics of friendliness and leisure, and tempered it with a Latin approach to life."[22]

Hemingway once referred to Key West as "the San Tropez of the poor." In the 1920s, Key West boasted telephone service, electric trolley cars, and automobiles. The island's relative prosperity did not last, however, as its local economy suffered several setbacks. Hundreds of locals lost their jobs when the island's canning business closed and when the cultivation of sponges had been supplanted by its synthetic production elsewhere in Florida. But most damaging to thousand of workers was Key West's cigar industry's relocation to Tampa.[23]

Amid economic crisis, Key West received federal assistance in 1933 through the Federal Emergency Relief Administration (FERA) and the Civil Works Administration (CWA), programs that allocated money for projects and hired workers. This proved a temporary solution. Economically devastated, Key West declared bankruptcy in 1934 and called upon the federal government for assistance, resulting in FERA's taking charge of the city. This agreement enraged Hemingway, who disliked President Roosevelt's "alphabet programs," and the possibility that his out-of-the way island would be transformed into a tourist spot.[24]

During the mid–1930s, Hemingway enjoyed Key West's unpretentious surroundings and colorful locals, many who joined him drinking at Sloppy Joe's Bar. In Hemingway's 1937 novel *To Have and Have Not*, one his characters described Conch Town in the moonlight: its main street drug stores, five Jewish-owned stores, a large dime store, poolrooms and beer joints, the many ice-cream parlors, barber shops, the only decent restaurant, and a corner hotel where taxis parked next door.[25]

In 1934, the year of Key West's bankruptcy, Hemingway bought with his *Esquire* magazine's earnings his famed fishing boat, the *Pilar*, on which he often spent more time than on land. Since hooking his first marlin off the Cuban coast in 1932, Hemingway had found a new sport. "These Gulf Stream days," explains Michael Reynolds, "pursuing fish as large as his imagination, are the beginning of a new pursuit which will last him the rest of his life." Once the catch of commercial fishermen, marlin were now pursued by sportsmen who fought them with rod and reel.[26]

Pound, who once told Hemingway that lake fishing was a joke, now made snide remarks about his friend's sport of catching "tunny fish." Though Pound never had any intention of living in Key West, his longtime friend William Carlos William once suggested that he leave Italy for Hemingway's island home. "If you come to America," wrote Williams, "the only place I think of for you is Key West, FLA." Pound emphatically answered, "To hekll with Key West," and in reference to Hemingway's sport he lashed out, "I ain't a fish-killer NO how."[27]

As war clouds gathered in Europe, Hemingway's Key West life was disrupted. On Labor Day 1935, a massive hurricane wrought devastation in the Keys. The nearly 200 victims of this disaster were World War I veterans, bonus marchers who had been chased out of Washington, D.C., in 1932. When President Roosevelt came into office many of these vets reemerged in Washington. To placate the thousands of jobless men demanding their military bonus pay—due in 1935—Eleanor Roosevelt met with them at Camp Hunt, Virginia. To remove the threat of another march on Washington, Harry Hopkins conceived the plan to employ the vets for a dollar-a-day in FERA Rural Rehabilitation Camps in South Carolina and Florida. To assist in building the Overseas Bridge Project connecting Florida's mainland with the Keys, hundreds of vets were assigned to Islamorada and Lower Matecumbe Key. They were housed in makeshift quarters during hurricane season and on keys that were slightly above sea level. Their rescue depended on a special train that, due to miscommunication over the Labor Day holiday, never reached them in time.

In his informative study, *FDR and the Bonus Marchers*, Gary Dean Best concluded:

> Shipped to the camps by a Roosevelt administration eager to avoid incidents in Washington, the veterans were placed at the mercy of the elements on exposed keys, in flimsy shacks and tents during hurricane season, under administrators who were inexperienced in hurricanes, indecisive, and unresponsive to advice, who thought they could plot the hurricane and evacuate the men only when the camps were in imminent danger.[28]

Hemingway inspected the damage first-hand at Lower Matecumbe Key, discovering the dead, swollen bodies of the vets. Upon his visit to camp Five, Hemingway discovered a site of 187 dead bodies and wrote Max Perkins that he had not seen such death since "the Piave in June of 1918." Most of these workers were World War I veterans, down-and-outers living on the fringe of society, many of whom Hemingway had drunk with at Sloppy Joe's. Hemingway considered these men of makeshift camps sacrificed by an uncaring government which failed to rescue them by railroad car.

The left-wing publication *New Masses* invited Hemingway to write about the Matecumbe Key disaster. Years earlier, Hemingway had described *New Masses* to F. Scott Fitzgerald as "puerile and shitty." Enraged by the Matecumbe disaster, Hemingway put aside his dislike for the magazine—one that constantly faulted his art for lacking class-consciousness—and contributed an article entitled "Panic," which, unknown to its author, was published as "Who Murdered the Vets?"[29]

Hemingway's dislike for Roosevelt's Administration only increased as he saw federal money spent to transform Key West while it failed to properly house and look after Matecumbe Key's WPA workers. Raised in Oak Park by a mother who championed the progressive Republican values of his boyhood hero, Theodore Roosevelt, Hemingway came to adulthood little interested in politics. In Hemingway's poem "Roosevelt," which appeared in *Poetry*, he lauded TR as a legendary man of action. As for Theodore Roosevelt's cousin, Franklin Delano Roosevelt, Hemingway harbored a gut-driven dislike. Even after he met the president in the White House, his opinion did not change.

CHAPTER 10

United Fronts,
Divided Friendships

World events during the 1930s drove writers and artists into various causes and warring camps. Only a minority of American writers became communists. More became fellow travelers, while a larger number joined a United Front that brought together antifascists opposed to Mussolini and Hitler. Others, like Pound, supported Italian fascism by deed of the word—in letters, magazine articles, and, finally, radio broadcasts—praising Mussolini's stature as both a reformer and builder of a new nation, its pride restored.

By the early 1930s, Europe feared the increasing militarization of Nazism and Italian fascism. Stalin initially thought these fascist regimes, along with the governments of capitalist countries, would collapse. In 1928, he had ushered in what became known as the Third Period, the communists' unrelenting ideological war against capitalism. During the Third Period, communists were not to collaborate with social democrats or liberals, and any left-wing collaboration to salvage capitalism was considered the work of "social fascists." But Stalin, realizing Germany's and Italy's growing power, greatly altered his policy in 1935 by declaring a "Popular Front" that welcomed all antifascists.

Divergent as their politics became, Hemingway and Pound equally rejected social realism—the official aesthetic of Stalin's Soviet Union. Above all, social realism, as it permeated the arts, was to further class consciousness while revealing the maladies of capitalism. In 1936, Pound addressed Soviet literature when writing publisher James Laughlin: "No real literature will come out of people who are trying to preserve a blind spot. That goes equally for ivory tower aesthetes, ant-propagandists and communists who refuse to think: Communize the product."[1]

Pound considered proletarian literature as "literature of social significance as no significance ... pseudo-pink blah." For Pound, the leftwing working-class novel and poetry were empty vessels of art. Though Pound had aroused the American left's interest when he praised the 1926 debut of *New Masses* as "the liveliest wire now functioning," he did so at a time when the publication still represented an array of writers and modern literature in its political content.[2]

When Hemingway read the editorial response to Pound's commentary in *New Masses*—"Pound Joins the Revolution"—he heatedly responded: "So you joined the New Masses." Sharing Sherwood Anderson's sentiment at the time, Hemingway asserted: "Listen and Papa will tell you why Messrs. Rorty, Freeman, Mike Gold etc. etc. want a revolution. Because they hope that under some new order they would be men of talent." Hemingway concluded—"FUCK the new masses and their revolution. In case *you'd* mistaken my sentiments."[3]

But Pound's admiration for *News Masses* did not last, and despite the magazine's favorable reference to him, the poet never advocated revolution in Russia or any other European country. Yet he did believe Social Credit could benefit the Soviet Union. Pound wrote, "The true artist is the champion of free speech from the beginning." Yet in the same essay, Pound noted the limitations of this idealized role. "A work of art need not contain any statement of a political or of a social or a philosophical conviction, but it nearly always implies one."[4]

Despite his proclaimed individualism, Hemingway soon associated with the left in Spain. From 1936 to 1939, Spain was embroiled in civil war, what many antifascists called the struggle of darkness and light that pitted the Spanish Republic and its Soviet ally against General Francisco Franco's coalition of royalists, fascists, and right-wing Catholics and their allies, Nazi Germany and fascist Italy.

Not long after the establishment of the Second Republic in 1931, Spain's King Alfonso XIII went into self-exile. Torn between political factions and regional disputes, Spain was a country caught between tradition and modernity. Republican reforms reduced the role of the Catholic Church and called for the right of divorce, non-religious sanction of marriage, and secular schools, hospitals, and cemeteries. Up until 1931, the Spanish anarcho-syndicalists were stronger than the socialists. As historian Gabriel Jackson writes, the "attitude of the masses ranged from goodhumored iconoclasm to revolutionary bloodlust." By May that year, nearly thirty-five churches were burned.[5]

Hemingway arrived in Spain during the spring of 1931 to research his bullfighting book, *Death in the Afternoon*. The bullfighting-obsessed Hemingway devoted little public writing to the tumultuous events of the newly proclaimed republic, while privately telling friends he was closely following political events. In *Death in the Afternoon* he voiced his confidence that "the modern bullfight will continue in Spain." Hemingway stayed in Madrid, a city under martial law and then spent most of his time at bullrings. He then summered with Pauline in Santiago de Compostela.[6]

A land close to Hemingway's heart, Spain offered unique landscapes, food, and art. Edmund Wilson, in his review of *Three Stories and Ten Poems* and *in our time*, alluded to Hemingway's prose about bullfighting as possessing "the dry sharpness and elegance of bull-fight lithographs of Goya. And, like Goya, he is concerned first of all with making a fine picture." In the fall of 1925, Hemingway purchased Joan Miro's *The Farm* as a present for Hadley. Originally purchased for 5,000 francs by his friend Evan Shipman—who made the initial down payments—Hemingway later claimed that his enthusiasm for this work of modern Spanish art led a sympathetic Shipman to decide the painting's ownership by a roll of the dice. Having won, Hemingway took over the payment, drawing upon Hadley's finances.[7]

Apart from the bullring, one of Hemingway's favorite destinations was Madrid's Prado Museum. A building he considered from the outside as "unpicturesque" and coldly institutional, Hemingway praised the Prado's well-lit interior as an inviting place where he spent hours enjoying well-arranged great works of art. "The colors," he wrote in *Death in the Afternoon*, "have kept so wonderfully in the dry mountain air," their presentation so simple that gallery visitors, accustomed to ostentatious frames and plush rooms and "bad lighting," often come away with the impression that they must not be great masterworks.[8]

Beyond its art, people, and memorable landscapes, Hemingway was aware of Spain's darker aspects, elements that made it unique. In *Death in the Afternoon*, written in the year of the Republic's birth, Hemingway offered readers a glimpse into the Spanish character. A country passionately enamored with bullfighting, Spain was, for Hemingway, a nation of pride, common sense, and impracticality. "Because they have pride," wrote Hemingway, "they do not mind killing."[9]

Spain erupted into civil war in 1936 when Francisco Franco led his forces from Morocco to Spain to restore the monarchy and preserve the Catholic Church. Upon the outbreak of the civil war, Hemingway tried to remain neutral. Journalist and novelist Harry Sylvester remembered Hemingway's initial stance concerning the conflict. It was a "bad war in which nobody was right," Hemingway told Sylvester. "What mattered to him was relieving human suffering." Hemingway went on to explain that "it was neither Christian nor Catholic to kill the wounded in a Toledo hospital with hand grenades, or to bomb the working-class area of Madrid simply to kill poor people." He acknowledged that priests and bishops had been shot, but he wondered why the church sided with "the oppressors and not with the oppressed."[10]

Non-political as he tried to remain, Hemingway could not stand aside and watch Franco's coalition and its Italian and Nazi allies destroy the republic. Between March 1937 and November 1938, Hemingway made four trips to Spain where he perceptively foresaw the civil war as a dress rehearsal for a bigger conflict. His dislike for Roosevelt was heightened by America's joining Britain and France in declaring a noninterventionist policy in Spain that gave extensive military advantages to Germany and Italy, while making the Soviet Union the only major backer of the Republican cause.

Hemingway's passion for Spain failed to resonate with Pound, who came to consider the country barbarous and backward. Pound had traveled to Spain in 1906 to study the work of playwright Lope de Vega, and made a ten-day Spanish trip in 1908, after which he considered writing a novel set there. But it would be the troubadours and southern France that captured his imagination. In 1936, Pound voiced his contempt for Spain and the republic's ally, the Soviet Union. "Europe ENDS with the Pyrenees," thundered Pound. "Neither Spain nor Russia has ever contained more than a handful of civilized individuals." He went on to call Spain "a damn'd nest of savages/ and Russia shall not haa/a/AV Bar/Bar/Bar Barcelonah!!!" In *Guide to Kulchur*, Pound pontificated: "Russia is not a civilized nation. Russia was a nation with a few cultivated persons near its apex. Ditto Spain. A few chaps in Madrid read Rémy de Gourmont. These literati were neither numerous enough, nor vigorous enough nor sufficiently 'all round' men to 'save Spain.'"[11]

Pound claimed to have no interest in Spain's civil war, and informed William Carlos Williams that it was "of no more importance than the draining of some mosquito swamps in deepest Africa." He also sarcastically observed, "Spain is an emotional luxury to a gang of sap-headed dilettantes." In November 1936, Pound wrote Hemingway on this subject, insisting, "Why don't you use yr. celebrated bean another 24 minutes and got to it that *all* the buggarin massacres are CAUSED by money.... You seen a lot, and unpleasant; but WHY WAS IT? Because some sodomitical usurer wanted to SELL the goddamn blankets, and airplanes." As to the bankers, Pound further ranted that "god rot their testicles—in their *wallet*, in the buggarin bunk account."[12]

Hemingway was aware of the role of banks, the military and industrialists during the First World War. He shared the prevailing mood of Americans during the 1930s, who looked with distrust upon financiers and munitions makers they believed had drawn the United States into war. He could agree with Pound, who, in 1935, wrote, "Pacifists who refuse to investigate the economic causes of war make common cause with the gun sellers." But with the civil war in Spain, Hemingway, while seeking military aid for the Spanish Republic, was at odds with the Roosevelt administration's refusal to intervene.[13]

In August 1935, Roosevelt anticipated Italy's invasion of Ethiopia and signed The Neutrality Act that prohibited arms trade with any belligerent nation whenever the president proclaimed a state of war existed. This bipartisan bill passed with the assurance that it would be in effect for only six months, long enough to be enforced against Italy in its Ethiopian war. In the end, the act had no affect on Italian aggression in Ethiopia.

After the outbreak of civil war in Spain, America followed the isolationist policy of British Prime Minister Stanley Baldwin's government and that of the Popular Front of French Premier Léon Blum. Aware of isolationist public opinion, President Roosevelt, no matter how much he wanted to assist European democracies, could not act alone. Instead, he cooperated with Congress to pass several neutrality laws. In February 1936, Roosevelt signed the Neutrality Act, known as the moral embargo, which called upon American manufacturers and arms makers to refrain from shipping war materiel to Spain. But this act did not apply to countries engaged in civil war. Additional legislation was needed to prevent such shipment of arms, resulting in a second moral embargo—the Neutrality Act of 1937, passed in January by a Congressional joint resolution which forbade shipment of arms to any country engaged in civil war. In March, still another neutrality law was enacted. As historian F. Jay Taylor explained:

> The new legislation retained the same provisions as the old, the main difference being that the President was given considerably more discretionary power. One new feature of the act, the so-called "cash and carry" plan, provided that nonmilitary commodities could be paid for upon delivery and taken away from American ports by the foreign power.[14]

Hemingway first aided the Loyalist cause by raising funds to buy ambulances, but it would not be long before he saw the conflict firsthand.

Knowing it to be the subject of a good story, Hemingway had several reasons for going to Spain, including his dollar-a-word contract with the North American Newspaper Alliance "that would help to pay off the money he had borrowed for the ambulances." The trip also afforded escape from domestic troubles with his wife, Pauline, and a continued liaison with a talented fellow overseas correspondent and novelist, the blonde and beautiful Martha Gellhorn.[15]

Gellhorn entered Hemingway's life in late December 1936, when she walked into Sloppy Joes Bar in Key West. Accompanied by her mother and brother, she caught Ernest's eye. Tall, stylish and blonde, Gellhorn was an experienced and talented freelance correspondent and had worked for FERA, writing dispossessed and about out-of-work Americans. Gellhorn's experience among the depression-ridden poor resulted in her well-received novel, *The Trouble I've Seen*, also praised by family friend Eleanor Roosevelt. After her mother and brother left, Martha stayed behind in Key West—meeting Hemingway on several occasions and reading the unrevised manuscript of *To Have and Have Not*. Both passionate about the Spanish Civil War, they soon began a love affair in Madrid.

In 1936, Hemingway's novelist friend John Dos Passos sought to help the Republican cause by rallying fellow artists in the making of a documentary which would reveal the hardships of everyday Spaniards. Initially based in New York and intended to arouse public opinion that would pressure the Roosevelt Administration to change its non-interventionist policy in assisting the Spanish Republic, the film brought together supporters including Hemingway, Archibald McLeish, and Lillian Hellman. Hemingway arrived in New York in mid–February and immediately argued with Dos Passos's wanting the film to portray the plight of the people; he demanded it concentrate on the combatants. Their differences settled for the time being, Dos Passos and Hemingway met with their film group, Contemporary Historians, among them Communist party member Joris Ivens. Bound to his job at *Fortune* magazine, McLeish stayed behind to raise money and collect film segments as they arrived from Spain.

Hemingway arrived in Spain on March 14, 1937, and spent two months observing and assisting the making of *The Spanish Earth*. While continuing his love affair with Gellhorn in Madrid, Hemingway visited the front, feeling as if, writes Carlos Baker, returning "to scenes not unlike those he had known in Italy long ago." Back among comrades in arms in a fight worth fighting for, Hemingway found himself reinvigorated as he cultivated what would become the basis for forthcoming literature.[16]

Daily artillery bombardments from nearby Garabitas heights fell upon

Madrid, occasionally hitting the hotel. Located on high ground, Madrid was not initially overrun by Franco's troops because it would be a costly uphill struggle for them that would inevitably turn into fierce street-by-street fighting. The Nationalists followed German theories of war and attempted bombing the inhabitants into surrender. But not having formidable airpower, they employed nearly a dozen planes in daily raids that, in each sortie, killed fewer than fifty inhabitants.

Never blind to the atrocities committed by all sides, Hemingway spoke out about Christians killing wounded Republicans, and the abuses suffered by Spaniards at the hands of absentee landlords. He openly admitted that he sympathized with the workers' struggle against the landlords, with whom he spent time drinking and shooting—the same class of landowners he would just as soon shoot "as the pigeons."[17]

While based at Madrid's Hotel Florida, Hemingway frequented the Soviet-occupied Gaylord Hotel. There he found good company. Hemingway believed his Soviet guests offered "true gen," the journalistic term for inside intelligence. Gaylord's entrance was guarded by bayonet. Inside, Hemingway spent hours drinking and eating. At the same time, he visited members of International Brigades and got to know many of their volunteer soldiers. At the same time, he developed a respect for many of the Soviet officers and advisors. In *For Whom the Bell Tolls* (1940) the American explosives expert Robert Jordan, working with a small band of pro–Republican peasants, ruminates: "You're not a real Marxist and you know it. You believe in Liberty, Equality and Fraternity. You believe in Life, Liberty and the Pursuit of Happiness. Don't ever kid yourself with too much dialectics."[18]

Back in America, the pro-communist left, always looking for allies among well-known writers, lost hope in John Dos Passos and anticipated that Hemingway might see the light. But Hemingway never let respect for his Soviet friends in Spain politicize his art. In 1936, he informed his Soviet friend, the perceptive critic Ivan Kaskin, about writers and critics who threatened to marginalize writers who had no interest in Marxism or communism. "I would rather have one honest enemy," stated Hemingway, "than most of the friends that I have known."[19]

Defiant in his individualism, Hemingway saw the Soviets as allies and admired their organizational skills. Committed to the United Front against fascism, Hemingway, nevertheless initially underestimated or looked askance at the extent of Moscow's influence in and among the supporters of the republic, and its motives and abuses in defeating Franco's coalition. But he also knew more than he let on at times. Hemingway later told Joe

North of *New Masses*, "I like Communists when they're soldiers; when they are priests, I hate them." As for the Spanish fascist Falangists fighting under Franco, he also saw them as brave but politically misguided and later commented, "Listen, arrows are o.k. taken separately, but I don't like them in bunches."[20]

Hemingway's close association with Soviet officers in Spain bolstered his belief that he was better informed than most of his colleagues. Antony Beevor's history of the Spanish Civil War insightfully discusses Hemingway's involvement: "It is difficult to ascertain how much Hemingway was influenced by the privileged information he received by senior party cadres and Soviet advisors. Being taken seriously by experts distorted his vision. It made him prepared to sign moral blank cheques on behalf of the Republic: hence his absurd claim that 'Bruheuga will take its place in military history with the decisive battles of the world.'" Adding to the confusion of biographers on the subject of Hemingway and Gellhorn's supporting the Soviets, Gellhorn's biographer, Caroline Moorhead, raises a valid point. "Exactly how much Martha and Hemingway actually knew about the torture and assassinations is impossible to say," wrote Moorhead. "Certainly, they did not want to know."[21]

Hemingway's friend John Dos Passos had already passed through the stage of sympathizing with the Stalinist left and thus remained distrustful of Hemingway's new comrades. Arriving in Madrid in the spring of 1937, Dos Passos stayed at the Hotel Florida that housed fellow writers, journalists, and the makers of *The Spanish Earth*. Tension between Hemingway and Dos Passos grew heated when the latter's Spanish friend Robles, a Johns Hopkins University instructor, was summarily executed. One of those occasions when Hemingway showed no compassion for his friend's feelings, he related to Dos Passos the news of Robles's death, wrongly claiming that he must have deserved such a fate at the hands of their communist allies. Dos Passos warned Hemingway about the Soviet's growing influence. As Dos Passos's biographer noted, "A friendship was ended, one casualty of the political turbulence of the decade."[22]

After several months in Spain, Hemingway returned to the United States. In June 1937, he and Gellhorn spoke at the left-wing–sponsored American Writer's Congress in New York City. The first Writer's Congress had been held two years earlier and gave rise to the communist-oriented League of American Writers. In *New Democracy*, Pound reacted to the league as "the offspring of a bigoted sect" that needed to bring its "Marxism up to date." He thundered: "If the congress proposes to reform society, let

at least the executive committee contain a few members who know something about economic history, outside the dogmas of some bigoted sect."[23]

While the first Writer's Congress had concentrated on capitalism's
overthrow, reflecting Stalin's Third Period ideology, its second gathering
was a Popular Front antifascist rally. Held at Carnegie Hall June 4–6, the
Second Congress designated twenty-two well-known writers to speak, and
featured USA Communist party leader Earl Browder and fellow travelers—Joseph Freeman, Malcolm Cowley, Granville Hicks, and several new
attendees, including Hemingway and the Congress's chairman of the opening session, Archibald McLeish. "By the time of the second congress,"
explains Daniel Aaron, "the party felt it expedient to push aside open Communists like Freeman, Gold, and Hicks in favor of illustrious fellow travelers
whose appearances would dramatize the Popular Front."[24]

At the Friday-night opening, 358 writers and 3,500 spectators gathered, while another thousand were turned away. Fortified by strong drink
from a nearby bar, Hemingway, the star of the Congress, delivered his first
major public speech at 10 p.m., subsequently published by the League of
American Writers as "The Writer and War" and in *New Masses* as "Fascism
Is a Lie." Before Hemingway spoke, Joris Ivens talked and showed two
sequences from *The Spanish Earth*. The stage set for his speech, Hemingway delivered, nervously, a diatribe that dealt with atrocities suffered at
the hands of the Spanish rebels and their Italian and German allies. Hemingway's most memorable lines stated: "There is only one form of government that cannot produce good writers, and that system is fascism. For
fascism is a lie told by bullies. A writer who will not lie cannot live or work
under fascism."[25]

In her address, Gellhorn asserted that the solidarity among writers in
Madrid was so strong that none of them competed for "a scoop or to beat
anyone else." It is unlikely that the competitive Hemingway adhered to this
ethical principle. If Gellhorn evoked the words of Popular Front rhetoric,
she appeared to some writers at the Congress, like Dawn Powell, as a privileged want-to-be traveler dressed in a gray fox coat. At evening's end, Powell recalled how Hemingway left the hall pursued by his female "pack of
foxes" en route to the Stork Club.[26]

Hemingway and Gellhorn then went on a nationwide tour to promote
The Spanish Earth, which featured his narration. On July 8, 1937, Hemingway and Gellhorn visited the White House for a private showing of the
film. It was shown on a sweltering Washington, D.C., evening to the president and his wife, Eleanor. Also present was Harry Hopkins, FDR's head
of the WPA—Hemingway's despised government agency that was respon-

sible for transforming Key West. Ironically, Ernest liked Hopkins, as he did Eleanor. Though the Roosevelts enjoyed the film, Hemingway's White House visit did nothing to change U.S. policy in assisting Spain and only reaffirmed his dislike of the president, whom he described to his mother-in-law as "very Harvard charming and sexless and womanly."[27]

Hemingway's dislike of Roosevelt was shared by those on the left, many of whom, ready to welcome major writers into their ranks, saw the possibility of Hemingway's coming over to their cause. One sign of this occurred with the October publication of Hemingway's 1937 novel *To Have and Have Not*. Though poorly received by the mainstream critics, the novel attracted the favorable notice of some leftwing reviewers in the now-famous last dying words of its protagonist Harry Morgan—"No matter how a man alone ain't got no bloody fucking chance." This utterance of a dying one-armed charter boat captain was, for some, a sign that Hemingway had shed his individualism. Yet, as literary scholar Scott Donaldson explains, Hemingway's alternatives to individualism throughout the novel were represented by even more abhorrent alternatives, in that "big government oppresses, revolution brutalizes, communism attracts the fashionable and insincere, politics ruins art, and there is precious little any man can do for his fellows." In his landmark work, *On Native Grounds*, Alfred Kazin, views *To Have and Have Not* as the work "of an angry and confused writer who had been too profoundly disturbed by the social and economic crisis to be indifferent, but could find no clue in his education by which to understand it. Inevitably, he lapsed into melodrama and sick violence."[28]

Hemingway contrasts the novel's wealthy haves—those sleeping, or trying to sleep, on their yachts on a quiet Key West night, with the have nots, army veterans with whom Hemingway drank at Sloppy Joe's—Freddy's Bar in the novel. These Florida Key survivors of war had been chased out of Anacostia Flats by President Hoover and sent south by Roosevelt, who, as one vet says as a way "to get rid of us." There were forty communists among the 2,000 vets working for FDR's "alphabet program" in Key West. But as one of the vets asserts, "A rummy can't be a communist." Hemingway then mocks the fashionable writers of the left. *To Have and Have Not*'s Robert Gordon—based upon Dos Passos—is a leftist, writing a novel about a textile strike in Gastonia. Gordon's wife lashes out at her husband as an opportunist who changes politics "to suit the fashion" of current trends.[29]

In the novel's portrayal of Cuban revolutionaries who rob a Key West bank to provide money for their cause, Hemingway reveals the irony of how the robbers kill several workingmen in the process. A student of revolutions, Hemingway was well aware of the bloodshed that typically arises in their wake—that the innocent can fall victim; that exploiters can go on the take; that the zealous can kill without mercy. Faced with a similar situation in Spain, Hemingway could only hope for a short conflict with a worthy outcome.

In April 1938, Pound wrote the young publisher James Laughlin that if the latter went to Paris, he should do his "best to annoy Ernest [Hemingway]. Mebbe he is still in Paris. If so better get both SIDES." Hemingway had been in Paris with Martha Gellhorn during March. While in Paris, before leaving for his third trip to Spain, Hemingway wrote Dos Passos, denying the Soviet domination of the Republican cause, since most of the officers that Dos Passos had met in Spain were non–Russian European communists. In Barcelona, Hemingway attended a showing of *The Spanish Earth*.[30]

The war in Spain was straining other friendships as well. By 1938, Pound's correspondence mentioning the war antagonized his friend William Carlos Williams. Chairman of the local Committee for Medical Help to Loyalist Spain, Williams informed Pound, "I detest your bastardly Italy today." He went on to comment that "Hemingway, with all his faults, is in Loyalist Spain. Wish you were there." Pound responded by stressing that Hemingway was there because of the need for "subject matter." As far as the communist threat in Spain, Pound lectured Williams, "EUROPE never intended Russia to get Barcelona." Pound ended this letter with an insulting, "HEIL Hitler." Williams candidly responded: "I think you're wrong about Spain. I think you're letting yourself be played for a sucker by the party in power in the country in which you happen to be living. As for Hemingway, his face is objectionable, I agree there, but he's far from being the issue in Spain or from representing it in his philosophy." Williams, concluded, "It is you, not Hemingway, in this case who is playing directly into the hands of the International Bankers."[31]

Hemingway made his last trip to Spain in November 1938. March 1939 saw the defeat of the Spanish Republic. Back in Key West and ready to leave for Cuba—his home for the next twenty years—Hemingway wrote his editor Max Perkins, "Am going to stay in one place now and work no matter what." Memories of war left him with numerous stories to write and the genesis of a great novel—*For Whom the Bell Tolls*.[32]

Published in 1940, *For Whom the Bell Tolls* caught the attention of William Carlos Williams, who noted the strong connection between Hemingway's craft and the lessons of Pound. Williams wrote James Laughlin:

"I'm starting to read Hem's novel. I'll bet he got his title out of a book of quotations, damned good lead off with the quotation from [John] Donne—which is itself something. The book teaches me one thing: a novel is not only a story but News, the kind of news newspapers can't sell and that you've got to feed 'em the bunk—love and war all the old fuck stuff.... Perhaps some of us lay too much stress on the value of literature as excellence in itself. You got to have a message, a MESSAGE! You ask ol' Ez, he'll tell you that."[33]

CHAPTER 11

Wordsmiths in Wartime

In *For Whom the Bell Tolls*, the death of Hemingway's Robert Jordan symbolized the death of 70,000 combatants killed during Spain's Civil War. After the Republic's defeat, Hemingway lost interest in political causes. Years later he reflected on his involvement: "I became involved in what was happening to the world and I had stayed with the better and for worse.... It had not been easy to get back and break the chains of responsibility that are built up, seemingly, as lightly as spiderwebs but that hold like steel cables."[1]

War in Spain proved to Hemingway the inevitability of Mussolini and Hitler thrusting Europe into another massive conflict. In stark contrast, Pound believed that Mussolini had no such intentions, he continued to praise him as a great statesman. Writer Kay Boyle and her husband, Lawrence Vail, visited Pound in Rapallo in 1938 to hear the poet laud Mussolini and Hitler. "I saw him desperate for power," recalled Boyle, "thirsting and starving for power, no matter how demeaning the conditions for attaining them might be."[2]

Long having given up fostering an artistic American Risorgimento, Pound turned to the possibility of converting his native land to his version of Social Credit that fused stamp script with Douglas's underconsumptionist theory. Pound hoped the Roosevelt Administration would embrace his monetary theory and guide America into a new, prosperous age. To carry out this messianic mission, Pound arrived in New York City on April 21, 1939, and told a reporter: "Nothing but devilment can start a new war west of the Vistula.... But the bankers and the munitions interests, whoever and wherever they may be, are more responsible for the present talk of war than are the intentions of Mussolini or anyone else." When asked about

116

Hemingway, Pound responded, "Hemingway is a good guy, but I don't suppose we'd want to meet personally. Spain." After Franco's victory in Spain nearly two months before, this comment insensitively slighted Hemingway, whom Pound thought was on the wrong side of history.[3]

After a brief stay in New York, Pound went to Washington, D.C. Though he did not see Roosevelt, Pound attained private audiences with a number of officials, anyone who would hear him out about monetary reform. This included senators John Bankhead, William Borah, Robert Taft, Arthur H. Vandenberg, James F. Byrd, Hamilton Fish, Jr., Martin Dies, and H.J. Voorhis. He attended a session of Congress and urged Voorhis, one of the most cooperative senators, to have all legislative hearings broadcast by radio to the American public.

During his American visit, Pound stayed at William Carlos Williams's home. Williams had witnessed Pound's many phases of life. He now encountered a Pound consumed by conspiracy theories. "The man is sunk, in my opinion," Williams wrote James Laughlin, "unless he can shake the fog of fascism out of his brain during the next few years, which I seriously doubt that he can do. The logicality of fascist rationalization is soon going to kill him." Williams thought Pound a "misplaced romantic" and "batty in the head," presciently seeing the dangers awaiting a man Hemingway had also judged mentally unstable.[4]

Pound's Social Credit–based ideas fell on deaf ears. Once again, he saw himself as rejected by his home country, a country in which leading universities had refused him a teaching position. He lashed out against banks and bankers as a Jewish conspiracy. He called President Roosevelt "Rossenfeld" and vilified the Jewish members of his administration's brain trust. Convinced that America had no need for a true poet who offered sound economic advice, Pound saw the Italians as respectful of his art and ideas.

Pound, inflamed by Social Credit, crusaded to save the Western world from bolshevism and utilized radio to spread his message. (He had used the medium in 1935 when he broadcast on shortwave radio in Rome.) In his 1938 work, *Guide to Kulchur*, Pound championed the possibilities of radio by reminding his readers: "Lenin won by radio, Roosevelt used it. Coughlin used it as minority weapon."[5]

By the mid–1930s, state-controlled Italian radio broadcast Mussolini's speeches, along with programs of art and entertainment. It featured more classical music, operas, full-length dramas, and live-theater performances than its American counterpart. By 1938, Italy boasted one million listeners who tuned into Ente Italiano Audizione Radiofoniche (EIAR), the company that controlled the country's programming. In his book *The Fascist Experience* Edward R. Tannenbaum notes that "few Italians seemed to have listened to foreign broadcasts, which were easy to receive at night." Tannenbaum explained that Italians "were so used to the tone and rhetoric of their own broadcasts that, unconsciously, they rejected other broadcasts." It is understandable that Pound's broadcasts in English, intended for American and British troops, would not have interested Italians.[6]

America's entrance into the war in late 1941 cut off Pound from America and Britain, countries he most wanted to influence. He took to the airwaves in talks influenced by Canadian-born Father Coughlin, known by his detractors as the "father of hate radio," whose 1930s broadcasts from Royal Oak, Michigan, attracted a nationwide audience. As Pound scholars have asserted, Pound possessed many of the same political leanings of the rightwing populism that bred such anti–Semitic firebrands. "Father Coughlin speaks regularly to millions of Americans, and that means he speaks also *for* them," stated Pound; he admired Coughlin's "great gift for simplifying vital issues to the point that the populace can understand their main factor if not the technical detail."[7]

Inspired by Coughlin, Pound entered what he called the "microphone war." In his droning, authoritative voice that slipped into a "folksy drawl of a plainsman from the Western United States," Pound became a deluded messiah, the great poet, and Social Credit Confucian, who believed that he offered an economic and ethical vision that could put entire nations' houses in order.[8]

As Europe headed closer to war, Hemingway's letters to Pound remained friendly. Hemingway once sent Pound the jawbones of a shark that his poet friend dubbed "The Grave of the Unknown Sailor." Impressed by this object's "power and tenacity," "Pound hung them on his living room wall," explained literary scholar John Tytell, as "a lesson in Imagism, the concrete object acting as visible symbol and existing entirely without discourse."[9]

Hemingway's gift was a calling card from the Caribbean, where he was spending much of his time in Cuba during his failing marriage to Pauline. Hemingway's Key West home had become a tourist destination. Listed in the 1939 WPA Florida guide, the house is described as enclosed by a high wall that "encloses the entire landscaped premises." But, by this time, Ernest had moved on to Cuba; he could no longer tolerate the changes on the island. Thousands visited by way of the recently completed Overseas Highway. The island's five hotels offered accommodations. Guests swam, fished, played shuffleboard, or frequented the two local motion-picture houses.[10]

Since 1940, the Hemingways' Key West home had remained empty. Pauline filed for divorce in March on grounds of desertion and secured a settlement that included the earnings of her ex-husband's next novel. Ernest lived in a Havana hotel room at the Ambos Mundos. Martha, searching for a permanent residence, found, not far from Havana, suitable quarters in a rundown house on the outskirts of the village of San Francisco de Paula. "It was a sprawling, one-story Spanish structure," wrote author Bernice Kert, "with some good features—a sixty foot living room, fifteen acres of lush farmland, a swimming pool filled with unfiltered greenish water, and a fenced-in area, overrun with weeds, that once had been the tennis court." In April, Ernest and Martha moved into the Finca Vigia. After his divorce with Pauline was finalized in May, Hemingway married Martha on November 2 and, by Christmas, he had purchased the Finca Vigia for $12,500.[11]

Through correspondence Pound was kept up to date on Hemingway's latest achievements and personal life. Published in October 1940, *For Whom the Bell Tolls* emerged as Hemingway's best-selling book up to that time. Sounding much like his correspondent, James Laughlin wrote Pound that his "friend Hemingway is having prodigious success with his book on spinach, which is hailed as THE great novel of all time since Homer—and was sold to hollywood for $150,000 ect etc. He deevorced Pauline and married the blonder girl I was telling you about, you recall?"[12]

In September, Ernest and Martha ("the blonder woman") vacationed as non-paying guests at the Sun Valley Lodge in central Idaho, a place they enjoyed since first visiting several years before. There, they relaxed at one of the earliest established "multi-use western resorts catering to the moderately wealthy, the famous, those on the rise." Guests arrived by train and were "driven up the valley past smooth brown hills," then passed through Pound's birthplace of Hailey on their way to the resort that accommodated numerous activities, from tennis and horse riding to bird hunting and trout fishing. Guests were offered a heated swimming pool, shops, and restaurants. There were parties and dances and gambling tables and a roulette wheel in nearby Ketchum.[13]

On December 3, Ernest and Martha went to Arizona. Some say that while they were passing through Texas they heard a radio broadcast announcing the Japanese attack on Pearl Harbor. Another account claims that they heard the broadcast in San Antonio, when a young Native American, selling newspapers, yelled out that America was at war. Hemingway angrily responded to the attack. He wrote Maxwell Perkins—in a letter he demanded to remain private—that it was imperative Secretary of the Navy Henry Knox be fired along with the other Americans responsible for the Pearl Harbor attack.

Germany and Italy declared war on the United States on December 11. President Roosevelt urged that Western hemisphere countries join in mutual protection from outside aggressors. A former Cuban dictator recently elected Cuban president in 1940, Fulgencio Batista entered the war on the Allied side. Batista's government established a new constitution and vowed to oppose the fascist powers.[14]

Hemingway had no interest in fighting under the Cuban flag. If he had such intentions, a 1907 American law—again enforced in 1937 during the Spanish Civil War—prohibited citizens from taking an oath of allegiance to a foreign government, with the penalty of loss of citizenship. Hemingway utilized his ties to the American ambassador to Cuba in forming a Havana-based counterespionage service. The main thrust of Hemingway's unit was to report on Nazi sympathizers among Spanish fascist Falangists. Though Spain remained neutral during the Second World War, the Allies found it important to keep watch on a country that had been courted by Hitler to join the Axis cause. Given approval by the U.S. State Department to form his undercover unit, Hemingway named it The Crook Factory, and made the Finca his headquarters. This caused dissension between the State Department and the FBI that opposed Hemingway's service. FBI chief Herbert Hoover personally disliked the hard-drinking Hemingway, whom he condemned as participating in the communist-led Republican cause. Hemingway eventually turned over his counterespionage operation to Gustavo Durán, a fellow Republican in the Spanish Civil War.

Hemingway then commissioned his thirty-eight-foot fishing boat, *Pilar*, in the search for German U-boats in the Caribbean. The shipping of Venezuelan oil and bauxite from French and English Guiana became prime targets for German U-boats. Close to Hemingway's maritime territory, U-boats began attacking oil tankers and merchant ships in the Caribbean. When war broke out, American and Cuban naval capability to patrol the U.S. Atlantic coast and the Caribbean was so scant that the Navy called upon civilian volunteers and their vessels to assist in this effort, thus resulting in the numerous commissioning of small civilian vessels.

Hemingway answered this call. As a maritime volunteer he became a member of what was informally called "The Hooligan Navy." More than a thrill-seeking spree with friends and comrades, the *Pilar*'s patrols involved dangerous risks. By the summer of 1942, twenty-two U-boats sank seventy-two merchant ships in the Gulf of Mexico; in the Caribbean, losses of Allied ships numbered 153 vessels. The Caribbean patrols placed Hemingway in the role of independent combatant. At the head of his handpicked crew—along with a required Marine gunner/radio operator—he plotted his own strategy, even daringly taking with him at times his teenaged sons, Gregory and Patrick.

Because the *Pilar* could not be outfitted with on-deck machine guns, the crew was limited to using Thompson machine guns, grenades, and an improvised explosive fashioned by Hemingway. The *Pilar* served deceptively as a boat conducting research for the American Museum of Natural History. It patrolled Cuba's north coast to the Old Bahamas Channel, one of three main approach routes of U-boats into the Caribbean. Unable to reach the speed to approach a U-boat that was moving away from it, the *Pilar* acted as decoy in luring the enemy close enough in an effort to damage its conning tower by machine-gun fire and light explosives. Though most experts agree that this tactic would prove ineffective in an actual confrontation with a U-boat, Hemingway went out into open waters hoping for such an encounter.

But the U.S. Navy viewed auxiliary craft like the *Pilar* most useful in spotting U-boats. Because it was rumored that fascist collaborators had set up covert fueling and food supply stations on the Cuban coast, the *Pilar* and its crew could be of service in sighting—and even attacking—these positions. But these supply operations were nothing more than rumor, and Hemingway's claim to have sighted a U-boat was another myth among many. In his book, *The Hemingway Patrols*, Terry Mort deals in depth with the writer's maritime service. "The patrols were a privateering adventure," explained Mort, "as well as a romantic quest, and of course, they were also an exercise in realism, a genuine attempt to serve and fight."[15]

As the Allies took control of the Atlantic in 1943, the U.S. government ended all auxiliary anti–U-boat service. Hemingway's service had its cost. Coming at the end of a failing marriage, it caused severe conflict with Martha, who never wavered in her belief that these activities in the Caribbean were a good-time spree of hard drinking and fishing at the government's expense. There were other consequences as well. In 1943, the FBI had opened a file on Hemingway's anti-submarine activities, a file that would continue in its surveillance until 1955. By war's end, both Hemingway and Pound would be on the FBI's list, the former as a suspected leftist, the latter as a supposed fascist enemy of the state.

While Hemingway searched for German U-boats, he learned about Pound's Radio Rome broadcasts. After the Pearl Harbor attack, Pound's broadcast on January 29 was entitled "On Resuming," in which he insensitively referred to the Pearl Harbor attack as "Arbour Day." He told his listeners that America was "ILLEGALLY at war, through what I consider the criminal acts of a President whose mental condition was NOT, as far as I could see, all that could or should be desired of a man in so responsible a position or office." Pound also alluded to Japan's cultural achievements, as if defending the country from its barbarous acts.[16]

With regards to Italy, Pound asserted: "For the United States to be makin' war on Italy AND on Europe is just plain damn nonsense and every native born American of American stock KNOWS it is plain damn nonsense." As he had in *Jefferson and/or Mussolini*, Pound referred to the virtues of his host country. Trains ran on time. Grain yield was up, the water supply improved, and the swamps drained. All supposedly led to the superior health of its citizens and made fascist Italy superior to the slums of America.[17]

Fortunately for Pound, several Americans looked out for his welfare. Archibald McLeish—the director of the Library of Congress—emerged as the most active supporter in Pound's cause, a charitable gesture given that in earlier years Pound's had, by way of correspondence, dismissed McLeish's poetic talent. Several months before Pearl Harbor, in October 1941, President Roosevelt appointed McLeish head of the new agency Office Facts and Figures (OFF). McLeish remained head of OFF until June 1942, when he headed the newly established Office of War Information (he resigned from OWI in January 1943). As McLeish's biographer Scott Donaldson writes: "In his view it was the proper and necessary function of OWI to provide this channel by helping the American people to decide what they were fighting for, what kind of world they wanted to live in after the war was over."[18]

At complete odds with the OWI's vision, Pound took to Radio Rome to tell the American people and their British Allies the "truth" behind what he viewed as an unnecessary war. Several of his broadcasts had harsh words for McLeish. This occurred when many leading American newspapers negatively treated FDR's choice of McLeish—a poet with ties to the left—in heading a federal information-gathering agency. In April 1942, Pound's broadcast responded to remarks made by McLeish in the media: "He has been given a gangsters brief; that is, he has been entrusted with the defense of a gang of criminals, and doin' his damnedest." McLeish's service in the Roosevelt Administration made him even more disreputable to Pound. In the same broadcast, Pound argued "that any man who submits to Roosevelt's treason to the Republic commits a breach of citizen's duty." Thus, according to Pound, McLeish was complicit in a treasonous gang that had plunged America into an unjust war. On another occasion during the same year, Pound called McLeish "Frankie's most faithful UNhappy warrior," someone who would "admit that reformers, the monetary reformers, the men who wanted honest functioning of the treasuries and finance in England and America, did NOT prevent this war."[19]

Nevertheless, McLeish recognized Pound as a great poet and sent Hemingway's letter of support to literary scholar and writer Allen Tate, who had just been appointed as the Library of Congress consultant in poetry. As head of the OWI and the Library of Congress, McLeish used his credentials to help Pound. He contacted his old friend Harvey Bundy, assistant secretary of war, alerting him to the fact that if Pound were to be incarcerated by the military authorities he could very well be tried and summarily executed. It was crucial that Pound be guaranteed a civil trial.

Pound's Jewish friend and fellow poet Louis Zukofsky, aware of the Radio Rome broadcasts, wrote William Carlos Williams after the latter forwarded a letter sent from Pound. Zukofsky wrote Williams: "He seems a we bit lonely between the lines—but why he should expect not to be, broadcasting for Muss. and writing for Social Justice—& expect civil life to continue under the circumstances beats me." Zukofsky added, "I wonder when Ez will realize the hole he's in—if ever."[20]

On occasion some Americans heard the Radio Rome broadcasts. One evening, a bank teller in New Jersey heard Pound's broadcast, which included a mention of local bank customer William Carlos Williams. When the teller encountered Williams's wife, Floss, there was a question regarding her husband's connection to Pound. Suspicion had also been aroused among investigators, resulting in Williams being twice visited by the FBI. In April 1942, the Department of Justice began an investigation into Pound's broadcasts. Agents were ordered to bring the recordings so that Williams could identify Pound's voice. This never occurred. Already outraged at Pound's earlier support of Franco, Williams was incensed that Pound's radio talks had led the FBI to investigate his own loyalty during wartime.

Other writers and poets took note of Pound's overseas activities. Writing in *Poetry* in 1942, Eunice Tietjens demanded that it was time "to put a formal end to the countenancing of Ezra Pound" and his attempt "to undermine the country of his birth through enemy propaganda." During late 1942, a friend of Alfred Kazin showed him transcripts of foreign broadcasts that included copies of Pound's Radio Rome broadcasts. "The first thing I saw reference to Mrs. Roosevelt consorting with 'niggers.' I felt amazement more than anything else as I read these pronouncements by one of the original poets and master critics of the twentieth century, the writer most responsible for making modernism in literature part of our lives." Kazin would never forget the shock of reading Pound's racist and antisemitic remarks. "Pound was to say after the war that no man named Ezra could be an anti–Semite," commented Kazin. "And that he had not known about the gas chambers." Kazin added that he well knew about such Nazi atrocities, and that he, like Pound, could also "personalize history."[21]

During the previous year, Nancy Cunard encountered Hemingway on the streets of Havana and recalled "nearly tripping over his great big foot stuck out on the sidewalk," only to be "greeted by Hemingway's broad smile." In a sidewalk café over drinks, Cunard asked Hemingway about Pound's reported pro-fascism. In her memoir, Cunard recalled Ernest explaining to her:

> Ezra had been ridiculed and paid no attention to first of all his native country, the United States. Next, living in England, he had not encountered sufficient respect for his work and ideas. Thirdly, it was more or less the same when he went to live in France. But it Italy, where he settled in the mid-twenties, he was considered of importance increasingly as the years passed. There he was a figure, perhaps even "a great man."[22]

Hemingway's concern about Pound's broadcasts prompted him to write Archibald MacLeish in early April 1943, asking about his friend's broadcasting schedule and radio wavelength. Certain that Pound would eventually have to stand trial, Hemingway wanted to hear the broadcasts so that he would be well informed if the U.S. government called upon him to testify. In a letter written on May 5, Hemingway requested from MacLeish photostats of Pound's broadcasts and confided that Ezra "should shoot himself." In this letter, Hemingway expressed his mistaken belief that Italy had treated Pound seriously as a poet. This so-called veneration, according the Hemingway, drew Pound into Mussolini's orbit. Hemingway concluded that Pound's punishment should be based upon his pathological mental state.[23]

On July 26, 1943, the day the transcripts arrived, a United States grand jury indicted Pound for treason. Reading the transcripts, Hemingway reviewed some of the crucial evidence that the U.S. government was using to accuse Pound of treason. Pound's radio rants only confirmed Hemingway's long-held belief that the poet was mentally unstable. Hem-

ingway voiced to MacLeish the main argument that he would repeatedly stress over the next decade—that Pound should be punished, not mar-
tyred.

Writing to poet Allen Tate, Hemingway reemphasized his remarks to
McLeish, and asserted that his old friend had slipped into madness. He
urged Tate to read the Radio Rome photostats and stressed that it was the
responsibility of all who had known Pound to inform the U.S. government
about his ignominious descent into mental illness.

It is not known if Hemingway was aware of Pound's mentioning him
on the air. On July 26, 1942, Pound's broadcast, briefly addressing unique
Americans, commended Hemingway as one who had stayed on top of the
most innovative currents in literature and society. With regard to most
young writers, Pound predicted, "They will not be tomorrow's Hemingways, or even today's Clark Gables." Pound most likely made reference to
For Whom the Bell Tolls. "I hear a million Americans have taken advantage
of Mr. Hemingway's last production, and so they ought to. TWO million
ought to read it (probably ... I haven't yet seen a copy but that is due to
conditions of Atlantic transport)."[24]

On March 14, 1943, Radio Rome aired Pound's talk, "Anglophilia."
In this rambling diatribe, Pound attempts to explain the latent English origins in America that now owe nothing to its European source, and therefore, he reasons, the United States should not fight for Britain's empire.
He speaks about the hostile treatment to which he was subjected while living in England and in Paris: "A truly representative American, the well
known and very widely read writer, Mr. E. Hemingway, considered me, in
1922, the ONLY American who ever got out of England alive." Pound goes
on to say: "That was a perfectly sincere opinion, given in a decade when
neither Hemingway nor I were being political. Mr. Hemingway is hardly
ever political. I believe his father was English." Again, Pound stresses his
friend's uniqueness: "The exceptional man, the, as Mr. Hemingway would
call him 'the good guy,' does NOT constitute the mass of the population.
He goes out and gets shot in the first months of 1914. His mass weight in
the democratic majority tends to diminish."[25]

But this kind of gossipy subject did not represent the majority of
Pound's broadcasts. More often, there were diatribes against the Roosevelt
administration, the bankers and usurers, communists, and supposed Jewish
plots to control finance and ruin modern nations. Pound began one program by stating, "Had I the tongue of men and angels I should be unable
to make sure that even the most faithful listeners would be able to hear
and grasp the whole of a series of my talks." Pound insisted that his talks

were presented in a coherent, logical order and thought them the best source for Americans to learn about art and economics.[26]

Despite Pound's admiration for Italy, he mentioned Hitler on the air more often than Mussolini. Though nothing was said about concentration camps, Pound had little or no sensitivity towards the Jewish people, who, he claimed, had wrought destruction in every country they inhabited. "Don't start a pogrom," demanded Pound. "That is, not an old style killing of small Jews. That system is no good whatsoever. Of course, if some man had a stroke of genius and could start a pogrom UP AT THE top, there might be something to say for it." Even Pound could excuse selective genocide as a means of removing Jewish bankers from places of power. But any talk of pogroms in 1942—the same year the Nazis adopted the "final solution"—is very disturbing in hindsight. Though Pound may have been ignorant of Nazi atrocities against the Jews, he would have much to answer for later. Even after he was imprisoned, he recommended that younger writers read Hitler's *Mein Kampf.*[27]

All of Pound's radio talks were thematically intended for American or British audiences. For those in London, he described their island as an outpost of "Yankee Judea," and told his British listeners that when Germany invaded the USSR in June 1941, they had their chance to get out of the war—a conflict that the Allies might not win. America and Britain had also made a monumental mistake in allying with the Soviet Union—"the Muscovite Terror" led by a "Georgian train robber."[28]

Pound's talks often centered upon Jewish financiers supposedly controlling the U.S. and the U.K. and a duplicitous American-Anglo media that had polluted their citizenry, blinding them to their political and economic histories. In Nazi fashion, he referred to President Roosevelt as "Rosenfeld" or "Frankie Finklestein Roosevelt," and his administration as "a gang" of "misleaders."[29]

Pound reminded listeners that he was first and foremost a poet, then an economist conversant with history. He repeatedly referred to his native land as a fallen country, stating, "America was promises," because it had forsaken its founders like Adams and Jefferson. But if Pound had learned anything from reading American history, he should have been aware of executive power during wartime. By denouncing the president he was also questioning the powers of the commander in chief. This is an interesting contradiction from a man who admired strong and imperious leaders and mistakenly believed Jefferson ruled over America from 1800 to 1826. Pound suggested that the president, if found mentally unstable for his actions, be jailed. "Keep Roosevelt's gang in office," he warned, "and you will not

ONLY lose the war abroad in both oceans but you will LOSE everything worth having at home." Given Pound's fate of imprisonment it was with a profound sense of irony when he boldly announced: "I think Roosevelt ought to be jailed, if a committee of doctors thinks him responsible for his actions, and I think he ought to be in a high-walled gook house, or insane asylum if he is NOT."[30]

Disgusted by Pound's diatribes against the U.S. government and his deluded anti–Semitism, Hemingway admitted to McLeish that the outspoken poet deserved "punishment and disgrace." Hemingway believed Pound's theories about predatory Jewish bankers to be especially absurd. Brought up in Oak Park, Illinois, Hemingway had been accustomed to mocking Jews and referred to himself as "Hemenstein," or added the suffix "stein" to the nicknames of friends. This prejudice appeared in letters to Pound, as Hemingway labeled certain individuals "Celto-Kike" or "Bloomsbury kike intellectual." Hemingway's cruel mockery and name-calling ended when he learned about the Nazis' barbarous treatment of the Jews.

Hemingway must have wondered, What had become of the apolitical poet of 1922? Always ready to help an old friend, Hemingway told McLeish that he would do "anything an honest man should do."[31]

By June 1943, the U.S. government suspended Hemingway's Q-boat operation after the battle of the Atlantic had greatly reduced German submarine warfare in the Caribbean. A month later, Pound's indictment for treason made international headlines. The news of this charge reached Pound in Rapallo, where for the past two years he had placed the blame for the war on banks and financiers. Pound had his chances to leave Italy or at least escape indictment for treason. Had he suspended his radio talks after Germany and Italy declared war on the United States, his case would have been one of a broadcasting eccentric poet spewing vitriolic nonsense, crank economics, and racist hate talk. Since this was not the case, he could have avoided the government's charges of treason by becoming an Italian citizen, something he never considered.

When war broke out in Europe, Pound may have tried to return to America. In May 1940, the embassy in Rome advised all Americans to leave Italy. The American embassy offered financial assistance for travel and sent several ships to evacuate Americans. According to Hugh Carpenter, Pound went to renew his passport at the Consulate General in Rome, which instead confiscated it, and informed Pound that the matter had to be reviewed in Washington, D.C. Federal authorities authorized a passport, allowing Pound's return to America for the duration of the war on the stipulation that his broadcasting cease.

In the interim, Pound had the option of taking a Pan-Am clipper from Rome to Lisbon in neutral Portugal—presumably with Dorothy. But this came too late as Pound's father fell ill and could not make the trip through occupied France. On November 11, 1941, eighty-three-year-old Homer fell and broke his hip. The Pounds' inability to leave was also due to Olga's refusal to abandon her daughter Mary in Italy. Whatever the circumstances, the Pounds stayed in Italy, where Ezra continued broadcasting over Radio Rome.

By 1943, Pound's daughter Mary recalled how Rapallo had "become a resort for the German army." She observed her father watching closely the stiff mannerisms of the uniformed German visitors and his ambivalent attitude towards them. "Emotionally, he had no leanings towards Germany," wrote Mary. "The same Boches who had killed some his best friends during the First World War, were lurking in the background." At the same time, Mary explained how her father respected German discipline and some aspects of the Nazi economic system.[32]

On July 25, 1943, Mussolini was forced to resign and was replaced by Marshal Pietro Badoglio. Under Bagdolio's new government the Fascist Party was dissolved, ending its twenty-one year rule. The Germans subsequently occupied Italy as the Allies invaded Sicily and then landed at Salerno, south of Naples. Preparations by the Allies in Great Britain to make a cross-channel invasion limited the number of troops in Italy and hindered their northward advance; that quickly became bogged down as they faced fierce German resistance. Pound saw the Allied invasion as a direct attack on Italian art and architecture that ended Il Duce's chance to establish a modern Risorgimento.

In August, Badoglio attempted to negotiate peace with the Allies. At this time, Pound went to Rome, where, at the American embassy now managed by the Swiss, he sought out the official reasons for the charges against him, only to learn that the embassy's contact with Washington had been cut. Back in Rapallo in early August, Pound wrote a letter to United States attorney general Francis Biddle to explain that the Italians never asked him to broadcast "anything contrary to his conscience, or contrary to his duties as an American citizen." He denied that he had spoken directly to the troops and argued that he was exercising his right to free speech by calling out "the facts" responsible for the entire conflagration.

In early September 1943, Anglo-American forces landed at Salerno. Thinking that the Allies had landed at Genoa, poet Louis Zukofsky wrote

William Carlos Williams about their friend Pound: "By the way, if the Am. army has really landed in Genoa, that's not far from Rapallo & Ez is in the Am. Army's arms? Unless he's escaped to 'barbaric' Spain or noortal Switzerland. Or 'Ezra in Sweden' for the title of ??? The comedy vies with the tragedy. I suppose Shakespeare could have written a tragedy on the fall of Mussolini, with Ez. as minor counsellor, but even that would have been Richard the Thirdish."[33]

In 1943, the new Bagdolio government declared war on Germany, but a Mussolini-led fascist regime was declared that September in the northern Italian town of Salò near Lake Garda—The Repubblica di Salò. Rescued by the Germans, Il Duce now ruled under their authority. Pound contacted the new regime and, at its invitation, visited Salò and met officials. Pound pledged his loyalty to the Salò Republic and planned returning to the airwaves, this time from Milan. As Leonard W. Doob, complier of Pound's Radio Rome speeches, asserts, "No evidence exists to indicate that any of the material was ever broadcast to America in Pound's name from Radio Milan while that station remained under the regime's control."[34]

On October 10, Pound visited friends in Rome, then embarked alone on foot north to visit his daughter Mary in the Tyrol. As in days past, he traveled with a rucksack on a route that avoided German troops, an estimated fifty miles from Rome to Rieti. From there, he took a train north. After managing to obtain clearance from German military authorities, he continued on foot. Another train took him from German-occupied Bologna to Verona, from which he walked to his daughter's town of Gais.

This journey Pound envisioned as part Homeric, part Hemingway adventure. In unpublished lines intended for Canto 84, he wrote about this trek:

> One night under the stars
> one on a beach at Retiti
> one on Bologna platform
> after food at the cab-driver's friend's trattoria
> Lo sfacelo, understood why Hem had written.
> that is, his values.

Pound's old friend inspired his arduous northern trip, proving that at nearly sixty years of age, he, too, was a man of action, still vigorous, and willing to take to the road.[35]

Halfway across the world, Hemingway, his Q-boat duty having ended, spent lonely days at the Finca surrounded by his cats and drinking friends. Urged on by Martha, Hemingway became a *Collier's* frontline war correspondent—a job the War Department reserved exclusively for men, as women journalists were not allowed at the battlefront. Hemingway took a plane to England, while Martha sailed eighteen days on a dynamite-carrying freighter. Ernest arrived on May 17, 1944, weeks earlier than his wife—an interval of time in which he collected information for an article on the Royal Air Force. He met and became the lover of fellow American war correspondent Mary Welsh. When Martha arrived in London she found her wounded husband recovering from injuries sustained when his Jeep hit a water tank during a nighttime blackout. Martha entered Ernest's hospital room to find him cheerfully drinking with friends. In London, she learned that her husband had taken up with a married female journalist.

Hemingway spent D-Day, June 6, 1944, in a landing craft in the English Channel, observing the Omaha Beach landing. On D-Day +1, Martha, attaining Red Cross credentials, preceded Ernest in reaching Normandy.

Back on the war front, Hemingway took advantage of being close to the fighting in France. Assigned to the 22nd regiment of the Fourth Infantry Division, he fulfilled the role of journalist while working closely with the Office of Strategic Services (OSS) and as an irregular combatant with the Free French, all of which led to a military investigation. Able to talk his way out of the possible charges against him that would have resulted in his removal from Collier's and sent home, Hemingway remained close to the front and followed the Free French forces during the reoccupation of Paris.

Hemingway claimed that he and his irregulars had freed the Ritz Hotel and Sylvia Beach's bookstore—a legend of his own making. Once in Paris, Hemingway and a few of his Free French Allies visited the shop. Greeted by Beach and her companion, Adrienne, Hemingway found the store emptied of its vast amount of books and papers, including the photos of himself and Pound that once adorned its walls. The shop had closed nearly four years earlier when a German officer threatened to confiscate Beach's entire inventory if Beach did not give him the store's only copy of Joyce's Finnegan's Wake. He returned once more with the same demand. In fear of imprisonment and the confiscation of her store, Beach, assisted by friends, moved everything, including the furniture, to a fourth-floor storage spot.

Staying at the Ritz, Hemingway ate sparingly from the hotel's limited food supply, but enjoyed an abundance of wine. Ernest spent time with Mary Welsh, a new lover who reinvigorated Ernest's lust for life. He joined Mary in touring Paris, seeing old haunts he had once visited with Hadley. Their walk in Montparnasse would have taken them to the Notre Dame de Champs, site of his second Paris apartment and Pound's studio. The fate of his poet friend must surely have crossed his mind. But the thrill of love and liberating Paris overshadowed concern for a man Hemingway still respected but would repeatedly call "a stupid traitor."

As Hemingway accompanied the 22nd Regiment of the Fourth Infantry Division into Germany, witnessing the brutal fighting in the Hürtgen Forest, Pound lived under German occupation in Rapallo, translating Confucius. In May 1944, the Germans strengthened coastal defenses, making Italian life in seaside towns more difficult as food became scarce. Pound's daughter Mary recounted that the family never "lingered on the beach, for there were soldiers stationed along the railroad close by, and on the beach itself cement walls had been set up. All the coast was heavily guarded."[36]

That same month, Ezra and Dorothy were forced by the Germans to leave their apartment within a twenty-four-hour period. They took up Olga's invitation to live with her in the nearby small village of Sant'Ambrogio. There, Ezra, his wife, and his mistress maintained an uneasy but quiet existence. This required the relocation of a cache of paperwork collected from the last twenty years—hundreds of books, papers and manuscripts, including letters from such friends as Hemingway. Transported by briefcase and knapsack, the material was carried to several locations in town.

Life for the three proved difficult. The long trek from the bottom of the hill to Olga's Sant'Ambrogio apartment took nearly an hour as they walked a "broad cobbled path, on narrow stone steps," past "gray holding walls" and olive, eucalyptus, and lemon trees. Sometimes they bought dried figs and chestnuts from the peasants. Inside Casa 60, accommodations were adequate, but the atmosphere was one of strained tolerance. Dorothy later recalled it as a form of hell.[37]

When Rome fell to the Allies on June 4, 1944, Rapallo had seen minimal damage by Allied planes that indirectly hit the town during the bombing of Genoa. Pound's daughter, Mary, recalled "bombers over Genoa and all along the coast to destroy bridges at Aurelia road," and that in Rapallo "only the church and the schoolhouse were hit." By the end of the war many houses like that of Pound's parents sustained slight structural damage.[38]

On May 2, German envoys signed an unconditional surrender of Italy. Shortly after, Pound, dressed in his finest, wandered down the hillside and presented himself to American troops—his head filled with delusional plans of helping negotiate peace with Japan or learning to speak Georgian for a personal meeting with Stalin. Making no sense to the Americans, Pound returned to his apartment.

During the war several Italian communist partisans had been shot in Rapallo by German troops. Their roles now reversed, partisans combed the area for fascists and their collaborators. On May 3, Dorothy left the apartment on her weekly visit to Ezra's mother, Isabel, and Olga went shopping. At his desk, working, Pound heard a knock on the door and encountered several machine-gun-carrying partisans. When forced to leave his apartment, Pound pocketed a Confucian translation of Mencius and a Chinese dictionary and, crossing the grounds, picked up several eucalyptus seeds that he would keep throughout his imprisonment. When Olga returned, a neighbor informed her that Ezra had been led away. She went immediately to partisan headquarters at Zoagli. She stayed at Ezra's side when he was taken to Lavagna, where they saw a wall bloodied by the victims of summary executions. When his captors learned that Pound brought no bounty, they let him go free.

Still thinking he could be of great use to the State Department and not giving much thought to his indictment, he sought out U.S. military headquarters in at Lavagna. He and Olga were then taken to U.S. Counter Intelligence Corps headquarters in Genoa. Finally identified, Pound was questioned by FBI agent Frank Amprim, who had been assigned to investigate war crimes. Afforded the use of a typewriter and treated well in Genoa, Pound persisted in believing that he would be called upon to negotiate a postwar peace in Asia or in Moscow, and, though it was not permitted, he requested to write a letter to President Truman to assist in communicating with the Japanese.

Taken by military police to the U.S. Army Disciplinary Training Center near Pisa, Pound entered a makeshift, one-and-a-half-mile-square camp, holding 3,600 court-martialed military criminals and murderers. Those who had gone AWOL could return to service after successfully undergoing fourteen-hour-a-day training. Surrounded by barbwire, the camp had several guard towers. Small pup tents held prisoners, and larger ones accommodated the guards and officers; other light wood structures were covered with chicken wire and tar paper.

At the DTC, Pound was placed in one of the cages known as "death cells" that held prisoners awaiting death sentences. Welding torches were used to reinforce Pound's six-by-six-foot cage, and curious prisoners wondered at this extra security measure, unaware that it would hold a captured poet. In a row of these cages, Pound's place of confinement exposed him to the elements. Inside what Pound called his "gorilla cage," bright lights shone down on him in the darkness, paining his sensitive eyes. When given a small pup tent, he erected it inside the cage in many clever ways for protection.

Sixty-year-old Pound finally collapsed under the strain of his outdoor confinement and was transferred to the medical section, where he spent the summer. Many prisoners, even several African Americans, liked this avuncular eccentric, dressed in army fatigues—no shoe laces or a belt were issued for reasons of preventing suicide—as he engaged in imaginary fencing and tennis matches. On the dispensary typewriter Pound worked six hours a day, translating Confucius.

In the meantime, investigators under the direction of the FBI searched Pound's Rapallo apartment and confiscated his papers. Headlines back in America alerted readers to the imprisoned poet. As *Time* magazine celebrated victory in Europe, it reported: "As the political prison camps of Germany are emptied, the political prison camps of the allies are filled, included among the latter prisoners was Ezra Pound ... a star Axis propagandist ... arrested near Genoa." This brief mention was accompanied by Pound's photograph—hat tipped back on his head, bespectacled, smiling, his shirt opened to reveal a bare chest.[39]

The Cantos written at DTC, notes Hugh Kenner, were the work of a Pound more at "peace with himself, the great poet forcing the angry propagandist to surrender all but a few cragged redoubts." Many critics have considered this section, known as the *Pisan Cantos*, the finest of Pound's epic poem. Hemingway later admired them as proof that the great master had not slipped into aesthetic oblivion.[40]

CHAPTER 12

An Exile's Return

On November 18, 1945, Pound was extradited to Washington, D.C. Upon leaving the DTC's medical dispensary, he put his hands around his neck and jerked up his chin in a gesture suggesting a gallows fate. While held in Genoa, Pound wrote in a sworn statement in his defense: "Life consists in taking the million to one chance when instinct bids, and the stake is worth it, and when it can, in any case do no harm." Pound would soon discover the consequences of following his instincts in realms far beyond that of poetry.[1]

In another statement in May 1945, Pound held firm to his Confucian principles: "Whenever a Chinese dynasty has lasted three centuries it has been founded on the principles ascertained by Confucius.... Dynasties not so founded have flopped, as have the systems of Mussolini and Hitler." Thus, Pound, the would-be sage counselor to world leaders, believed the European Axis failed from ignoring his brand of Confucian wisdom and Social Credit. As Robert Spoo astutely explains: "Ezra's worldview was essentially a static one, a time lag of the mind. Circumstances might change, years elapse, but his stock themes and characters remained the same.... Now, under the strain of events, he more than ever dreamed of playing a world-historical role as the sane economist, the Confucian super ambassador." Upon this deluded premise, Pound thought he would be judged in a U.S. federal court. Hemingway believed Pound's Radio Rome transcripts would be evidence enough to prove Pound's foolish utterances as those of a deluded poet.[2]

At this time, Pound's publisher, James Laughlin, stepped up efforts to alter Pound's image, reminding the literary community of his worth as a major poet. As a Harvard graduate, Laughlin made the pilgrimage to

Rapallo. Laughlin had taken Pound's advice and became a publisher, founding New Directions Books. In 1938, Laughlin's small firm became Pound's major source of reissuing his books of poetry and essays.

Laughlin also came to Pound's assistance by retaining Julien Cornell as the poet's attorney. Cornell based his defense strategy upon proving Pound's insanity. He collected his client's personal history, and among this evidence was a letter from Hemingway referring to the 1933 dinner with Pound in which he and James Joyce judged the poet to be mentally unstable. But as Pound biographer Hugh Carpenter points out, "There was a considerable difference between calling him 'cracked' in private letters and publicly claiming, as a legal defense, that he was clinically insane." In 1944, William Carlos Williams confided to Robert McAlmon that he had made up his mind to "defend him if I am ever called as a witness in his trial." Little suggests, however, that Hemingway and other writers once close to Pound would have testified in court as to the poet's mental state.[3]

Pound maintained that his broadcasts were not treasonous but intended to save the American Constitution. The poet offered his services to the Allies, claiming that his knowledge of Asian culture would prove vital in the postwar negotiations with the defeated Japanese; he also volunteered to learn Georgian so as to speak directly with Joseph Stalin in his native language.

Held in the District of Columbia Jail, Pound awaited indictment. He thought that by acting as his own counsel he could set the record straight in a high-profile trial. Judge Bolitha Laws denied this request. After a fit of claustrophobia, Pound was transferred to the jail infirmary. On November 26, the original 1943 indictment of treason was revised upon the "question as to the sufficiency of the available evidence to sustain the charges in their original form, owing to the requirement in the American constitution of two witnesses to each overt act of treason."[4]

The next morning, Cornell met privately with Pound about the Grand Jury indictment, and suggested that his client remain mute. Stunned at this suggestion and in fear of the trial, Pound remained speechless, struggling for words that failed to come forth. That afternoon in court, Cornell entered a plea of innocence for his client, whom he requested be allowed to stand mute. Cornell then submitted to Judge Laws the affidavit describing Pound's loss of memory and recent breakdown, and entered an insanity plea. Judge Laws requested that Pound be moved to a hospital where mental health professionals could observe and perhaps treat the accused. Pound was then transferred from the district jail to a private room in the psychiatric ward of Gallinger Municipal Hospital.

In early December, Pound and Hemingway's Paris publisher, Bill Bird, visited Ezra. During his fifteen-minute visit, Bird tried to speak of personal matters, but Pound remained obsessed with politics. Bird reported to Dorothy that her husband "appeared disillusioned" over Mussolini's defeat and execution, and talked of persuading Stalin of the superiority of the U.S. Constitution to the Soviet Constitution.[5]

To assess Pound's mental state, the court required the findings of four psychiatrists—three appointed by the prosecution and one chosen by counsel—as "delusions of grandeur." On December 14, the trial continued with the presentation of evidence by the four psychiatrists, each of whom judged Pound as unfit to plead. Judge Laws then demanded that Pound be moved from Gallinger to St. Elizabeths Hospital, Washington, D.C.'s, federal hospital for the criminally insane.

In 1945, James Laughlin wrote T.S. Eliot: "There has been so much publicity about his being (not being accused of being) a traitor that we must go to work here with a campaign to reestablish his standing. If we can get Hemingway to let us use publicly what he said privately in letters to Julien [Cornell] we will have something to work with. Hem states that bitter ant-fascist as he was he never hated Ezra because he realized he was not responsible for what he was doing. If we can get that around it will start something."[6]

Hemingway refused to support any such extra-legal efforts to free his friend. But in correspondence and in the media, Hemingway repeatedly urged Pound's release and deportation to Italy, where the poet could write freely. Several days before Pound was judged mentally unfit, Hemingway wrote Malcolm Cowley describing Ezra as a mentally unbalanced traitor whose head should be shaved as a collaborator. He also mentioned the 1933 dinner with Pound and Joyce as evidence of his friend's madness.

On December 21, 1945, Pound was admitted to St. Elizabeths, occupying a hill in Washington, D.C. Built in 1855 as the Government Hospital for the Insane, it later housed wounded Civil War soldiers. Three hundred Union and Confederate dead were buried on its grounds. It was at this time that soldiers, not wanting to write home that they were being held in a hospital for the insane, referred to it as St. Elizabeths—the colonial name for the tract where the institution now stood and from which the hospital took its name in 1916. Located on three hundred lush acres, St. Elizabeths had numerous red-brick gothic-style buildings, some of which were old and dilapidated. At the time of Pound's confinement, its maximum capacity of 6,500 had exceeded that number.

Confined to Howard Hall while awaiting trial, Pound was not allowed to wander beyond its surrounding dry moat and high wall. One of the hospital's oldest buildings, Howard Hall held the criminally insane under strict supervision. Pound's small cell—his "hell hole" behind an iron door—made him claustrophobic and left him longing for the comfort of a tub bath. As literary scholar Robert Spoo writes: "At the DTC he had been able to study nature as a way of persuading himself that the eternal ordinary persisted despite madness raging through man's world. During the first months of St. Elizabeths, however, there was no green katydid to offer lessons in sanity, no infant wasp to show that nature's courses ran undisturbed, no sunset to chide the vanity of man-made beauty."[7]

Indicted on nineteen counts of treason, Pound appeared on February 13, 1946, before a sanity hearing to determine if he was fit to stand trial. In the District of Columbia courthouse, Cornell acted as Pound's defense lawyer, opposing two Department of Justice prosecutors. After three minutes of deliberation the jury handed down its verdict—Pound was of unsound mind. It is still argued that Pound was either feigning madness, was temporarily ill, or was suffering from megalomania. During the courtroom proceedings Pound rose to his feet and shouted, "I never did believe in Fascism. God damn it; I am opposed to Fascism." Quieted by his lawyer, Pound sat dejectedly, his head resting on the table.[8]

On February 14, 1946, the *New York Times* carried the byline, "Pound's Mind 'Unsound.'" The federal court judged him as being "mentally UNSOUND" and therefore "unfit for a treason trail." A number of newspapers and magazines carried various opinions regarding Pound— some condemning him as dangerous and his crimes equal to Nazi propagandists; others, like the *Washington Post*, considered Pound's wartime role as never important enough "to make it necessary to exact the price of his treason in blood." The *Post* voiced the same view as Hemingway: that Pound not be made a martyr.[9]

Others had their opinions. Pound's old friend Joe Gould, the famous Greenwich Village bohemian most remembered for attempting to write his epic "History of the World," responded to the government's judgment of Pound's mental state. In a letter to William Carlos Williams, Gould included a poem about Ezra Pound. Williams considered Pound "a jackass," but "not a traitor," because he "had it in him to be what he's turned out to be from the beginning." Pound's friend Louis Zukofsky wrote Williams that he thought the trial and Pound's treatment "a mad way out – typical of our time: glib psychiatrists, willing judges etc." but did not want to see him suffer. Zukofsky, nevertheless, addressed the vital point that Pound was "certainly willing to see millions suffer <while he> ranted."[10]

Hemingway publicly called Pound a traitor, mentally imbalanced if not mad. According to Hemingway's son Gregory, he later took a more contradictory view, telling him that he had convinced himself that Pound "was crazy when insanity was his only defense against treason.... That was uppermost in our minds when a group of us tried to get the treason charge dropped—and we succeeded—so poor Ezra was committed to St. Elizabeths Hospital in Washington." The accuracy of this account—written more than a decade after Ernest's death—may cast some light on Hemingway's loyalty; but, in private correspondence, Hemingway maintained that Pound was undoubtedly not the same man he had known back in early Paris days.[11]

In Pound's early years of confinement at St. Elizabeths, visitors saw him for fifteen-minute intervals, and were allowed access only upon his approval. Pound did not allow reporters interviews. Daily three-hour exercise periods were required. During his incarceration, Pound was given no drugs, no psychiatric sessions, no occupational therapy. Ironically, Pound did not contest his being judged mentally unfit; his main concern was being found guilty of treason, which he wholeheartedly denied.

In his study, *The Roots of Treason*, E. Fuller Torrey argues that Pound was considered by most of the staff and hospital psychiatrists as not mentally ill—that Dr. Winfred Overholser led the way in misleading the Justice Department about Pound's mental condition. More recent scholarship counters Torrey's contention that Pound feigned mental illness. Wendy Stallard Flory points out that Overholser assessed Pound's mental state according to psychiatric categories and research of the day. "Overholser was wise enough to know that diagnostic categories are often clumsy attempts at systematization of complex patterns of mental activity, that they are subsequent to the intuitive insights that lead to their formalization."[12]

Pound made the best of his confinement. Biographer Hugh Carpenter perceptively summarized Pound's life at this time: "Confinement at St. Elizabeths, though undoubtedly a severe ordeal, was entirely without blessings. It is hard to imagine what way of life, what role, would have remained for him in Rapallo—or elsewhere—if he had been allowed to go free at the conclusion of the war. To play the noble sufferer, the maligned but uncomplaining sage, the wise man in the madhouse, offered far more potential than that of the elderly and not very popular poet still exiled in a Europe that had seen the defeat of his ideas."[13]

Dorothy's arrival in Washington, D.C., made Pound's life more tolerable. Through Archibald McLeish's assistance, Dorothy secured a passport and traveled from Italy to America in 1946. Taking a simple apartment in Washington, D.C., Dorothy visited Ezra daily. Pound depended upon his wife—the committee of one responsible for his affairs—to write many of the letters sent to defend his name and reputation. When still in Rapallo, Dorothy wrote Pound's friend, U.S. House Representative George Holden Tinkham. In one of the many letters Dorothy sent defending her husband, she emphasized to Tinkham: "E. was never under anybody's order at the Radio—The stuff was all his own. He was trying to teach them a little history, U.S. history: Adams, Jefferson, points on the Constitution. He always has worked for inter-communication to understanding as per. continuing nonparty and nonpolitical work after the fall of Mussolini."[14]

As if one mind with her husband, Dorothy defended Ezra and saw him wrongly judged and confined. At this early stage of his confinement, poet Charles Olson visited, but soon discovered a man still speaking out against Jews and defending the fallen fascist regimes. Olson thought the poet as not mentally ill, and stated, "He is a fascist, the worst kind, the intellectual fascist."[15]

In February 1946, H.L. Mencken visited St. Elizabeths and brought his friend four pounds of candy. "Inasmuch as he is charged with treason," wrote Mencken in his dairy, "he is in the strictest confinement, and all visitors must see him in a barred room in the presence of a guard." Mencken went on to write that he would send Pound a "small sum for minor needs." Mencken recorded that Pound complained of suffering from lethargy, that he was not fit to write poetry for another three years.[16]

During the following month, E.E. Cummings and his wife, Marion, visited Pound, "bringing flowers and good cheer." Cummings's biographer wrote, "Marion (against hospital regulations) photographed Pound reclining in a government chair, carnation in his button hole, half a smile on his face." Cummings also wrote about Pound in his dairy, revealing his disgust for the political Pound: "Some of his raving was apt; some merely bizarre—anyhow, all was tasteless (frantic).... But America *did* "win this war": therefore, P (having bet a thousand percent on the completely wrong horse) is in trouble."[17]

In February 1947, Pound was moved from Howard Hall to the Center Building. A year later he occupied a room in the building's Chestnut Ward, where slipper-wearing male inmates, known as "Chestnuts," "drifted along linoleum floors." Pound was allowed the use of an area outside his room where he received a steady flow of visitors. Laughlin described it as an "alcove by a window in the long hall with fairly comfortable chairs." Pound snapped his fingers to make some of the ward inmates fetch an extra chair or to shoo them away. Now that he was receiving visitors and constantly sending out correspondence, Pound wrote his mother, in a mood of dark humor: "You might like it better than Rapallo, at least the steam heat and the morning coffee."[18]

There was the reason at this time for Pound's regarding his confinement as a refuge rather than imprisonment. He believed that his release would place him in danger of being exterminated by imagined enemies, notably Roosevelt's economic advisor Bernard Baruch and columnist Walter Winchell, who were supposedly responsible for his confinement. In St. Elizabeths, Pound feared Baruch—whom he had frequently maligned on his Radio Rome broadcasts—had plotted a conspiracy to poison him.[19]

By 1948, Pound was allowed access to St. Elizabeths' grounds. Summer days were spent with Dorothy, relaxing under a large oak, in folding chairs; newspapers were offered to guests to sit or lie upon the grass. Tea was served from a thermos, and fruit handed out. Once having enjoyed giving food scraps to Rapallo's stray cats, Pound now fed birds and teased squirrels by tying a string to pieces of food then drawing it away.

At this time, poet Robert Lowell frequently visited, bringing friends such as Randall Jarrel and John Berryman. On one occasion he brought publisher Robert Giroux, and found the imprisoned poet "full of gay obscenities, funny nutty jokes on notables." Pound sang songs for his guests, read from some translations, and made out a list of books he thought worth reading.[20]

William Carlos Williams visited as well. In 1946, Williams had written President Truman, suggesting that his friend Ezra Pound, though admittedly "a fool" for his wartime broadcasts, be allowed to go free. A friend who had known Pound since college days, William was "Old Bull," a tough-minded individual who traveled from nearby New Jersey to see Pound. When he first visited Williams in the summer of 1946, he marveled at how outwardly content Pound seemed in confinement. At the sight of Williams on the tree-shaded grounds, Pound rose up from his beach chair to greet him. Williams thought his friend looked much the same—"same beard and restless twitching of the hands, shifting of the shoulders about as he lay back in the chair studying me." Out of Pound's broken sentences and wandering train of thought—the "short, swift words"—Williams listened for nearly an hour to theories, conspiracies, and world remedies—the duty of artists, even if imprisoned, to set the record straight and spread the truth.[21]

Another visitor, Marianne Moore, sent ten dollars to Pound and admonished her old friend, "Don't be embittered. Embitterment is a sin—

a subject on which I am an authority." A poet of strong will and immense talent, Moore could offer wise words. "You have scores of friends," she later wrote, "not scores of good as your animal friends, but scores who somewhat sweeten their environs. You must not be profane, Ezra, without cause; or penny wise (no pun intended). Not to be in context where one belongs is misleading."[22]

As he watched friends grow old and die, Pound took on the role of elder poet sage, referring to himself as "grand pa." Now gray-bearded, Hemingway also played up his image as "Papa," fishing the Caribbean. Both men had passed through many phases of life. Pound, once the poet rebel of London, Parisian-based promoter of young artists and deluded visionary of Rapallo—now held forth to younger hospital visitors. Louis Dudek remembers Pound taking on the "grand pa" role when he first visited him around 1950. In his diary, Dudek describes a "huge and animal-like" Pound with a shaggy beard that pointed "outward in three directions"—the round, highly flushed face, with glasses that of a "Chinese sage."[23]

CHAPTER 13

"A good year
to release poets"

Unlike many of Pound's longtime friends, Hemingway did not visit St. Elizabeths. Those who did were disturbed by the conditions and their friend's mental state. T.S. Eliot encountered Pound in St. Elizabeths to find an unbearable megalomaniac and "a very sad case." St. Elizabeths and its imprisoned poet was such an unpleasant experience that Eliot visited only occasionally while in Washington. As he told John Malcolm Brinin: "From what I could tell, he seemed capable of rational discourse in the early part of the day but grew less so as the day went on. To be in his company was less to attend him that to observe him—the deterioration, painful for the visitor and of no earthly help to Ezra."[1]

Living in Cuba, Hemingway never considered a visit. Some writers like Michael Reck—a later visitor to St. Elizabeths—believed that guilt kept Hemingway from visiting Pound, that a being inside a mental institution did not fit his "he-man world-sportsman" role. But Hemingway had his own mental problems, bleak dark moods intensified by excessive drink. This only increased his reasons for not visiting. Having undergone psychiatric examination during World War II, Hemingway, like Pound, despised mental-health specialists. His dislike for psychiatrists was shared by Pound who, in his antisemitic conspiratorial mind, referred to them as "kikiatrists" given to Vienna gutter thinking—Jewish science"—that was determined to undermine Western civilization.[2]

For Hemingway mental illness was a sign of weakness. Later, in need of clinical help he refused treatment in a mental hospital. In the end, it is ironic that the confined Pound never experienced electroshock, while

Hemingway later underwent this procedure several times at the Mayo Clinic.

One telling sign that Pound understood Hemingway not visiting or overtly campaigning to free him was revealed when he told Eustace Mullins at St. Elizabeths: "Hem tried to do all he could and still work *within* the system." Pound knew well how much Hemingway despised bureaucracies and feared further federal government investigation. Pound hoped to see his old friend, but knew it would be outside the walls of St. Elizabeths.[3]

In 1949, several years after the death of Gertrude Stein, Alice B. Toklas expressed a profound insight into Pound's later path in life. Writing Thornton Wilder, she observed: "If the war had only lasted longer he would have turned against Italy—the way he did against France twice and England— and he'd be free now to find a more varied audience—which is what one always most wished for him."[4]

If most Americans had largely forgotten Pound, they soon encountered his name in newspaper headlines. On January 20, 1949, the front page of the *New York Times* announced: "Pound, in Mental Clinic, Wins Prize for Poetry Penned in Treason Cell." That year, Pound was awarded the Bollingen Award for the *Pisan Cantos*. Established and endowed by Paul Mellon, the non-profit Bollingen Foundation bestowed its $1,000 award under the auspices of the Fellows in American Letters of the Library of Congress. Published by New Directions in 1948, the *Pisan Cantos* (Nos. 74–84)—considered by the majority of the fellows as the best poetic work published that year—caused a national controversy. Among panelists casting their votes for Pound's work, T.S. Eliot and Alan Tate thought it well deserved, even more than William Carlos Williams's nominated work, *Patterson (Book Two)*.

Panelists like Eliot and Tate defended their vote upon the formalist assumption that a work of art be understood solely by its structural elements—that biographical or historical influences had little to do with its intrinsic value. As reported in the *New York Times*, the panelists were well aware of the controversy surrounding the award to Pound, but stressed that an "objective view" had to prevail. "To permit other considerations," stated the judges, would undermine the "poetic achievement to sway the decision [and] would destroy the significance of the award and would in principle deny the validity of the objective perception value on which any civilized society must rest."[5]

This aesthetic viewpoint outraged many Jewish writers. Dissenters among the Bollingen panelists, notably Karl Shapiro, represented those who could not separate the poetry from the poet. News of the prize caused a split among writers and intellectuals. As Irving Howe later recalled, "We were forced back to a reconsideration of what could be meant by aesthetic autonomy."[6]

Many writers in the press spoke out against giving the award to a poet whose work had been composed while imprisoned in a U.S. military detention camp. Robert Hillyer's article in a June edition of the *Saturday Review of Literature* carried the headline, "Treason's Strange Fruit: The Case of Ezra Pound the Bollingen Award." In his article, Hillyer supposedly revealed a fascist conspiracy that ran through the work of Pound, Eliot, Carl Sandburg, W.H. Auden, and others. This evoked a number of editorial responses that defended Pound. William Carlos Williams thought Hillyer's article a "disgusting attack."[7]

The furor caused by the 1949 Bollingen Award culminated in what has been termed "The Pound Question" and the controversy it raised has been viewed by scholars like Karl Frederick as "a crisis in Modernism." Frederick considers Pound a fallen modernist, a cultural rebel turned antisemite and political elitist. For most Jewish writers and critics Pound had perverted language by sacrificing the human element for ideological and racist rants. Though modernism was founded on the irreverent, the need to attack the aesthetic commonplace, Frederick asserts that the Bollingen Award had opened the way for the sacrifice of moral responsibility in the name of poetry. The question remains: did a supposed poet madman, in the name of freedom of expression, have the right to voice his anti–Semitism in the immediate aftermath of the Holocaust? It was one thing for Pound to write poetry expressing pro-fascist and anti–Semitic sentiments and quite another for his receiving a prestigious national literary award for its composition.

Marred by mention of Mussolini and anti–Semitic references, the *Pisan Cantos*, nevertheless, contain many fine lines dealing with the imprisoned poet's possible redemption as he contemplates nature—seeing the local terrain through a Chinese sage's eyes—sifts through history, and addresses his fellow prisoners, most of them African American. Mentioned in the *Pisan Cantos* (no. 74) alongside George Antheil, Hemingway considered the section as some of the epic's finest verse. Though he never voiced his opinion about the Bollingen Award in the media, Hemingway upheld the formalists' view amid the heated debate, and his consistent urging that Pound receive the Nobel Prize more than revealed where he stood. Later, Ernest wrote Dorothy to congratulate Ezra upon winning the Bollingen Award, telling her how he admired his recent poetry and glad that his friend was not hanged like the 1916 Irish rebel Roger Casement. Never one to value literary awards, Pound irreverently called the Bollingen Award the "Bubble-Gum Award."

In the aftermath of the Bollingen Award, Hemingway paid tribute to Pound in New Direction's anthology *An Examination of Ezra Pound* (1950). First published in England, this work brought Hemingway together with other internationally known writers and critics, including T.S. Eliot, Allen Tate, and Marshall McLuhan, a longtime admirer of Pound, who in 1948 visited St. Elizabeths with a young student, Hugh Kenner.

All the while, Hemingway repeatedly stated in the press that Pound be released and allowed to live in Italy. He well knew his visit could work against his friend since a celebrity like himself would attract reporters who might goad Pound into commenting on politics or race. Most of all, Hemingway no doubt feared that visiting a federal institution would also bring attention from the FBI. Hemingway revealed uneasiness about his support of Pound when later writing to his friend A.E. Hotchner, "Actually laying it on the line for bloody Ezra Pound. Knowing all the trouble will get in for it."[8]

Over the years Hemingway was often called upon to help free Pound. South American poet Gabriela Mistral conceived of a petition to gather signatures of Nobel Prize winners to request the dismissal of the charges against Pound. This was to be sent to President Truman. Though Hemingway had not yet won a Nobel Prize, Mistral contacted Hemingway in 1951 through a letter sent to Pound by scholar D.D. Paige. Suspicious of this scheme, Hemingway wrote Paige, expressing his many misgivings. He differentiated between Pound, the poet, and Pound, the radio propagandist. He asserted that President Truman was unlikely to support such a controversial issue—especially with an upcoming election year—while being attacked by Republicans for being "soft" on communism.

Hemingway further warned Paige that if Pound was judged not insane, he would be required to stand trial. He warned about his friend's fate if released. Was Mistral prepared to offer asylum to Pound in her native country or secure his going back to Italy? Hemingway then wrote Dorothy Pound, explaining his position about this ongoing campaign and expressing his concern about people like Mistral, whose careers can be advanced by "Ezra's trials and misfortunes."[9]

Hemingway's concern about sensational publicity emerged when Pound's longtime mistress, Olga Rudge, living in Italy, drummed up support for Pound's release. Olga vowed to "not give E. up" and wrote letters to Dr.

Overholser at St. Elizabeths, inquiring about Ezra's health. Olga considered her role as crucial and thought Dorothy—her longtime rival for Ezra's affection—as lacking aggressiveness to rally support on Ezra's behalf. In October 1948, she distributed a petition in Rapallo for the locals to sign, proving that Ezra never "took part in fascist activities," "never committed anti–Semitic acts," and that he was a friend of America.[10]

Rudge's next attempted to clear Pound's name came with the publication of six transcriptions of Pound's Radio Rome broadcasts—*If This Be Treason* (1949). Mostly literary in content, this booklet, according to Olga, was proof of Ezra's innocence. Learning of Rudge's efforts to free Pound, Hemingway informed Paige about what he negatively referred to as "the Rudge business," which only added to the hysteria surrounding the case. Hemingway expressed this to Dorothy Pound as well. Again, Hemingway saw the danger in too much publicity, especially when drummed up by those not prepared to handle the matter effectively, legally or otherwise.

Hemingway was never a friend of Olga. In turn, she did not share Pound's fondness for Hemingway, whom she had considered in the 1920s as "the most unpleasant man in Paris." "The Rudge business" grated on Hemingway. In 1950, he received a letter from Olga. What concerned Olga was Dorothy's seeming inability to take direct action in freeing Ezra. Younger, bolder, and more outspoken, Olga saw herself as fully capable in helping the cause. After extending her appreciation in the recent republishing of Hemingway's 1923 "Homage" to Ezra, she asserted that such tributes did nothing to free him. Olga's 1950 letter to Hemingway expressed: "Of course the easy way is for E.'s friends to leave him where he is and salve their consciences with tributes to his literary worth—he is simply crawling with literary parasites—none of whom, in the States at least, compromise themselves by touching on the subject of treason ... it is surely time for his friends, if he has any, to see what can be done." She coldly concluded by asking, "[W]hat else have you done for E?"[11]

Hemingway answered Olga in a controlled, teeth-gritting response:

Dear Miss Rudge: I will try to be as short, and ... as blunt as you were.... You ask what I actually have done for Ezra. I obtained monitorings of Ezra's broadcasts during the war—Ezra was my true friend, and I wanted to see what sort of an ass he was making of himself, so that I might come to his aid when it was necessary. His broadcasts, which contained occasional pieces of excellent sense and brilliance, were really awful, and I saw that there would be a difficult problem whenever the war was over and he was a prisoner.

At the time ... I was in Germany fighting, my oldest boy Jack was wounded and a prisoner, and I knew nothing of Ezra's fate. When his attorneys wrote me ... I made a statement ... that he was of unsound mind when he made his broadcasts after the U.S. entered the war ... if Ezra is released at this moment, as of unsound mind, to be tried, he would receive a sentence of from ten to fifteen years.... He made the rather serious mistake of being a traitor to his country, and temporarily he must lie in the bed he made.

If I were a King or a President or even a divisional commander, I would pardon Ezra instantly, kick him in the ass, ask him to have a drink and tell him to use his head if he has one. But I am only his friend, and can only use my head in his behalf. I hope this answers your questions bluntly as they were put. To be even more blunt, I have always loved Dorothy, and still do.[12]

Olga's persistent fight to free Pound was also taken up by their daughter, Mary, who lived in Brunnenberg Castle in the Tyrol and was married to a half–Italian, half–Russian, Boris de Rachewiltz. Assisted by Olga, Mary attained a passport and arrived in America in 1953, naively determined to free her father. Before coming to St. Elizabeths, Mary visited several officials to plead her father's innocence, including those in the State Department, who warned that stirring up the case could lead to his execution.

Disillusioned, she was driven to St. Elizabeths by Pound's old friend and publisher Caresse Crosby. Escorted to the Chestnut Ward, Mary followed a staff member up a flight of spiral metal stairs. The ring of an electric bell allowed entrance into a dirty-walled, foul-smelling interior, with dark corridors where radios and televisions echoed. In an area blocked off by a folding screen, Pound greeted her. He had gained some weight and wore a Chinese-sage like beard. Mary marveled at how he seemed almost oblivious "to the poor driveling empty husks rocking with vacant stares in front of the blaring televisions, to the frightful leering of younger shades."[13]

Mary returned to find her father accompanied by Dorothy and her half-brother Omar. Besides the appalling conditions, she detested the younger visitors fawning over her father. She described these proto-beat types as "a new species of human beings in appearance and behavior: sloppy and ignorant." Though Mary considered these visitors crude, her father consoled in Confucian fashion that in time of war "'make use of all men, even dolts.'"[14]

After being awarded the 1953 Pulitzer Prize for *The Old Man and the Sea*, Hemingway won the Nobel Prize for literature in October 1954. On December 13, *Time* depicted on its cover Hemingway's white-bearded face. Its feature article traced Hemingway's lifetime accomplishments and described firsthand Hemingway's activities at the helm of his fishing boat,

Pilar. A reporter described Hemingway's unkempt "grey-white hair escaping beneath a visored cap" and the Caribbean "glare that induced a sea-squint in his brown, curious eyes set behind steel spectacles."[15]

In the article, Hemingway explained that the serious injuries suffered during two plane crashes in Africa the year before still ailed him. Thus, he would not be able to attend the Nobel Prize acceptance ceremony in Stockholm. He well knew, however, what he wanted to say. The article stated that Hemingway "would talk about a half-forgotten poet and great stylist Ezra Pound." After giving much credit to Pound in the editing and guidance of Hemingway's early work, the article turned to the poet's incarceration in St. Elizabeths and featured a photograph of the young Pound, cane in hand.

Though Hemingway recounted a story about Joyce—whose picture also appeared in the article—he reserved his most respectful words for his poet friend: "Ezra Pound is a great poet, and whatever he did he has been punished greatly and I believe should be freed to go and write poems in Italy where he is loved and understood. He was the master of T.S. Eliot. Eliot is a winner of the Nobel Prize. I believe it might well have gone to Pound.... I believe this a good year to release poets." Hemingway continued: "There is a school of thought in America which, if encouraged enough, could well believe that a man should be punished for the simple error against conformity of being a poet. Dante, by these standards, could well have spent his life in St. Elizabeths Hospital for errors of judgment and of pride."[16]

In Hemingway's 1954 Nobel Prize acceptance speech read before the Swedish Academy in his absence, he gave a nod to Pound and others who were never awarded, what Yeats called "The Bounty of Sweden." Hemingway expressed: "No writer who knows the great writers who did not receive the prize can accept it other than with humility. There is no need to list these writers. Everyone here may make his own list according to his knowledge and his conscience."[17]

Writer Dawn Powell regarded Hemingway's suggestion to give Pound the Nobel Prize as a noble gesture. Powell wrote to Hemingway's longtime friends Gerald and Sarah Murphy: "I thought Ernest H.'s use of the Nobel Prize to defend E Pound was probably the bravest thing he ever did—and in *Time,* too. Nobody in a powerful position ever seems to dare use it for anything controversial."[18]

Around this time, Pound responded to Hemingway's comments about him in the *New York Times,* by writing to E.E. Cummings that the "grape vine tells me that Hem wuz baulderized [sic] by the New York Slimes and current spewlitzer orgumz. ie. that the old runt is more of a man than the press lets the public know." Though Pound despised most popular magazines, *Time* favorably reviewed his 1954 *The Classic Anthology Defined by Confucius*. In this article, published a few months before Hemingway's Nobel Prize award, a book reviewer praised Pound's translation. Million of readers were made aware of the latest work of a "half-forgotten poet." The review, entitled "Confucius to Pound," stated: "Poet Ezra Pound makes a free and brilliant translation, even to use a few jazz idioms and hillbilly dialect." The article concluded, "Although Pound, 68, was charged with wartime sedition in 1945 and confined to St. Elizabeth's Hospital as 'mentally incompetent,' he proves once again that he is one of the finest U.S. poets alive."[19]

His name surfacing once more in the media, Pound nevertheless faced everyday realities. He contacted Hemingway and urged him to write an article about how asylum reform should give patients "more opportunities for sun and fresh air." In 1956, Hemingway sent Pound a check for $1,000 "on the old Chinese principle ... that no one possesses anything until they have given it to another." Pound later remarked, "Somehow I didn't like to cash it—didn't know how hard up he might be, too."[20]

At this same time, Pound's publisher, James Laughlin, called upon Hemingway to help free the poet. Hemingway responded by suggesting that since Laughlin was an heir to a steel fortune he should try "to buy Pound out of trouble." Laughlin replied that he "could find no 'hand to grease.'" Laughlin wrote T.S. Eliot that he had suggested Hemingway to call upon President Eisenhower "reminding him two old soldiers could surely see eye to eye."[21]

To boost the sale of Pound's New Direction editions and to further the cause of the poet's freedom, Laughlin's assistant editor composed an eight-page pamphlet, *Ezra Pound at Seventy*, including contributions by Hemingway, T.S. Eliot, Archibald McLeish, W.H. Auden, Marianne Moore, and Dame Edith Sitwell. In March 1956, New Directions managing editor, Robert M. MacGregor, wrote Dorothy Pound about Hemingway's comments in the pamphlet. "The only statement," informed MacGregor, "which even leans towards the controversial is Hemingway's, and he says, 'I believe he (Pound) made a bad mistake in the war in continuing to broadcast for that sod Mussolini after we were fighting him. But I also believe has had paid for them in full and his continued confinement is a cruel and unusual punishment." In his study of Laughlin's crucial role in resurrecting Pound's postwar literary image, Gregory Barnhisel explains how the publication of *Ezra Pound at Seventy* contributed to "New Directions strategy, emphasizing literary accomplishment, linking Pound with the important writers of the day, and downplaying his political works."[22]

In October 1956, Laughlin again asked for Hemingway's contribution to another New Directions promotional eight-page pamphlet of six poets and excerpts from Pound's Canto 90. Hemingway gladly contributed, but stressed the importance of Pound's release and permanent residence in Italy. Unfortunately, neither Hemingway nor any of the other contributors were quoted in regard to Pound's confinement or release.[23]

In the meantime, Hemingway's once close friend—poet and statesmen Archibald McLeish—took greater interest in "the Pound case." Although McLeish respected Pound, the artist, he was an unlikely candidate for taking on a leading role in freeing him. Over several decades, Pound never offered any positive comments about McLeish's poetry and even condemned him— a member of FDR's Wartime Office of Information—during a 1942 Radio Rome broadcasts as a member of "Roosevelt's gang." In turn, McLeish thought little of the *Pisan Cantos* and did not think they deserved the 1949 Bollingen Award. Yet he did not want Pound to perish inside St. Elizabeths and, in 1950, wrote an article in the poet's defense, published in *Poetry and Opinion*.

In his campaign to free Pound, McLeish became frustrated by the poet's repeatedly lashing out at President Roosevelt. Though his trial and incarceration occurred under the Truman administration, Pound irrationally demanded an apology from the U.S. government for his treatment under FDR. McLeish warned that he could see no way of helping Pound if the poet continued attacking President Roosevelt. In 1955, McLeish wrote Pound and received a response so confused that he wondered if Pound wanted his help at all. It was apparent that a visit was necessary.

In 1955, McLeish's glimpse at Pound's life inside St. Elizabeths appalled him and left him feeling "sick." Afterward, McLeish wrote to Hemingway vowing that he "wouldn't rest" until Pound was released. "Not only for his sake," emphasized McLeish, "but for the good name of the country: after ten years it was beginning to look like persecution and if he died there we'd never get the stain out." McLeish made public his view of Pound's incarceration. In November 1956, he wrote in the *New York Times*: "Not everyone has seen Pound in the long, dim corridor inhabited by ghosts of men who cannot stand still, or who can be still too long." McLeish concluded, "You carry the horror away with you like the smell of the ward in your clothes, and whenever afterward you think of Pound or read his lines a state of sorrow afflicts you."[24]

A Roosevelt Democrat during a Republican administration, McLeish sought out possible political allies for the cause. His Harvard friend, Under Secretary of State Christian Herter expressed interest in the case, and United Nations Secretary General Dag Hammarskjöld—an admirer of Pound's poetry—agreed to play a vital behind-the-scenes role in securing the poet's release.

McLeish gathered written support from leading literary figures. He first considered several names, including William Faulkner, but settled upon Hemingway, T.S. Eliot, and Robert Frost—three literary giants who benefited from Pound's early promotion of their careers. No friend of Pound, Frost initially thought the poet deserved imprisonment, but through McLeish's persuasion, lent his name to the cause, becoming its media front man. Frost was the nation's most famous living poet, someone who could be effective within the Eisenhower administration. Frost had not seen Pound since 1915, while in England, when the poet praised and promoted Frost's first work, *A Boy's Will*. Frost disliked Pound's overbearing manner, his politics, and his wartime activities, and he considered *The Cantos* "as those lengthy things," unintelligible but liked by some. However, when recruited in Pound's cause, Frost became its leading public figure.[25]

At the same time, Pound was slowly attracting media attention. In February 1956, *Life* magazine offered a plea for Pound's release, emphasizing that several war criminals had been released, including Tokyo Rose and SS General Step Dietrich. "Attention is surely due," stated *Life*, "the case of Ezra Pound.... Pound's room at St. Elizabeths has been called a 'closet which contains a national skeleton.' ... The arguments for quashing the indictment ... should be publicly considered." Later that same year, Hemingway spoke out in *Look*—"Some erudite midshipman had been by in early afternoon to ask my views on Ezra Pound. These views are succinct, although the subject is complicated. Ezra, I told them, should be released from St. Elizabeths hospital and allowed to practice poetry without let or hindrance."[26]

In January 1957, a letter signed by Frost, Eliot, and Hemingway was sent to Attorney General Herbert Brownell, Jr., and stressed that a number of Nazi war criminals had been released from imprisonment "and in many cases rehabilitated." It also argued that mental-health experts evaluating Pound had concluded that he was not fit to stand trial and that his mental state might never change, thus resulting in permanent confinement. Hemingway defended signing the statement on Pound's behalf, informing the

New York Post: "Sure I signed it. Pound's crazy. All poets are…. They have to be. You don't put a poet like Pound in the loony bin. For history's sake we shouldn't keep him there."[27]

Hemingway's concern about Pound's attracting negative media attention became a reality when the poet befriended, among his sycophantic visitors, a number of virulent racists and cranks. In 1957, the *New York Herald Tribune* announced, "SEGREGATIONIST KASPER IS EZRA POUND'S DISCIPLE." It was just as Hemingway feared. In almost blatant disregard of his case, Pound befriended John Kasper, a Columbia graduate and admirer of the Nietzschean figures of *The Cantos*. Kasper first visited St. Elizabeths during the summer of 1950 and, under Pound's influence, abandoned his academic studies to become a man of action. At Kasper's Greenwich Village bookshop, Make it New (after Pound's 1934 book), he initially welcomed, as Pound biographer Humphrey Carpenter emphasizes, a diverse crowd that included "several Negro friends and not to have excluded Jews from his acquaintance." But in time Kasper became a virulent anti–Semite and segregationist. Together with another Pound admirer, David Horton, Kasper launched the "Square $" booklet series, conceived by Pound and printed by James Laughlin.[28]

Around this time, McLeish called upon Hemingway to write to Frost. In June 1957, Hemingway reiterated to Frost his detestation of Pound's politics and his belief that the poet's dying in confinement would nevertheless be a black mark on America. Again, he stressed that Pound belonged in Italy, a country that Hemingway mistakenly claimed had honored him as a poet, and therefore clouded his judgment and drew him to fascism. That summer, Hemingway offered to contribute $1,500 dollars to Ezra's resettlement in Italy with his daughter, Mary.

Meanwhile, McLeish's behind-the-scenes efforts were bearing fruit. Deputy Attorney General William P. Rogers—soon to replace Brownell as attorney general—called for a meeting to discuss Pound's case with Frost and "his co-signers, Eliot, and Hemingway." By April, Rogers once more urged a conference with Frost, Eliot, and Hemingway. While gladly lending his name to the cause, Hemingway never went to Washington.

On July 19, MacLeish and Frost met in Washington with Attorney General Rogers. McLeish reported on the meeting to Hemingway: "The Department of Justice 'would apparently be willing to drop the indictment' if somebody could come forward with a sound plan for taking care of Pound outside St. Elizabeths." At this time, however, with the Kasper affair still not settled, the State Department opposed Pound's returning to Italy, where he could live with his daughter Mary's family. But the State Department also expressed concern over the media's sensationalizing Pound's return to the country where he had embraced fascism.[29]

As Pound attracted controversy, Hemingway sent letters to cheer up his old friend—thematic missives he referred to as "The Unknown Tongue." Pound wrote back in April, "Archie [is] still pickin lilies in the valley of asphodel ... but yr letters lighten captivity."[30]

On June 19, 1957, MacLeish asked Hemingway to write another letter in support of Pound and then stated: "Ezra has been in there for eleven years; that you understand the psychos say he can never be brought to trial; that his continued incarceration under those circumstances had already done us considerable damage abroad ... that he is a very great poet ... which raises considerations which ... should be kept in mind since one of the great pastimes abroad is nailing our asses to the barn door as bloody materialists who care nothing for art or artists."[31]

Hemingway wrote the requested letter in which he explained the threat of Kasper and Pound's other racist sycophants, the "fawning jerks" who crowded around his old friend. Hemingway once more insisted that Pound be returned to Italy, but should be prohibited from writing about or engaging in politics. Hemingway warned that if Pound were freed he should be kept from the media, for the need of expressing his views might find him on the Mike Wallace show.

McLeish then asked Hemingway to accompany Frost to Washington where they were to meet with Deputy Attorney General William P. Rogers. Hemingway responded that he could not make the trip but would assist in the case. On July 19, 1957, Frost traveled to meet with Deputy Rogers.

On August 19, 1957, Representative Usher L. Burdick, of North Dakota, introduced House Resolution 403 that required a full-scale investigation into the Pound case. That fall, Hemingway commented in the media about Pound's wartime activity. This reached Pound in St. Elizabeths. Incensed when reading that Hemingway referred to him as a traitor, Pound wrote E.E. Cummings, "Hem talking about EP's errors/as if his red idiocy in Spain was the answer."[32]

As in the past, private conversations differed from public comments. Pound typically avoided media references about Hemingway. But there were instances when he let slip unflattering comments. Pound once told James Laughlin that "the trouble with Hem is that he can't keep two ideas in his head at the same time." When Michael Reck visited Pound at St. Elizabeths he handed Ezra a Rheingold Beer magazine advertisement, showing a "burly, hairy" Hemingway in tropical surroundings, contentedly holding a full glass. "Pound instantly folded part of the ad over, recounted

Reck, and "handed it back to me, a mischievous glimmer in his eye. Now you saw only Hemingway in shorts and the big black print of the slogan: Purity—Body—Flavor."[33]

On September 9, 1957, *Time* carried a story based upon an article in the Italian publication *Il Tempo*, which quoted Pound as saying, "In America, well, Papa Hemingway knows how to write, but he's dishonest." Concerned that this would reach Hemingway, Pound wrote Harry Meacham, an American literary friend who worked diligently for the poet's release from St. Elizabeths. In his letter to Meacham, Pound requested: "If you write to Hemingway, Finca Vigia, San Francisco di Paula, Cuba, do say that you have been here and that D.P. [Dorothy Pound] and I were both very indignant about the lie in 'Tempo' the Italian weekly." When Meacham complied, Pound thanked him for clearing up the situation. Meacham assured Pound that Hemingway claimed to have seen the quote in *Time*, but paid no attention to it. Pound informed Meacham that the validity of his making such comment about Hemingway was as if "to believe that we did not live in Rue Notre Dames des Champs in the old days."[34]

As these events unfolded, Frost made important strides in the Pound case. In late February 1958, Frost was invited by President Eisenhower to an informal White House stag dinner. Before this event, he met with Rogers and Eisenhower's chief of staff, Sherman Adams. In regard with the Pound case, Rogers commented, "Our mood, is your mood, Mr. Frost."[35]

In spring 1958, George Plimpton discussed Pound's case with Hemingway in the *Paris Review*. Plimpton asked if Pound's ties to Kasper had any influence on his willingness to involve himself in the poet's release. Hemingway denied that Kasper had any relevance in his involvement in the case; once again, he urged that Pound be released and allowed to return to Italy and abstain from politics. Hemingway informed Plimpton, "Great poets are not necessarily girl guides nor scoutmasters nor splendid influences on youth"—among them, he named Verlaine, Rimbaud, Shelley, Byron, Baudelaire, Proust, and Gide as those as having questionable morals.[36]

Absent on April 18, 1958, the day of the dismissal of Pound's indictment, Frost, Eliot, and Hemingway were represented by Frost's statement read aloud in court: "I feel authorized to speak for my friends, Archibald McLeish, Ernest Hemingway, and T.S. Eliot. None of us can bear the disgrace of our letting Ezra Pound come to his end where he is. It would leave too woeful of a story in American literature." After hearing hours of testimony, Judge Bolitha Laws dismissed Pound's indictment, freeing the poet after nearly twelve years of confinement.[37]

Free once more, Pound spent time with friends in Richmond, Virginia, and visited his boyhood home in Wyncote, Pennsylvania. In *The Richmond News Leader*, Pound simply referred to Hemingway as "one of the best." Pound stayed a night in Rutherford, New Jersey, with Williams and his wife, Floss. Few words were exchanged between the fellow poets. Pound's son, Omar, a World War II Army veteran turned scholar, came to the house and greatly impressed his hosts. After the visit, Floss wrote Louis Zukofsky: "Well – the famous Erza Pound has come and gone. – we survived – but it was quite an ordeal. – Ezra terribly jittery – Dorothy uncommunicative – she looked very tired." Both Floss and Bill wrote how they managed to keep away reporters and media photographers. They did, however, allow a visit by famed photographer Richard Avedon, whose series of photographs of Pound's agonized expressions have become iconic images.[38]

On July 9, 1958, Pound returned to Italy. His ship landed in Naples, where, during a brief stop, he stood before reporters and photographers and proudly gave a fascist salute. He informed them that America was a country of pervading ignorance—"a madhouse"—ruled over by a Congress of lunatics. The following day, American newspapers carried the headline: "Pound, in Italy, Gives Fascist Salute; Calls America an 'Insane Asylum.'" Descending the gangplank in Genoa, Pound greeted a crowd and told reporters that he was back on "sacred ground" and said that a madhouse is the finest place to live in America.

Ezra and Dorothy stayed in the Italian Tyrol with his daughter's family. As Noel Stock observed, "Pound very badly wanted to see old friends, and a large empty room at the castle was repaired and made ready as a reception-room in case Hemingway or others should come." In mid–July 1958, Hemingway, concerned about Pound's welfare, sent him a check for $1,000. The poet never cashed this gift and instead made it a keepsake by encasing it inside a Plexiglas paperweight. Pound's friend Brigit Patmore recalled him receiving some money from Hemingway. Whether it was the $1,000 check sent that July or another sum sent before Hemingway's death, it was intended, as Patmore noted, to pay for "a well deserved holiday."[39]

Fearful of the FBI and its surveillance during these last years, Hemingway had reservations when writing about Pound or mentioning him in the press. He asked his friend A.E. Hotchner, "Will I be boiled in Congressional oil for being kind to poor old Ezra?"

Hotchner replied: "No that's all over. I don't think this Congress knows who Ezra Pound is."

At the height of the Cold War most American politicians, fearing the spread of communism, were little concerned over the spent forces of fascism.[40]

When asked by an Italian reporter about Hemingway, Pound blatantly stated that his old friend had "sold himself to the god dollar." Taken aback at this comment, the reporter wrote, "Thus Uncle Ez spoke of Hemingway, who wanted to renounce the Nobel Prize in his favor." Both no doubt had their misgivings about each other and at times let slip unflattering comments. But when the press reported such comments, Pound again blamed the media for stirring up animosity between him and Hemingway. As Pound biographer J.J. Wilhelm noted, "For even though journalists unconsciously kept trying to stir up trouble between the two writers, especially by quoting Pound making unfavorable comments about Ernest, the two former sparring partners of Montparnasse did not allow this to break up their friendship."[41]

Early in 1959, Pound informed Hemingway of a possible joint speaking engagement in Munich. This engagement offered "swank" accommodations for two, and paid airfare for Hemingway's traveling from his residence in Cuba to Munich. Hemingway never accepted. In October, Hemingway's island home was on the verge of Fidel Castro's ouster of Batista. Around this time, Pound wrote a letter explaining his financial troubles and, in his verbal shorthand, stated, "Old man him tired."[42]

In 1959, Hemingway immersed himself in writing his "Paris book"— the posthumously published *A Moveable Feast*—recalling events from 1921 to 1926. Hemingway settled old scores in his book, satirized former friends, and sometimes disparaged them. Writing his Paris book Hemingway also took retributive aim at Gertrude Stein and recast in part-myth his times with F. Scott Fitzgerald. Often cruel after breaking with friends, Hemingway was not troubled when speaking ill of the dead—he once unsentimentally uttered that "a live son of a bitch is a dead son of a bitch."

Hemingway would not live to see his Paris book reach his old friend in Rapallo. On July, 2, 1961, a shotgun suicide ended Hemingway's life in Ketchum, Idaho—twelve miles from Pound's birthplace of Hailey. On the morning of July 6, Hemingway's funeral service was held at the small Episcopal Church in Ketchum. At the gravesite, a Catholic priest eulogized in Latin, then in English, reading from the book of Ecclesiastes. Uninvited participants crowded around the periphery of the cemetery. Mary Hemingway wore all black, and Ernest's brother, Leicester, attended as did his sisters Marcelline, Madeleine and Ursula; however, the youngest, Carol, wished to pay her last respects in private. The hillside service, held in a vast mountain range, had a serenity that was spoiled by reporters, who photographed and recorded it from a distance. Mourners heard a newsman providing a play-by-play update, giving the event a feeling of a commercial spectacle.

At the time of Hemingway's death, Pound had been in a health clinic in Merano, near his granddaughter Mary's castle home in the Tyrol. Staying with friends in Rome, Pound suddenly lost his appetite. When Mary arrived she and Olga decided, without Ezra's knowledge, to take him back to the clinic. "When news of Hemingway's suicide reached Merano," writes J.J. Wilhelm, "everyone agreed to keep silent about this, since it would only increase Ezra's depression. However, a thoughtless nurse mentioned the subject." A friend visiting the hospital recalled how Pound "went into a terrible tantrum, said American writers are all doomed and the USA destroys them all, especially the best of them."[43]

Learning of Hemingway's suicide, Edmund Wilson—the first eminent critic to review Hemingway's first Parisian-published books—confided in his diary: "This upset me very much. Absurd and insufferable though he often was, he was one of the foundation stones of my generation, and to have him commit suicide is to have a prop knocked out." Aware of Hemingway's electroshock treatment at the Mayo Clinic, Wilson thought his death by shotgun as undignified for a writer who urged his fellows to "last and get their work done." Also a man of the twenties, Wilson recalled the greatness of a writer exploited by *Life* magazine—"The desperation in his stories had always been real: his most convincing characters are always a few jumps ahead of death. It is a wonder that this was not more noticed. Instead, the press and the public mainly took their cue for their conception of him from his show of full-blooded vitality."[44]

More than his writing, Hemingway's full-blooded vitality has come to define him. But he presented another side of himself in the posthumously published *A Moveable Feast* (1964). In his Paris book, Hemingway spared Pound the usual vitriol when recalling most former companions, remembered him instead for unrelenting generosity, with kind words reserved for so few. *A Moveable Feast* presents an affectionate portrait of Pound, a friend that Hemingway considered "kinder and more Christian" than himself—a kind poet "sincere in his mistakes, an "irascible saint" as so many saints have been.[45]

In a *New York Times* review of *A Moveable Feast*, Louis Gallantière—one of the first Americans Hemingway met in Paris—wrote that Ernest "loved Ezra Pound." Gallantière further commented that although Hemingway "has little to tell about him—there is no portrayal, no record of his ideas or singularities—it is clear that this was a good and innocent man, able to disarm Hemingway's suspicion, which was the only path to his affection."[46]

The Snows of Yesteryear

Engrossed in the history of Paris when first arriving there, Hemingway imagined the wolves of Villon's fifteen-century stalking the streets. After Hemingway's death, Pound may have recalled Villon's line also admired by his late friend: "But where are the snows of yester-year." Hemingway, another lost companion, joined in death Ford Maddox Ford, Joyce, and others of the 1920s Paris scene.

Hemingway's persistent admiration for Pound, the poet, was revealed in a posthumous inventory of his private library. Of the poetry in the collection Pound's works were the most numerous, ranging from *Gaudier-Brzeska* (1916) to a 1958 edition of *Pavannes and Divagations*. After years of Hemingway publicly ranking Eliot as a lesser poet, it is telling that next to Pound's work, the second-most represented works by a poet in Hemingway's library were Eliot's.

Pound once explained that, in his artistic friendships, he never bothered to look at their "complete character and personality.... Wyndham Lewis always claimed that I never saw people because I never noticed how wicked they were, what SOB's they were. I wasn't the least interested in the vices of my friends, but their intelligence." Not long after Hemingway's death, Pound recalled that he "did not disappoint me.... I never saw him save at his best."[1]

Pound outlived Hemingway by more than a decade. Despite his severe bouts with depression and physical ailments, he did have periods of mental acuity. In 1962, the *Paris Review* published a perceptive and clear-minded interview with Pound. When he came across this interview, Edmund Wilson wrote that Pound "still seems to make more sense than I should have supposed he did; talked without bogus Americanese and with surprising absence of egotism about the events of his life."[2]

That same year, after undergoing an operation due to ureamic poisoning, Pound recuperated in Rapallo. Still responsible for Pound's finances and business arrangements, Dorothy, tired of Olga and Ezra's continuing relationship, agreed to her husband's living with Olga in nearby San' Ambrogio. Dorothy's marriage had taken her from England to Paris to Italy. She had lived nearly a decade in a cramped Washington, D.C., apartment and daily visited St.Elizabeths. Dorothy believed that Olga—nearly ten years her junior—was better prepared to care for Ezra. After decades of waiting, as Hugh Carpenter noted, Olga "had her prize."[3]

Dorothy stayed in Rapallo, rarely taking notice of her husband and his mistress. Ezra annually wintered with Olga at her Venice apartment, The Hidden Nest. In Venice, the old poet, typically dressed causally, once more donned his wide-brimmed hat and loosely strung tie. Cane in hand, he took long walks, often with friends and visitors, sometimes without saying a word. In his last decades, Hemingway had made Harry's Bar in Venice a favorite Italian hangout. Yet, in this city of art and decadence, the two friends never crossed paths.

Living between Rapallo and Venice, Pound remained unrepentant about his role in the war. In the *Paris Review*, he once more reiterated his wartime motives: "I thought I was fighting for a constitutional point.... Seeing the folly of Italy and America being at war—! I certainly wasn't telling the troops to revolt.... And if any man, any individual man, can say he has had a bad deal from me because of race, creed, or color, let him come out and state it with particulars. *The Guide to Kulchur* was dedicated to Basil Bunting and Louis Zukofsky, a Quaker and a Jew."[4]

But over time, Pound slipped into depressive states—dark moods and pangs of regret about the validity of his art and the possible misguided ventures into economics and right-wing politics. In these early years of readjusting to life in Italy, his spirits were sometimes brightened by letters from younger writers and poets. In 1962, poet Robert Lowell wrote: "Ezra, I think you should feel happy about your life, and the thousands of kindnesses you have done your friends, and how you've been a fountain to them. So you've been to me, and I miss the old voice."[5]

Eventually, Pound spoke so rarely that the media reported he had become mute. When he did wish to speak, Pound often confessed failure, as a poet led down paths of ideological delusion. At the same time, literary scholar Alfred Kazin had feared a new generation would lionize the aging poet rebel. Though Kazin recognized Pound's talent and his role in the arts, he feared that the "poet and madman" could "re-emerge as an aged hipster and clown, a man who all his life has defied conventional authority and been against the government."[6]

Though cranks and would-be poets visited Pound, a new generation of brilliant poets and writers venerated his art. The 1950s poets—Charles Olson and Robert Creeley—of Black Mountain College, North Carolina, revered Pound, as did Robert Duncan. Olson held Pound in high regard until the elder poet's anti–Semiticism drove him away from St. Elizabeths. At nineteen, Creeley experienced a revelation reading Pound's *Make it New* and later consulted the poet about publishing a little magazine.

Since forming a literary circle in New York City, Jack Kerouac's beat companion poet Allen Ginsberg greatly admired Pound. Attracted to art and criminality, the beats found the imprisoned poet a modern example of the artist at odds with the state. In 1952, Jack Kerouac, downhearted as a literary establishment outsider, wrote to a friend: "For my position in this generation is a whole lot like Ezra Pound in his—It was Pound [who] influenced Stein, and she influenced Hemingway; it was Pound [who] influenced T.S. Eliot; but where is Pound? In the madhouse."[7]

Ginsberg lauded Pound as "the one who," in the twentieth century "single-handedly had to drag literature out of sort of a metronomic, automatic desensitization it had fallen into because of the overuse of iambic." Ginsberg saw the connection between the early moderns in Paris—"the preoccupation in all literature since 1905, meaning since Pound and Stein. In a rough way, this problem of natural-speech mind," emphasized Ginsberg, "occupied everybody interesting in America one way or another.... Hemingway was also involved in the same problem."[8]

On the pilgrimage to meet Pound in 1967, Ginsberg and friends visited San'Ambrogio—"a small modest house which overlooked the great blasts of blue Mediterranean spaciness and shore." Ginsberg and his companions sang to a harmonium outside Ezra's apartment. Olga thought Ginsberg's longhaired entourage filthy-looking, but Pound found them amusing. Later that year, Ginsberg and Michael Reck visited Pound in Venice. During this encounter, Ginsberg introduced himself as a "Buddhist Jew." Obviously, the aged Pound did not reveal that he had long thought the Buddha as the "Indian Circe of negation and dissolution." Pound told Ginsberg that his worst mistake in life and art, beyond that of writing a lot of "double talk," was "that stupid, suburban prejudice of anti–Semitism." When Reck inquired about Pound's influence on Hemingway, he tried to respond, but his pursed lips brought forth no response.[9]

At this same time, Hemingway's influence was still prevalent among younger writers. Author of *One Flew Over the Cuckoo's Nest* (1962) and

Sometimes a Great Notion (1964)—set in the rural Northwest—Ken Kesey admired the young Hemingway. Kesey reminded readers of the brilliant young Hemingway:

> Don't be misled by the bodies of bullfighters or riddled remains of soldiers; look instead for live trout on the bottom vibrating against the clean current, or bacon fat going cold on a veteran's breakfast plate, or old boards going into sharp focus through a pair of binoculars; in those delicate transitions where nothing actually moves you may find something of the slow and gentle old giant.[10]

Two years before his death, Pound affectionately told one of his biographers that "Hemingway has never disappointed me." Hemingway once warned about a writer's destiny—that if "the rewards come early, the writer is often ruined by them. If they come too late, he is probably embittered." One could say that Hemingway lived out this path while the feeble and elderly Pound—his fiery persona dampened—became humbled and virtually mute.

In his mid–1960s popular study of Italy, Luigi Barzini observed the fate of expatriates like Pound: "A day comes when these old people grow ill and helpless, far from the familiar sights and sounds of their youth, self-exiled for reasons which have become dim in their memories, in an alien place which they never saw as it is and quite understood.... Many die every year and are buried hurriedly in the corner of an Italian cemetery reserved for heathens and heretics." On November 1, 1972, nearly two days after his eighty-seventh birthday, Pound died in Venice.[11]

Olga feared Pound's funeral would turn into a publicity event and thus kept it a quiet affair. Funeral rites were conducted by the Benedictines who owned San Giorgio—a nearby island outside Venice—where Pound was laid to rest. Taken by gondola across the lagoon from San Marco to San Giorgio, Pound, the pagan poet, was given a Protestant service, and buried among non–Italian Christians in the cemetery's Protestant section, near the graves of Diaghilev and Igor Stravinsky. Pound's simple marble tombstone bears only his name. Not long after, Olga found a cache of Hemingway's letters among Ezra's documents stored in a safe deposit box—those cherished "life savers" of correspondences that kept close two immensely different individuals in times of triumph and despair.

Chapter Notes

Preface

1. William Cookson, ed., *Ezra Pound Selected Prose 1909–1965* (New York: New Directions, 1973), 117; Pound to Hemingway, October 13, 1923, Pound Mss., Lilly Library.

2. B. L. Reid, *The Man from New York: John Quinn and His Friends* (New York: Oxford University Press, 1968), 435; James Mellow, *Hemingway: A Life Without Consequences* (New York: Houghton Mifflin, 1992), 159.

3. Carlos Baker, ed., *Ernest Hemingway: Selected Letters 1917–1961* (New York: Scribner's Sons, 1981), 383.

4. Donald Hall, "Interviews—Ezra Pound: The Art of Poetry," *Paris Review* 28 (Summer/Fall 1962), 9; Matthew J. Bruccoli, *Scott and Ernest: The Authority of Failure and Success* (New York: Random House, 1978).

Chapter 1

1. Walter B. Rideout, *Sherwood Anderson: A Writer in America Volume 1* (Madison: University of Wisconsin Press, 2006), 407.

2. David D. Anderson, *Sherwood Anderson: An Introduction and Interpretation* (New York: Holt, Rinehart, Winston, 1967), 171.

3. Sylvia Beach, *Shakespeare and Company* (Lincoln: University of Nebraska Press, 1991), 30.

4. Thomas Scott, *et al.*, eds., *Pound/The Little Review: The Letters of Ezra Pound to Margaret Anderson: The Little Review Correspondences* (New York: New Directions Book, 1988), 279, 249; Charles E. Modlin, ed., *Sherwood Anderson Selected Letters* (Knoxville: University of Tennessee Press, 1984), 25; Walter B. Rideout, *Sherwood Anderson: An American Writer Volume 1* (Madison: University of Wisconsin Press, 2006), 413.

5. Donald Gallop, ed., *The Flowers of Friendship: Letters Written to Gertrude Stein* (New York: Alfred A. Knopf, 1953), 141–42.

6. Robert Forrest Wilson, *Paris on Parade* (Indianapolis: Bobbs-Merrill, 1925), 206; *Ezra Pound to His Parents: Letters 1895–1929*, ed. Mary de Rachewiltz, A David Moody, and Joanna Moody (New York: Oxford University Press, 2010), 490.

7. Wyndham Lewis, *Blasting and Bombardiering* (Berkeley: University of California Press, 1967), 277; Edmund Wilson, ed., *The Collected Essays of John Peale Bishop* (New York: Charles Scribner's Sons, 1948), 328.

8. Reid, *Quinn*, 199; Charles Norman, *Ezra Pound* (New York: MacMillan, 1960), 254.

9. Malcolm Cowley, *Exile's Return: A*

Literary Odyssey of the 1920s (New York: Penguin Books, 1976), 121.

10. Williams in Louis Simpson, *Three on the Tower: The Lives and Works of Ezra Pound, T. S. Eliot and William Carlos Williams* (New York: William Morrow, 1975), 216; Ezra Pound, *Personae: The Shorter Poems,* ed. Lea Baechler and A. Walton Litz (New York: New Directions, 1990), 185; Victoria Glendinning, *Rebecca West: A Life* (New York: Alfred A. Knopf, 1987), 41.

11. Sherwood Anderson to Lewis Gallantière, November 28, 1921, Anderson Papers, Newberry Library.

12. Pound in Reid, *Man from New York,* 285; Eustace Mullins, *This Difficult Individual, Ezra Pound* (New York: Fleet, 1961), 110–11; Ezra Pound, *Jefferson and/or Mussolini* (New York: Liveright, 1970), 56.

13. Charles Baudelaire, *The Painter of Modern Life and Other Essays,* trans. and ed. Jonathan Mayne, unabridged (New York: Da Capo, 1964), 27.

14. Alan Judd, *Ford Maddox Ford* (Cambridge: Harvard University Press, 1991), 23; Loeb in Denis Brian, *The True Gen: An Intimate Portrait of Ernest Hemingway by Those Who Knew Him* (New York: Grove Press, 1988), 48, 49; Scott Donaldson, *By Force of Will: The Life and Art of Ernest Hemingway* (New York: Viking, 1977), 68.

15. Robert McAlmon, with Kay Boyle, *Being Geniuses Together: A Binocular View of Paris in the '20s* (Garden City, NY: Doubleday, 1968), 180; *Hemingway: Selected Letters,* 62, 65.

16. Charters in J. J. Wilhelm, *Ezra Pound London and Paris 1908–1925* (University Park: University of Pennsylvania Press, 1990), 290; Humphrey Carpenter, *A Serious Character: The Life of Ezra Pound* (Boston: Houghton Mifflin, 1988), 73, 401.

17. Al Laney, *Paris Herald: The Incredible Newspaper* (New York: D. Appleton-Century, 1947), 165; Ezra Pound to Dorothy Pound, July 13, 1923, Pound Mss., Lilly Library; Janet Flanner, *Paris Was Yesterday 1925–1939,* ed. Irving Drutman

(New York: Viking Press, 1972), viii; Putman, *Paris,* 98.

18. Sisley Huddelston, *Paris, Salons, Cafes, Studios* (New York: Blue Ribbon Books, 1928), 121; Caresse Crosby, *The Passionate Years* (New York: Ecco Press, 1979), 265.

19. *Hemingway: Selected Letters,* 420.

20. Virgil Thomson, *Virgil Thomson By Virgil Thomson* (London: Weidenfeld and Nicholson, 1967), 110.

21. Wyndham Lewis in *T. S. Eliot: A Collection of Critical Essays,* ed. Hugh Kenner (Englewood Cliffs, NJ: Prentice-Hall, 1962) 30; Pound, *Selected Prose 1909–1965* (New York: New Directions, 1973), 117.

22. Pound to Dorothy, July 23, 1922, Pound Mss., Lilly Library.

23. Michael Reck, *Ezra Pound: A Close-Up* (New York: McGraw-Hill, 1973), 85; Carpenter, *Serious Character,* 241.

24. Hadley in Gioia Diliberto, *Hadley* (New York: Ticknor & Fields, 1992), 108; Hadley in Bernice Kert, *The Hemingway Women: Those Who Loved Him, the Wives and Others* (New York: W. W. Norton, 1983), 113; Margaret Anderson, *My Thirty Years War: The Autobiography, Beginnings and Battles to 1930* (New York: Horizon, 1969), 244; Harriet Monroe, "Ezra Pound," *Poetry* (May 1925), 90.

25. Hadley in Diliberto, *Hadley,* 1992, 108; Margaret Anderson, 244.

26. Matthew Josephson, *Life Among the Surrealists: A Memoir* (New York: Holt, Rinehart & Winston, 1962), 318.

27. Hadley in Diliberto, *Hadley,* 108–09.

28. Pound, *Pavannes & Divagations,* 203; Pound in Carpenter, *Serious Character,* 393.

Chapter 2

1. Eliot quoted in Russell Kirk, *Eliot and His Age: T. S. Eliot's Moral Imagination in the Twentieth Century* (Wilmington: ISI Books, 2008), 63.

2. Malcolm Cowley, "The Heming-

way Legend," reprinted in *Ernest Hemingway: A Literary Reference*, ed. Robert W. Trogdon (New York: Carroll & Graf, 2002), 95.

3. Williams in Simpson, *Three on the Tower*, 213.

4. McAlmon, *Being Geniuses Together*, 10; Ernest Hemingway, *A Moveable Feast*, 15th printing (New York: Charles Scribner's Sons, 1979), 132.

5. Ezra Pound, *ABC of Reading* 1934 (New York: New Directions Paperbacks, 1960), 28, 32, 37.

6. Edmund Wilson, ed., *The Collected Essay of John Peale Bishop* (New York: Charles Scribner's Sons, 1948), 328.

7. Ernest Hemingway, *Death in the Afternoon* (Scribner's Sons, 1932), 51.

8. Ezra Pound to Dorothy Pound, July 20, 1922, Pound Mss., Lilly Library.

9. Simpson, *Three on the Tower*, 68; Frederick Karl, *Modern and Modernism: The Sovereignty of the Artists, 1885–1925* (New York: Athenaeum, 1985), 117.

10. Ezra Pound, *Personae, The Shorter Poems of Ezra Pound*, 19–21.

11. Ezra Pound, *Antheil and the Treatise on Harmony* (New York: Da Capo, 1968), 52.

12. Ezra Pound, *The Letters of Ezra Pound, 1907–1941* (New York: Harcourt, Brace, 1950), 89; *Essays of John Peale Bishop*, 40.

13. Ernest Hemingway, ed., *Men at War* (New York: Wings Books, 1991), xviii; Spender in *Hemingway, Literary Reference*, 190; ibid, 173, 303.

14. *Hemingway in Literary Reference*, 41, 274; Kenneth Lynn, *Hemingway* (New York: Simon & Schuster, 1987), 246.

15. Van Wyck Brooks, *Days of the Phoenix: The Nineteen Twenties I Remember* (New York: E. P. Dutton, 1957), 163.

16. McAlmon, *Being Geniuses*, 258; Pound in Carpenter, *Serious Character*, 43.

17. Pound, *Antheil*, 37; Ezra Pound *Pavannes and Divagations* (New York: New Directions, 1958), 58, 70; Pound in E. Fuller Torrey, *The Roots of Treason: Ezra Pound and the Secrets of St Elizabeth's* (New York: McGraw Hill, 1984), 107.

18. Wilson, *Paris on Parade*, 287; Pound, *Pavannes and Divagations*, 70.

19. Pound, *Pound/The Little Review*, 248; Pound in Eustace Mullins, *This Difficult Individual, Ezra Pound*, 149.

Chapter 3

1. Beach, *Shakespeare & Company*, 26; Wyndham Lewis, 277; Samuel Putman in *America as Americans See It*, ed. Fred J. Ringel (New York: The Literary Guild, 1932).

2. Wilson, *Paris on Parade*; James Laughlin, *Pound as Wuz: Essays and Lectures on Ezra Pound* (St. Paul: Graywolf Press, 1987), 4–5, 175.

3. Bishop in *Ernest Hemingway: The Man and his Work*, ed. John K. M. McCaffey (Cleveland: The World Publishing Co.), 151.

4. Ezra Pound, *The Cantos of Ezra Pound* (New York: New Directions, 1979), 72.

5. Hemingway in Ezra Pound, *Gaudier-Brzeska: A Memoir* (New York: New Directions, 1970), 140.

6. Harold Stearns, *Confessions of a Harvard Man: A Journey Through Literary Bohemia, Paris and New York in the 1920s & 1930s* (Santa Barbara, CA: Paget Press, 1984), 164.

7. Pound, *Personae*, 188.

8. Malcolm Cowley, *A Second Flowering: Works and Days of the Lost Generation* (New York: Viking, 1973), 50.

9. Edward Burns, ed., *Staying Alone: Letters of Alice B. Toklas* (New York: Vintage, 1975), 150.

10. Richard Humphreys in *Pound's Artists: Ezra Pound and the Visual Artists in London, Paris and Italy* (London: The Tate Gallery, 1985).

11. Mary Rachewiltz, A. David Moody, and Joanna Moody, eds., *Ezra Pound to His Parents: Letters 1895–1929* (New York: Oxford University, 2010), 367; Pound mentioned Noh performances to Dorothy, July 7, 1922 and August 3, 1922, Lilly Library.

12. Pound in Carpenter, *Serious Character*, 384.

13. Pound, *Antheil*, 51, 61.

14. Ezra Pound to Dorothy Pound, July 17, 1923, Pound Mss., Lilly Library; Man Ray, *Self Portrait* (Boston: Little Brown & Co., 1963), 149.

15. Putman, *Paris*, 90.

16. *Pound/The Little Review*, 290; Carpenter, *Serious Character*, 399; Pound in Mark Polizzotti, *Revolution of the Mind: The Life of André Breton* (New York: Da Capo, 1997), 427.

17. Nicholas Joost, *Ernest Hemingway and the Little Magazines: The Paris Years* (Barre, MA: Barre, 1968), 100.

18. Hilda Doolittle, *End to Torment: A Memoir of Ezra Pound* (New York: New Directions, 1979), 49; William Carlos Williams, *The Autobiography of William Carlos Williams* (New York: Random House, 1951), 188.

19. Hemingway: Selected Letters, 102.

20. Pound, *Antheil*, 117.

21. Hugh Ford, *Four Lives in Paris* (San Francisco: North Point Press, 1987), 29, 28.

22. Virgil Thomson, *Virgil Thomson*, 83.

23. *Letters of Ezra Pound*, 172, 175.

24. James E. Miller, Jr., *T. S. Eliot: The Making of an American Poet, 1882–1922* (University Park: Pennsylvania State University Press, 2005), 404.

25. *The Letters of T. S. Eliot*, ed. Valerie Eliot, Gen. ed. John Hoffman (New Haven: Yale University Press, 2009), 707, 711.

26. Hemingway to Pound, *Letters of Ernest Hemingway* (Vol. 1), 364.

27. Natalie Clifford Barney, *Adventures of the Mind*, trans. and annotations John Spalding Gatton (New York: New York University Press, 1992), 118.

28. Williams, *Autobiography*, 228.

29. Diana Souhami, *Wild Girls—Paris, Sappho, and Art: The Lives and Loves of Natalie Barney and Romain Brooks* (New York: St. Martin's Press), 60.

30. Ibid., 61.

31. John Tytell, *Ezra Pound: The Solitary Volcano* (New York: Anchor Press, 1987), 180.

32. Williams, *The Autobiography*, 228: Hemingway, *Moveable Feast*, 110.

33. Janet Flanner, ed. Irving David *Paris Was Yesterday 1925–1939*, ed. Irving David (New York: Viking Press, 1972), xvi–xvii.

34. George Antheil, *Bad Boy of Music* (Garden City, NY: Doubleday, 1945), 146, 147.

Chapter 4

1. Hemingway to Pound, *Letters of Ernest Hemingway* (Vol. 1), 331.

2. Pound in *Pound, Thayer, Watson, and the Dial: A Story in Letters*, ed. Walter Sutton (Gainesville: University Press of Florida Press, 1994), 227.

3. *Pound/The Little Review*, 265.

4. Seldes in Norman, *Ezra Pound*, 256.

5. Josephson, *Life Among the Surrealists*, 89; Michael Reynolds, *Hemingway: The Paris Years* (New York: W. W. Norton, 1989), 64.

6. *Ernest Hemingway Complete Poems*, ed. Nicholas Gerogiannis, rev ed. (Lincoln: University of Nebraska Press, 1992), xxi, xxiv.

7. Ella Winter, ed., *The Letters of Lincoln Steffens Vol. II 1920–1936* (Westport, CT: Greenwood Press, 1966), 647.

8. David Cecil, *Max: A Biography of Max Beerbohm* (New York: Athenaeum, 1985), 303.

9. Ibid., 304; Carlos Baker, *Hemingway: A Life Story* (New York: Avon Books, 1968), 118.

10. Baker, Hemingway, 118; Hemingway to Pound, *The Letters of Ernest Hemingway* (Vol. 1), 364.

11. William White, ed., *Dateline Toronto: Hemingway's Complete Dispatches for the Toronto Star 1920–1924* (New York: Charles Scribner's Sons, 1985), 131.

12. Leon Surrette, *Pound in Purgatory: From Economic Radicalism to Anti-Semitism* (Chicago: University Chicago Press, 1999), 71.

13. Pound had first met James Joyce in Sirmione during the summer of 1920.

Pound suggested to Joyce that he move from Trieste to this city of villas and churches.

14. *Letters of Ezra Pound*, 183.

15. Wilson, *Paris on Parade*, 247.

16. Hemingway to Pound, *The Letters of Ernest Hemingway* (Vol. 1), 364.

17. Clarence Hemingway to Pound, in Michael Reynolds, *The Paris Years*, 80.

18. This news might have been misleading. The Lausanne Peace Conference began on November 21, 1922.

19. *Ezra Pound to His Parents*, 503, 504.

20. Mellow, *Hemingway*, 213–15.

21. Hemingway to Pound, *Selected Letters*, 77; Pound in *Ernest Hemingway: The Papers of a Writer*, 32.

22. Hemingway to Pound, *Letters of Ernest Hemingway* (Vol. 2), 10; Milton A. Cohen, *Hemingway's Laboratory: The Paris in Our Time* (Tuscaloosa: University of Alabama Press, 2005), 35.

23. Reynolds, *Paris Years*, 65.

24. Joost, *Little Magazines*, 37.

25. Monroe in Norman, *Ezra Pound*, 263; Ezra Pound, *Impact: Essays on Ignorance and the Decline of American Civilization* (Chicago: Henry Regenery, 1960), 151.

26. Virginia W. Johnson, *Genoa the Superb: The City of Columbus* (Boston: Estes and Lauriat, 1892), 64; Joseph Fattorusso, *Wonders of Italy: The Monuments of Antiquity, the Churches, the Palaces, the Treasures of Art* (Los Angeles: Medici Art Series, 1952), 43; Edgcumbe Staley, *Heriones of Genoa and the Rivieras* (New York: Charles Scribener's Sons, 1911), 299.

27. Hemingway to Pound, *The Letters of Ernest Hemingway* (Vol. 2), 4.

28. By the mid–1920s, Cunard became the lover of surrealist Louis Aragon. Cunard purchased William Bird's Three Mountains Press and founded Hours Press, which then printed Pound's *Draft of Cantos XXX*, in 1930.

29. Hemingway to Pound, *Hemingway: Selected Letters*, 78–79.

30. Ibid., 79.

31. Cohen, *Hemingway's Laboratory*, 34.

32. Reynolds, *The Paris Years*, 112.

33. Brian, *The True Gen*, 38.

34. Ibid., 43, 49.

35. In *True Gen*, Strater claims to have painted the portraits in Rapallo as well as another work of Ernest and Hadley. But Frederick Voss asserts, in *Picturing Hemingway: A Writer in His Time*, "Determining with certainty just where Strater did his portraits of Hemingway is almost impossible." They are dated 1922, but could have been completed in Strater's studio outside Paris.

36. For in-depth information about Pound and Malatesta, see Lawrence Rainey, *Ezra Pound and the Monument of Culture: Text, History, and Malatesta Cantos* (Chicago: University of Chicago Press, 1991).

37. Pound, *Gaudier-Brzeska: A Memoir*, 111; Jacob Burckhardt, *The Civilization of the Renaissance in Italy* (New York: Mentor Books, 1960), 60, 177; *Letters of Ezra Pound*, 239.

38. Gioia, *Hadley*, 147.

39. Cohen, *Hemingway's Laboratory*, 16.

40. Ibid., 36.

41. Huddleston, *Paris*, 122; Pound to Dorothy, June 21, 1923, Lilly Library.

42. *The Selected Letters of Marianne Moore*, Gen. ed. Bonnie Castello, assoc. ed. Celeste Goodridge and Christanne Miller (New York: Alfred A. Knopf, 1997), 202; Pound to Dorothy, July 23, 1923, Pound Mss., Lilly Library; James Mellow, *Hemingway*, 306.

43. Reynolds, *The Paris Years*, 140.

44. Pound and Hemingway in Cohen, *Hemingway's Laboratory*, 49.

45. Stein in *The Left Bank Revisited: Selections from the Paris Tribune 1917–1934*, ed. Hugh Ford (University Park: Pennsylvania State University Press, 1972), 257; Hemingway, *Moveable Feast*, 15.

46. Stendhal, *The Red and the Black* (New York: Penguin Books, 2002), 166.

47. Wilson, *Paris on Parade*, 311; Diliberto, *Hadley*, 154.

48. Virgil Thomson, *Virgil Thomson by Virgil Thomson* (New York: Alfred A.

Knopf, 1966), 76–77; Wilson, *Paris on Parade*, 238, 239.

49. Man Ray, *Portrait*, 184.

50. Ibid., 185.

51. Morley Callaghan, *That Summer in Paris: Memoir of Tangled Friendships with Hemingway, Fitzgerald and Some Others* (New York: Coward-McCann, 1963), 25.

52. David Donnell, *Hemingway in Toronto: A Post-Modern Tribute* (Windsor, Ontario: Black Moss Press, 1982), 51, 52.

53. William Burrill, *Hemingway: The Toronto Years* (Toronto: Doubleday Canada, 1994), 174.

54. Pound in Reynolds, *Paris Years*, 151; Burrill, *Hemingway, Toronto Years*, 153.

55. Hemingway to Pound, *Selected Letters*, 97.

56. *Letters of Ernest Hemingway* (Vol. 2), 54, 62.

57. Quoted in Charles A. Fenton, *The Apprenticeship of Ernest Hemingway* (New York: Viking Press, 1958), 253–54.

58. Hemingway to Pound, *Hemingway: Selected Letters*, 96.

59. Hemingway to Pound, *Letters of Ernest Hemingway* (Vol. 2), 83.

60. Callahan, *That Summer*, 30.

61. Pound in Burrill, *Hemingway, Toronto Years*, 202.

62. *Ezra Pound to His Parents*, 523.

Chapter 5

1. *Ezra Pound to His Parents*, 532; Brian, *True Gen*, 48.

2. Lynn, *Hemingway*, 250.

3. Brigit Patmore, *My Friends When Young: The Memoirs of Brigit Patmore* (London: Heinemann, 1968), 98, 100.

4. Hemingway to Pound, *Selected Letters*, 110, 111.

5. Carpenter, *Serious Character*, 56.

6. McAlmon, *Being Geniuses Together*, 179; Hemingway, *Death in the Afternoon*, 2.

7. Richard Ellmann, ed., *James Joyce* (New York: Oxford University Press, 1983), 695.

8. Pound, *Selected Prose*, 76, 109, 111, 113; *Letters of Ezra Pound*, 186.

9. *Ezra Pound to His Parents*, 543.

10. Reynolds, *The Paris Years*, 240.

11. Jolas in *The Left Bank Revisited*, 97–98.

12. Mencken, H. L. *H.L. Mencken: My Life as Author and Editor* (New York: Alfred A. Knopf, 1993), 63.

13. Fred Hobson, *Mencken: A Life* (Baltimore: Johns Hopkins University, 1994), 247.

14. Pound in Jeffrey Meyers, *Hemingway: A Biography* (New York: Harper Collins, 1985), 127.

15. Bunting in Judd, *Ford Maddox Ford*, 349–50.

16. Quoted in Bernard J, Poli, *Ford Maddox Ford and the Transatlantic Review* (Syracuse: Syracuse University Press, 1967), 143.

17. Hemingway: Selected Letters, 113.

18. Poli, *Ford Maddox Ford*, 116.

19. Ford in *The Left Bank Revisited*, 241–242.

20. Hemingway was paid for his contributions, whereas Pound most likely provided material without compensation.

21. Pound to Hemingway in Mellow, *Hemingway*, 252.

22. Wilson in Hemingway, *Literary Reference*, 35.

23. *Letters of Ezra Pound*, 199.

24. Hemingway in Mellow, *Hemingway*, 406; Pound, *Selected Prose*, 58.

25. Hemingway, *Movable Feast*, 107.

26. Forrest Read, ed., *Pound/Joyce: The Letters of Ezra Pound and James Joyce* (New York: New Directions, 1967), 230.

27. Wambly Bald in *The Left Bank Revisited*, 124.

28. Ezra Pound to Dorothy Pound, July 13, 1923, Pound Mss. III, Lilly Library; Hemingway in Jacqueline Taveneir-Courbin, *Ernest Hemingway's "Movable Feast": The Making of a Myth* (Boston: Northeastern University Press, 1991), 67–68.

Chapter 6

1. Eliot in Alfred Kazin, *Contemporaries* (Boston: Little & Brown, 1962), 118;

Kreymborg, *Troubadour: An Autobiography* (New York: Boni & Liveright, 1925), 370.

2. Ernest Boyd, "Aesthete: Model 1924," in the *The American Mercury Reader* (Philadelphia: Blakiston, 1944), 299.

3. Ezra to Dorothy Pound, July 20, 1923, Pound Mss., III, Lilly Library; Hemingway in Baker, *Hemingway*, 175, 758; Bowen in Mullins, *This Difficult Individual*, 187; Hemingway in Mellow, *Hemingway*, 264.

4. Pound, *Letters of Ezra Pound*, 189.

5. Bohun Lynch, *The Italian Riviera: Its Scenery, Customs & Food with Notes Upon the Maritime Alps* (Garden City, NY: Doubleday, Doran, 1928), vii, ix, 183, 197, 218, 248, 249.

6. Yeats, *A Vision* (New York: Collier Books, 1977), 3; Hugh Kenner, *The Pound Era* (Berkeley: University of California Press, 1971), 395.

7. Laughlin, *Pound as Wuz: Essays and Lectures on Ezra Pound* (St. Paul: Graywolf Press, 1987), 6; Simpson, *Three on the Tower*, 71.

8. Patmore, *My Friends*, 109.

9. Burckhardt, *Civilization*, 56.

10. Simpson, *Three on a Tower*, 65.

11. *Pound to His Parents*, 289. This reference appeared in a letter dated November 5, 1912.

12. Carpenter, *Serious Character*, 428; Cecil, *Max*, 484; *Ezra Pound to His Parents*, 624.

13. Surrette, *Pound in Purgatory*, 29.

14. Ibid., 34.

15. Pound 1933 essay, "Murder by Capital," in *Selected Prose*, 232: Humphreys, *Pound's Artists*, 15.

16. Wendy Stallard Flory, *The American Ezra Pound* (New Haven: Yale University Press, 1989), 87–88.

17. Surrette, *Pound in Purgatory*, 150.

18. Ezra Pound, "Mr. Pound on Prizes," *Poetry* (December 1927), 155, 156.

19. Hemingway Complete Poems, 71.

20. Hemingway, *The Torrents of Spring* (New York: Scribner, 2004), 18, 19, 74.

21. Bruccoli, *Scott and Ernest*, 57.

22. Matthew J. Bruccoli, with Judith S. Braughman, *F. Scott Fitzgerald: A Life in Letters* (New York: Charles Scribner's Sons, 1994), 7.

23. Mellow, *Hemingway*, 317–18; *The Letters of Ezra Pound*, 223.

24. Callaghan, *That Summer*, 48.

25. Brucccoli, *Scott and Ernest*, 25; Sherwood Anderson, *Selected Letters*, 80.

26. Mellow, *Hemingway*, 316.

27. Trogdon, *Hemingway: A Literary Reference*, 44.

28. Hemingway in Mellow, *Hemingway*, 474.

29. Hemingway in *Hemingway: A Literary Reference*, 155; William White, ed., *Dateline Toronto*, 153.

Chapter 7

1. Josephson in *The Left Bank Revisited*.

2. *Ezra Pound to His Parents*, 596; Ernest Hemingway, *The Sun Also Rises* (Charles Scribner & Sons, 1926), 42.

3. Pound in Mellow, *Hemingway*, 352.

4. Pound in Lynn, *Hemingway*, 167.

5. Hemingway in Mellow, *Hemingway*, 352; Pound in Lynn, *Hemingway*, 166.

6. Michael Reynolds, *Hemingway: An American Homecoming* (Cambridge: Blackwell, 1992), 109, 110, 113; Hemingway in Mellow, *Hemingway*, 347.

7. Pound, *Letters of Pound*, 205.

8. Carpenter, *Serious Character*, 461.

9. Yeats, *A Vision*, 26, 27.

10. Patmore, *My Friends*, 117–18.

11. Donaldson, *Archibald MacLeish: An American Life* (New York: Houghton Mifflin, 1992), 173; Hemingway: Selected Letters, 331.

12. *Pound/Joyce*, 227.

13. Left Bank Revisited, 244; David C. Heymann, *Ezra Pound: The Last Rower: A Political Profile* (New York: Viking, 1976), 60.

14. Pound in Reynolds, *Homecoming*, 82; Pound in Noel Stock, *The Life of Ezra Pound* (exp. ed.) (San Francisco: North

Point Press, 1982), 267; Reynolds, *Home-coming*, 112.

15. Callaghan quoted in Robert Crunden, *From Self to Society 1919–1941* (Englewood Cliffs, NJ: Prentice Hall, 1972), 51.

16. Frederick R. Karl, *Modern and Modernism: The Sovereignty of the Artist, 1885–1925* (New York: Athenaeum, 1985), 117.

17. Hemingway, *The Sun Also Rises*, 99–100.

18. Ernest Hemingway, *A Farewell to Arms* (Charles Scribner's Sons, 1957), 72.

19. Pound in J. J. Wilhelm, *Ezra Pound: The Tragic Years 1925–1972* (University Park: University of Pennsylvania Press, 1994), 24; *Pound to His Parents*, 215; Ezra Pound, *Jefferson and/or Mussolini* (New York: Liveright, 1970), 31.

Chapter 8

1. Grant Overton, ed., *Mirrors of the Year: A National Review of the Outstanding Figures, Trends, and Events of 1926–27* (New York: Frederick A. Stokes Co., 1927), 231, 249.

2. *Pound to His Parents*, 648; Aaron, 141; Townsend Ludington, ed., *The Fourteenth Chronicle: Letters and Dairies of John Dos Passos* (Boston: Gambit Inc., 1973), 368.

3. Josephson, *Life Among the Surrealists*, 89, 364.

4. Edmund Wilson, *Axle's Castle* (New York: Modern Library, 1996), 127.

5. Putman in *America as Americans See It*, 326, 328, 330.

6. Stock, *Pound*, 274.

7. Hemingway in *Ezra Pound: An Introduction to the Poetry*, ed. Sister Bernetta Quinn (New York: Columbia University Press, 1972), 23.

8. Root in *The Left Bank Revisited*, 275.

9. Stock, *Pound*, 306.

10. Baker, *Hemingway*, 302.

11. Ezra Pound, *ABC of Reading* (New Directions, 1930), 17–18.

12. Paul F Boller, *American Thought in Transition: The Impact of Evolutionary*

Naturalism, 1865–1900 (Chicago: Rand McNally, 1970), 13.

13. Kenner, *The Pound Era*, 167; Baker, *Hemingway*, 13.

14. Stock, *Pound* 311; Pound, *Jefferson and/or*, 98.

15. Pound in Carpenter, *Serious Character*, 487.

16. Pound, *Jefferson and/or Mussolini*, 24.

17. Ibid., 99, 128.

18. Ibid., 43, 107.

19. Fitzgerald in Norman, *Ezra Pound*, 310.

20. Michael Reynolds, *Hemingway: The 1930s* (New York: W. W. Norton, 1997), 146.

21. Pound, *Selected Letters*, 283. Reynolds, *Hemingway: The 1930s*, 146; Mellow, *Hemingway*, 426; Barry Ahearn, ed., *Pound/Cummings: The Correspondence of Ezra Pound and E. E. Cummings* (Ann Arbor: University of Michigan Press, 1996), 60.

22. Pound in Carpenter, *Serious Character*, 492.

23. Pound's biographers, Charles Norman, Hugh Carpenter, C. David Heymann, and John Tytell cite 1934 as the year this meeting took place. On their return to America, the Hemingways briefly returned to Paris, in March 1934.

24. Wilhelm, *Ezra Pound: The Tragic Years*, 94; *Hemingway: Selected Letters*, see letters to MacLeish and Tate, 548, 550.

25. *Hemingway Selected Letters*, 550; Ernest Hemingway, *Islands in the Stream* (New York: Scribner's Sons, 1970), 63.

26. It is interesting to note that the Liveright paperback edition of *Jefferson and/or Mussolini* (1970) carries a stamped disclaimer: "This book is being reissued under a contract which was executed in 1935 and does not necessarily reflect Pound's present views."

Chapter 9

1. Pound in Laney *Paris Herald: The Incredible Newspaper* (New York: D. Appleton-Century, 1947), 165.

2. Stein, *The Autobiography*, 293, 294; Woolf in Mellow, *Hemingway*, 357.

3. Mellow, *Hemingway*, 423.

4. Hemingway in *Hemingway: Selected Letters*, 384.

5. Tavenier-Courbin, *Ernest Hemingway's "A Moveable Feast,"* 7.

6. Stein in Mullins, *This Difficult Individual*, 134.

7. Ernest Hemingway, *Green Hills of Africa* (New York: Scribner Classics/Collier Edition, 1987), 19, 24, 196.

8. Stock, *Pound*, 306.

9. Pound in Carpenter, *Serious Character*, 497; Hemingway in Tytell, *Solitary Volcano*, 231.

10. Hemingway in Tytell, *Solitary Volcano*, 232.

11. *The Letters of Ezra Pound*, 252.

12. Tytell, *Solitary Volcano*, 234.

13. Carpenter, *Serious Character*, 491.

14. Joyce in Stock, *Pound*, 265.

15. Pound in Surette, *Pound in Purgatory*, 120, 214.

16. Nancy Cunard, *These Were Hours: Memories of My Hours Press, Reanville and Paris 1928–1931* (Carbondale and Edwardsville: Southern Illinois University Press, 1969), 129.

17. Pound in Mellow, *Hemingway*, 475.

18. Pound in Stock, *Pound*, 321; Pound quoted in Russell Kirk, *Eliot and His Age: T. S. Eliot's Moral Imagination* (Wilmington: ISI Books), 198.

19. Pound, *Kulchur*, 270.

20. Laughlin, *Pound As Wuz*, 4.

21. James Laughlin, *Byways: A Memoir*, ed. Peter Glassgold (New York: New Directions, 2005), 104. Laughlin, *Pound As Wuz*, 11.

22. *Florida: A Guide to the Southernmost State: Compiled and Written by the Federal Writer's Project of the Works Progress Administration for the State of Florida* (New York: Oxford University Press, 1965), 196.

23. Kirk Curnutt and Gail D. Sinclair, eds., *Key West Hemingway: A Reassessment* (Tallahassee: University Press of Florida, 2009), 92.

24. Norberto Fuentes, *Hemingway in Cuba* (Secaucus, NJ: Lyle Stuart, 1984), 97.

25. Hemingway, *To Have and Have Not* (New York: Charles Scribner's Sons, 1937), 193–194.

26. Reynolds, *Hemingway: The 1930s*, 92.

27. *Pound/Williams*, 190, 189.

28. Gary Dean Best, *FDR and the Bonus Marchers, 1933–1935* (Westport, CT: Praeger, 1992), 67.

29. *Hemingway: Selected Letters*, 216.

Chapter 10

1. *Letters of Ezra Pound*, 277.

2. *Ezra Pound to His Parents*, 606.

3. Hemingway in Mellow, *Hemingway*, 474.

4. Pound, "Patria Mia," in *Selected Prose*, 130.

5. Gabriel Jackson, *The Spanish Republic and the Civil War 1931–1939* (Princeton: Princeton University Press, 1972), 26.

6. Hemingway, *Death in the Afternoon*, 139.

7. Wilson in *Hemingway: A Literary Reference*, 36; Pound in Mellow, *Hemingway*, 322.

8. Hemingway, *Death in the Afternoon*, 27.

9. Ibid., 137.

10. Harry Sylvester in *True Gen*, 105.

11. Pound in Carpenter, *Serious Character*, 554; Pound, *Guide to Kulchur*, 158.

12. Williams, *Autobiography*, 316; Pound, *Guide to Kulchur*, 117; Pound in Antony Beevor, *The Battle for Spain: The Spanish Civil War 1936–1939* (New York: Penguin Books, 2006), 247; *The Letters of Ezra Pound*, 283.

13. Pound "History and Ignorance," *New English Weekly*, July 25, 1935, in *Selected Prose*, 267.

14. F. Jay Taylor, *The United States and the Spanish Civil War* (New York: Bookman Associates, 1956), 44.

15. Scott Donaldson, *By Force of Will: The Life and Art of Ernest Hemingway* (New York: Viking, 1977), 100.

16. Baker, *Hemingway*, 390.

17. *Hemingway: Selected Letters*, 456.

18. Ernest Hemingway, *For Whom the Bell Tolls* (New York: Charles Scribner's Sons, 1968), 305.

19. *Hemingway: Selected Letters*, 419.

20. Donaldson, *Force of Will*, 112; José Luis Castillo-Puche, *Hemingway in Spain: A Personal Reminiscence of Hemingway's Years in Spain by His Friend* (Garden City, NY: Doubleday, 1974), 95.

21. Beevor, *Battle for Spain*, 246–47; Caroline Moorehead, *Gellhorn: A Twentieth Century Life* (New York: Henry Holt, 2003), 127.

22. Townsend Ludington, *John Dos Passos: A Twentieth Century Odyssey.* (New York: E. P. Dutton, 1980), 374.

23. Ezra Pound, *Impact: Essays on Ignorance: The Decline of American Civilization*, ed. Noel Stock (Chicago: Henry Regenery Co., 1960), 232.

24. Daniel Aaron, *Writers on the Left: Episodes in American Literary Communism* (New York: Columbia University Press, 1992), 359.

25. Donaldson, *Archibald MacLeish*, 264–65; Henry Hart, ed., *The Writer in a Changing World* (Printed in the US: Equinox Cooperative Press, 1937), 207–08; *Hemingway: A Literary Reference*, 194.

26. Gellhorn in *The Writer in a Changing World*, 67; Tim Page, ed., *The Selected Letters of Dawn Powell 1913–1965* (New York: Henry Holt, 1999), 98.

27. *Hemingway: Selected Letters*, 460.

28. Hemingway, *To Have and Have Not*, 225; Donaldson, *Force of Will*, 109–10; Alfred Kazin, *On Native Grounds: An Interpretation of Modern Prose Literature* (New York: Harcourt, Brace, 1942), 336.

29. Hemingway, *To Have and Have Not*, 186.

30. *Pound to Laughlin*, 92; See letter to Dos Passos, *Hemingway: Selected Letters*, 463–64.

31. *Pound/Williams*, 197, 199–200.

32. *Hemingway: Selected Letters*, 482.

33. Hugh Witemeyer, ed., *Williams Carlos Williams and James Laughlin Selected Letters* (New York: W. W. Norton, 1989), 61.

Chapter 11

1. Ernest Hemingway, *True at First Light*, edited and introduction by Patrick Hemingway (New York: Scribner, 1999), 161.

2. Kay Boyle, "Pound in Rapallo," *The New York Review of Books* (May 7, 1987).

3. Heymann, *The Last Rower*, 85.

4. Williams in Heymann, *The Last Rower*, 87–88; Williams and Laughlin, *Selected Letters*, 49–54.

5. Ezra Pound, *Guide to Kulchur* (New York: New Directions, 1968), 241.

6. Edward R. Tannenbaum. *The Fascist Experience: Italian Society and Culture 1922-1945* (New York: Basic Books, 1972), 229.

7. Pound in Donald Warren, *Radio Priest: Charles Coughlin: Father of Hate Radio* (New York: The Free Press, 1996), 101.

8. Julien Cornell, *The Trial of Ezra Pound: A Documented Account of the Treason Case by the Defendant's Lawyer* (New York: John Day, 1966), 1.

9. Tytell, *Solitary Volcano*; Mullins, *This Difficult Individual*, 362.

10. *Florida: A Guide to the Southernmost State*, 201.

11. Bernice Kert, *The Hemingway Women: Those Who Loved Him, the Wives and Others*, 325.

12. Ezra Pound to James Laughlin, 123.

13. Michael Reynolds, *Hemingway: The Final Years* (New York: W. W. Norton, 1999), 31.

14. Fuentes, *Hemingway in Cuba*, 320.

15. Terry Mort, *The Hemingway Patrols: Ernest Hemingway and His Hunt for U-boats* (New York: Scribner, 2009), 218.

16. Leonard W. Doob, ed., *"Ezra Pound Speaking": Radio Speeches of World War II* (Westport, CT: Greenwood Press), 23.

17. *"Ezra Pound Speaking,"* 94.

18. Donaldson, *Archibald MacLeish*, 363.

19. *"Ezra Pound Speaking,"* 104, 188.
20. Williams and Zukofsky, 287.
21. Tietjens in Donaldson, *Archibald MacLeish*, 358; Alfred Kazin, *New York Jew* (New York: Alfred A. Knopf, 1978), 31, 34.
22. Nancy Cunard, *These Were the Hours: Memories of My Hours Press, Reanville and Paris 1928–1931*, ed. Hugh Ford (Edwardsville: Southern Illinois University Press, 1969), 128.
23. *Hemingway: Selected Letters*, 544, 545.
24. *"Erza Pound Speaking,"* 191.
25. Ibid., 245.
26. Ibid., 191.
27. Ibid., 115.
28. Ibid., 27, 49, 62.
29. Ibid., 50, 115.
30. Ibid., 84, 106.
31. *Hemingway: Selected Letters*, 548.
32. Mary de Rachewiltz, *Ezra Pound, Father and Teacher: Discretions* (New York: New Directions, 1975), 143, 161.
33. Barry Ahearn, ed., *The Correspondences of Louis Zukofsky and William Carlos Williams* (Middletown, CT: Wesleyan University Press, 200), 339.
34. Omar Pound and Robert Spoo, eds., *Ezra and Dorothy Pound: Letters in Captivity 1945–1946*, (New York: Oxford University Press, 1999), xi.
35. Poem in Carpenter, *Serious Character*, 628.
36. de Rachewiltz, 170.
37. Ibid., 115.
38. Ibid., 197.
39. "The Civilian Bag," *Time* (May 14, 1945), 21.
40. Kenner, *The Pound Era*, 474.

Chapter 12

1. Pound, *Letters in Captivity*, 73.
2. Ibid., 71, 10.
3. Carpenter, *Serious Character*, 703; Williams in Simpson, *Three on the Tower*, 296.
4. Stock, *Pound*, 417.
5. Bird in *Letters in Captivity*, 218.
6. Laughlin in Gregory Barnhisel, *James Laughlin, New Directions, and Remaking of Ezra Pound* (Amherst: University of Massachusetts Press, 2005), 102.
7. Pound, *Letters in Captivity*, 27.
8. Carpenter, *Serious Character*, 749.
9. William Van O'Connor and Edward Stone, eds., *The Casebook on Ezra Pound* (New York: Thomas Y. Crowell, 1959), 22.
10. Williams and Laughlin, *Selected Letters*, 89, 90; Correspondence of William Carlos Williams and Louis Zukofsky, 361.
11. Gregory H. Hemingway, M.D., *Papa: A Personal Memoir* (Boston: Houghton Mifflin, 1976), 103.
12. Flory, *American Ezra Pound*, 157.
13. Carpenter, *Serious Character*, 762.
14. Dorothy Pound to George Holden Tinkham, November 23, 1945, Pound Mss., III, Lilly Library.
15. Charles Olson, *Charles Olson and Ezra Pound: An Encounter at St. Elizabeths*, ed. Catherine Seelye (New York: Grossman, 1975), 17.
16. Charles A. Fecher, ed., *The Diary of H. L. Mencken* (New York: Alfred A. Knopf, 1989), 410–11.
17. Christopher Sawyer-Laucanno. *E. E. Cummings: A Biography* (Naperville, IL: Source Books, 2004), 467.
18. Kenner, *The Pound Era*, 506; Carpenter, 769; Laughlin, *Pound as Wuz*, 23; *Ezra Pound to His Parents*, xxiii.
19. Flory, *American Ezra Pound*, 171; Laughlin, *Pound as Wuz*, 23.
20. Paul Mariani, *Last Puritan: A Life of Robert Lowell* (New York: W. W. Norton, 1994), 169.
21. Williams, *Autobiography*, 336.
22. *The Selected Letters of Marianne Moore*, 461, 470.
23. Louis Dudek, ed., *D/K Some Letters of Ezra Pound* (Montreal: DC Books, 1974), 28.

Chapter 13

1. John Malcolm Brinin, *Sextet: T. S. Eliot & Truman Capote & Others* (New

York: Delta/Seymour Lawrence, 1981), 272.

2. Flory, *American Ezra Pound*, 172–73.

3. Mullins, *This Difficult Individual*, 341.

4. Gilbert Harrison Burns, ed., *Staying Alone: Letters of Alice B. Toklas* (New York: Vintage, 1975), 150.

5. "Pound, in Mental Clinic, Wins Prize for Poetry Penned in Treason Cell," *New York Times*, January 20, 1949, 1, 14.

6. Irving Howe, *A Margin of Hope: An Intellectual Autobiography* (New York: Harcourt, Brace, Jovanovich, 1982), 154.

7. Williams and Laughlin, *Selected Letters*, 172.

8. Albert J. DeFazio, ed., *Dear Papa, Dear Hotch: The Correspondence of Ernest Hemingway and A. E. Hotchner* (Columbia: University of Missouri Press, 2005), 173.

9. Ibid., 739–41.

10. Rudge in Carpenter, *Serious Character*, 785.

11. Wilhlem, *Ezra Pound in London and Paris 1908–1925* (University Park: University of Pennsylvania Press, 1994), 283; Rudge in Baker, *Hemingway*, 612.

12. Pound, *Letters in Captivity*, 193.

13. Mullins, *This Difficult Individual*, 21; de Rachewiltz, *Ezra Pound*, 293.

14. Ibid., 294.

15. "An American Storyteller," *Time*, December 13, 1954, 70.

16. Ibid., 72.

17. Hemingway in *Hemingway: A Literary Reference*, 297.

18. *Selected Letters of Dawn Powell*, 220.

19. "Confucius to Pound," *Time*, September 13, 1954, 114.

20. *Pound/Cummings*, 362. Baker, *Hemingway*, 676, 924.

21. Barnhisel, *Remaking of Ezra Pound*, 155.

22. Ibid., 154.

23. Ibid., 238.

24. Donaldson, *Archibald MacLeish*, 444; Harry M. Meacham, *The Caged Panther: Ezra Pound at Saint Elizabeth's* (New York: Twayne, 1967), 32–33.

25. Edward Connery Lathem, ed., *Interviews with Robert Frost* (New York: Holt, Rinehart & Winston, 1997), 183.

26. Carpenter, *Serious Character*, 819; Hemingway in Mullins, *This Difficult Individual*, 341.

27. Donaldson, *Archibald MacLeish*, 446; Baker, *Hemingway*, 680.

28. Stock, *Pound*, 446; Carpenter, *Serious Character*, 800.

29. Donaldson, *Archibald MacLeish*, 447.

30. Baker, *Hemingway*, 926.

31. MacLeish in Reynolds, *Hemingway: The Final Years*, 305.

32. *Pound/Cummings*, 373.

33. Laughlin, *Pound as Wuz*, 4; Pound in Meacham, *Caged Panther*, 39; Michael Reck, *Ezra Pound: A Close-Up* (New York: McGraw-Hill, 1973), 82.

34. Meacham, *Caged Panther*, 49, 53, 55.

35. Donaldson, *Archibald MacLeish*, 448.

36. Interview with Plimpton, *Hemingway: A Literary Reference*, 310.

37. Lawrence Thompson, ed., *Selected Letters of Robert Frost* (New York: Holt, Rinehart & Winston, 1964), 576.

38. Pound in Mullins, *This Difficult Individual*, 362; Correspondences of Williams and Zukofsky, 496.

39. Stock, *Pound*, 451; Patmore, *My Friends*, 150.

40. A. E. Hotchner, *Papa Hemingway: A Personal Memoir* (New York: Random House, 1966), 243.

41. Wilhelm, *Ezra Pound: The Tragic Years*, 314.

42. Stock, *Pound*, 453–54.

43. Wilhelm, *Ezra Pound: The Tragic Years*, 334.

44. Edmund Wilson, *The Sixties: The Last Journal, 1960–1972* edited and introduction by Lewis M. Dabney (New York: Farrar, Straus and Giroux, 1993), 47.

45. Hemingway, *Moveable Feast*, 108.

46. Lewis Gallantiére in *Hemingway: A Literary Reference*, 335.

Conclusion

1. Donald Hall, "Ezra Pound: An Interview," *Paris Review* 28 (Summer/Fall 1962), 22.

2. Wilson, *The Sixties*, 123.

3. Carpenter, *Serious Character*, 877.

4. Hall, *Paris Review* 28.

5. Saskia Hamilton, ed., *The Letters of Robert Lowell* (New York: Farrar, Straus and Giroux, 2005), 404.

6. Alfred Kazin, *Contemporaries* (Boston: Little Brown, 1962), 114–15.

7. Ann Charters, ed., *Jack Kerouac: Selected Letters 1940–1956* (New York: Penguin, 1996), 390.

8. Allen Ginsberg, *Spontaneous Mind: Selected Interviews 1958–1996* (New York: Harper Collins, 2001), 116, 375.

9. Reck, *Close-Up*, 153; Hall, *Paris Review* 28.

10. Ken Kesey, *Ken Kesey's Garage Sale*, with an introduction by Arthur Miller (New York: Viking Press, 1973), 181.

11. Lugii Barzini, *The Italians* (New York: Penguin Books, 1968), 28–29.

Bibliography

Aaron, Daniel. *Writers on the Left: Episodes in American Literary Communism.* With a new preface by Alan Ward. New York: Columbia University Press, 1992.

Ahearn, Barry, ed. *The Correspondence of Williams Carlos Williams and Louis Zukofsky.* Middletown, CT: Wesleyan Press, 2003.

_____. *Pound/Cummings: The Correspondences of Ezra Pound and E. E. Cummings.* Ann Arbor: University of Michigan Press, 1996.

Anderson, David D. *Sherwood Anderson: An Introduction and Interpretation.* New York: Holt, Rinehart & Winston, 1967.

Anderson, Margaret. *My Thirty Years War: The Autobiography, Beginnings and Battles to 1930.* New York: Horizon, 1969.

Anderson, Sherwood. Sherwood Anderson Papers. Newberry Library. Chicago, Illinois. Box 21, folder 1068.

Antheil, George. *Bad Boy of Music.* Garden City, NY: Doubleday, Doran & Co., 1945.

Ardizzone, Maria Luisa, ed. *Machine Art and Other Writings: The Lost Thought of the Italian Years/Ezra Pound.* With an introduction by the editor. Durham: Duke University Press, 1996.

Baker, Carlos. *Ernest Hemingway: A Life Story.* New York: Avon Books, 1968.

_____, ed. *Ernest Hemingway, Selected Letters 1917–1961.* New York: Charles Scribner's Sons, 1981.

Barney, Natalie. *Adventures of the Mind.* Translated, with an introduction, by John Spalding Gatton. New York: New York University Press, 1992.

Barnhisel, Gregory. *James Laughlin, New Directions, and the Remaking of Ezra Pound.* Amherst: University of Massachusetts Press, 2005.

Barzini, Luigi. *The Italians.* New York: Penguin Books, 1964.

Baudelaire, Charles. *The Painter of Modern Life and Other Essays.* Translated and edited by Jonathan Mayne. Unabridged Publication. New York: Da Capo, 1964.

Beach, Sylvia. *Shakespeare and Company.* New edition introduction by James Laughlin. Lincoln: University of Nebraska Press, 1991.

Best, Gary Dean. *FDR and the Bonus Marchers, 1933–1935.* Westport, CT: Praeger, 1992.

Bishop, John Peale. *The Collected Essays of John Peale Bishop.* Edited, with an introduction, by Edmund Wilson. New York: Bookman Associates, 1948.

Boller, Paul F., Jr. *American Thought in Transition: The Impact of Evolutionary Naturalism, 1865–1900.* Chicago: Rand McNally, 1969.

Boyle, Kay. "Pound in Rapallo." *The New York Review of Books*, May 7, 1987.

Breevor, Antony. *The Battle for Spain: The Spanish Civil War 1936–1939.* New York: Penguin Books, 2006.

Brian, Denis. *The True Gen: An Intimate Portrait of Hemingway by Those Who Knew Him.* New York: Grove Press, 1988.

Brinin, John Malcolm. *Sextet: T. S. Eliot & Truman Capote & Others.* New York: Delta/Seymour Lawrence, 1981.

Brooks, Van Wyck. *Days of the Phoenix: The Nineteen Twenties I Remember.* New York: E. P. Dutton, 1957.

Bruccoli, Matthew J., ed. *F. Scott Fitzgerald: A Life in Letters.* With the assistance of Judith S. Braughman. New York: Charles Scribner's Sons, 1994.

_____. Bruccoli, Matthew J. *Scott and Ernest: The Fitzgerald and Hemingway Friendship.* New York: Random House, 1978.

Burckhardt, Jacob. *The Civilization of the Renaissance in Italy.* Edited, with a new introduction, by Irene Gordon. New York: Mentor Books, 1960.

Burrill, William. *Hemingway: The Toronto Years.* Toronto: Doubleday Canada, Ltd., 1994.

Burns, Edward, ed. *Staying Alone: The Letters of Alice B. Toklas.* With an introduction by Gilbert Harrison. New York: Vintage Books, 1973.

Callahan, Morley. *That Summer in Paris.* New York: Coward-McCann, 1963.

Carpenter, Humphrey. *A Serious Character: The Life of Ezra Pound.* Boston: Houghton Mifflin, 1988.

Castillo-Puche, José Luis. *Hemingway in Spain: A Personal Reminiscence of Hemingway's Years in Spain by His Friend.* Trans. Helen R. Lane. Garden City, NY: Doubleday, 1974.

Cecil, David. *Max: A Biography of Max Beerbohm.* New York: Athenaeum, 1985.

Charters, Ann, ed. *Jack Kerouac: Selected Letters 1940–1956.* With an introduction by the editor. New York: Penguin Books, 1996.

Cohen, Milton A. *Hemingway's Laboratory: The Paris in Our Time.* Tuscaloosa: University of Alabama Press, 2005.

Conover, Anne. *Olga Rudge and Ezra Pound.* New Haven: Yale University Press, 2001.

Cookson, William, ed. *Ezra Pound Selected Prose 1909–1965.* With an introduction by the editor. New York: New Directions, 1973.

Cornell, Julien. *The Trial of Ezra Pound: A Documented Account of the Treason Case by the Defendant's Lawyer.* New York: John Day Co., 1966.

Costello, Bonnie, Goodridge, Celeste, and Christine Miller, eds. *The Selected Letters of Marianne Moore.* New York: Alfred A. Knopf, 1997.

Cowley, Malcolm. *The Dream of Golden Mountains: Remembering the 1930s.* New York: Penguin Books, 1981.

_____. *Exile's Return: A Literary Odyssey of the 1920s.* New York: Penguin Books, 1975. First published in 1934.

_____. *A Second Flowering: Works and Days of the Lost Generation.* New York: Viking Press, 1973.

Crosby, Caresse. *The Passionate Years.* New York: Ecco Press, 1979.

Crunden, Robert. *From Self to Society, 1919–1941.* Englewood Cliffs, NJ: Prentice-Hall, 1972.

Cunard, Nancy. *These Were the Hours: Memories of My Hours Press, Reanville and Paris 1928–1931.* Edited, with a foreword, by Hugh Ford. Carbondale and Edwardsville: Southern Illinois University Press, 1969.

Curnutt, Kirk, and Gail D. Sinclair. *Key West Hemingway: A Reassessment.* Tallahassee: University of Florida Press, 2009.de Rachewiltz, Mary. *Ezra Pound, Father and Teacher: Discretions.* New York: New Directions, 1975.

Diggins, John P. *Mussolini and Fascism: The View from America.* Princeton: Princeton University Press, 1972.

Diliberto, Gioia. *Hadley.* New York: Ticknor and Fields, 1997.

Donaldson, Scott. *By Force of Will: The Life and Art of Ernest Hemingway.* New York: Viking, 1977.

_____. *Archibald MacLeish: An American Life.* New York: Houghton Mifflin, 1992.

_____. *Hemingway vs. Fitzgerald: The Rise and Fall of Literary Friendship.* Woodstock, NY: The Overlook Press, 1999.

Donnell, David. *Hemingway in Toronto: A Post-Modern Tribute*. Windsor, Ontario: Black Moss Press, 1982.

Doob, Leonard W., ed. *"Ezra Pound Speaking": Radio Speeches of World War II*. Westport, CT: Greenwood Press, 1978.

Doolittle, Hilda (H. D.). *End to Torment: A Memoir of Ezra Pound*. Edited by Norman Holmes and Michael King. New York: New Directions, 1979.

Dudek, Louis, ed. *DK/Some Letters of Ezra Pound*. With notes by the editor. Montreal: DC Books, 1974.

Eliot, Valerie, ed. *The Letters of T. S. Eliot*. General editor, John Hoffman. New Haven: Yale University, 2009.

Ellmann, Richard. *James Joyce*. New and revised edition. Oxford: Oxford University Press, 1982.

Fattorusso, Joseph. *Wonders of Italy: The Monuments of Antiquity, the Churches, the Palaces, the Treasures of Art*. 11th ed. Madison: University of Wisconsin Press, 1952.

Fecher, Charles A., ed. *The Diary of H. L. Mencken*. New York: Alfred A. Knopf, 1989.

Federal Writer's Project of Works Projects Administration for the State of Florida. *Florida: A Guide to the Southernmost State*. New York: Oxford University Press, 1965.

Flanner, Janet. *Paris Was Yesterday: 1925–1939*. Edited by Irving Drutman. New York: Viking Press, 1972.

Fuentes, Norberto. *Hemingway in Cuba*. With an introduction by Gabriel Garcia Márquez. Secaucus, NJ: Lyle Stuart, 1984.

Flory, Wendy Stallard. *The American Ezra Pound*. New Haven: Yale University Press, 1989.

Ford, Hugh. *Four Lives in Paris*. With a foreword by Glenway Wescott. San Francisco: North Point Press, 1987.

_____. *The Left Bank Revisited: Selections from the Paris Tribune 1917–1934*. With a foreword by Matthew Josephson. University Park: Pennsylvania State University Press, 1972.

_____. *Published in Paris: A Literary Chronicle of Paris in the 1920s and 1930s*. With a foreword by Janet Flanner. New York: Collier Books, 1988.

Gallop, Donald, ed. *Flowers of Friendship: Letters Written to Gertrude Stein*. New York: Alfred A. Knopf, 1953.

Gerogiannis, Nicholas, ed. *Ernest Hemingway Complete Poems*. Revised edition. Lincoln: University of Nebraska Press, 1992.

Ginsberg, Allen. *Spontaneous Mind: Selected Interviews 1958–1996*. New York: Harper and Collins, 2001.

Glendinning, Victoria. *Rebecca West: A Life*. New York: Alfred A. Knopf, 1987.

Gordon, David M., ed. *Ezra Pound and James Laughlin: Selected Letters*. New York: W.W. Norton, 1994.

Gordon, Terrence W. *Marshall McLuhan: Escape to Understanding*. New York: Basic Books, 1997.

Hall, Donald. "Interviews—Ezra Pound: The Art of Poetry." *Paris Review* 28 (Summer/Fall 1962).

Hamilton, Saskia, ed. *Letters of Robert Lowell*. New York: Farrar, Straus & Giroux, 2005.

Hart, Henry, ed. *The Writer in a Changing World*. US: Equinox Cooperative, 1937.

Hemingway, Ernest. *Death in the Afternoon*. New York: Scribner's Sons, 1932.

_____. *A Farewell to Arms*. 1929. New York, Charles Scribner's Sons, 1957.

_____. *The Torrents of Spring*. 1926. New York: Scribner & Sons, 2004.

_____. *For Whom the Bell Tolls*. 1940. New York: Scribner, 1968.

_____. *Islands in the Stream*. New York: Scribner's & Sons, 1970.

_____. *A Moveable Feast*. 1964. 15th printing. New York: Scribner's & Sons, 1979.

_____. *The Nick Adams Stories*. New York: Scribner's & Sons, 1972.

_____. *The Sun Also Rises*. New York: Charles Scribner's Sons, 1926.

_____. *To Have and Have Not*. New York: Charles Scribner's Sons, 1937.

_____. *True at First Light*. New York: Scribner Paperback Fiction, 2000.

Hemingway, Gregory, M.D. *Papa: A Personal Memoir. Boston: Houghton Mifflin, 1976.

Hemingway, Mary Welsh. How It Was. New York: Alfred A. Knopf, 1976.

Heymann, David C. Ezra Pound: The Last Rower, a Political Profile. New York: Viking, 1976.

Hobson, Fred. Mencken: A Life. Baltimore: Johns Hopkins University Press, 1994.

Hotchner, A. E. Papa Hemingway: A Personal Memoir. New York: Random House, 1966.

Huddleston, Sisley. Paris, Salons, Cafés, Studios. New York: Blue Ribbon Books, 1928.

Humphries, Richard, Tate Gallery, and Kettle's Yard Gallery. Pound's Artists: Ezra Pound and the Visual Arts in London, Paris and Italy. London: The Tate Gallery, 1985.

Jackson, Gabriel. The Spanish Republic and the Civil War 1931–1939. 3rd printing. Princeton: Princeton University Press, 1972.

Jones, Howard Mumford, and Walter B. Rideout, eds. Letters of Sherwood Anderson. With an introduction by Howard Mumford Jones. Boston: Little, Brown, 1953.

Joost, Nicholas. Ernest Hemingway and the Little Magazine Years: The Paris Years. Barre, MA: Barre, 1968.

Josephson, Matthew. Life Among the Surrealists: A Memoir. New York: Holt, Rinehart & Winston, 1962.

Judd, Alan. Ford Maddox Ford. Cambridge: Harvard University Press, 1991.

Karl, Frederick R. Modern and Modernism: The Sovereignty of the Artist, 1885–1925. New York: Athenaeum, 1985.

Kazin, Alfred. Contemporaries. Boston: Little, Brown, 1962.

_____. On Native Grounds: An Interpretation of Modern American Prose Literature. New York: Harcourt, Brace, 1942.

_____. New York Jew. Alfred A. Knopf, 1978.

Kenner, Hugh. The Pound Era. Berkeley: University of California Press, 1971.

Kenner, Hugh, ed. T. S. Eliot: A Collection of Critical Essays. Englewood Cliffs, New Jersey: Prentice-Hall, 1962.

Kert, Bernice. The Hemingway Women: Those Who Loved Him, the Wives and Others. New York: W. W. Norton, 1983.

Kesey, Ken. Ken Kesey's Garage Sale. With an introduction by Arthur Miller. New York: Viking Press, 1973.

Kirk, Russell. Eliot and His Age: T. S. Eliot's Moral Imagination in the Twentieth Century. Wilmington, DE: ISI Books, 2008.

Kotynek, Roy, and John Cohassey. American Cultural Rebels: Avant-Garde and Bohemian Artists, Writers and Musicians from the 1850s through 1960s. Jefferson, NC: McFarland, 2008.

Kreymborg, Alfred. Troubadour: An Autobiography. New York: Boni and Liveright, 1925.

Laney, Al. Paris Herald: The Incredible Newspaper. New York: D. Appleton-Century, 1947.

Lathem, Edward Connery, ed. Interviews with Robert Frost. New York: Holt, Rinehart and Winston, 1966.

Laughlin, James. Pound as Wuz: Essays and Lectures on Ezra Pound. With an introduction by Hugh Kenner. Saint Paul: Graywolf Press, 1987.

_____. Byways: A Memoir. Edited and annotated by Peter Glassgold. With a preface by Guy Davenport. New York: New Directions, 2005.

Lewis, Wyndham. Blasting and Bombardiering. Berkeley: University of California Press, 1967.

Ludington, Townsend, ed. The Fourteenth Chronicle: Letters and Dairies of John Dos Passos. With a biographical narrative by the editor. Boston: Gambit, 1973.

_____. John Dos Passos: A Twentieth Century Odyssey. New York: E. P. Dutton, 1980.

Lynch, Bohun. The Italian Riviera: Its Scenery, Customs & Food with Notes Upon the Maritime Alps. Garden City, NY: Doubleday, Doran & Co., 1928.

Lynn, Kenneth S. Hemingway. New York: Simon & Schuster, 1987.

Mariani, Paul. *Last Puritan: A Life of Robert Lowell*. New York: W. W. Norton, 1994.

McAlmon, Robert, and Kay Boyle. *Being Geniuses Together: A Binocular View of Paris in the '20s*. Garden City, NY: Doubleday, 1968.

McCaffey, John K., ed. *Ernest Hemingway: The Man and His Work*. Second ed. Cleveland: The World Publishing Co., 1951.

McIver, Stuart B. *Hemingway's Key West*. Sarasota, FL: Pineapple Press, 1993.

Meacham, Harry M. *The Caged Panther: Ezra Pound at Saint Elizabeths*. New York: Twayne, 1967.

Mellow, James R. *Charmed Circle: Gertrude Stein and Company*. New York: Praeger, 1974.

_____. *Hemingway: A Life Without Consequences*. New York: Houghton Mifflin, 1992.

Mencken, H. L. *My Life as Author and Editor*. Edited and introduction by Jonathan Yardley. New York: Alfred A. Knopf, 1993.

_____. *The Diary of H. L. Mencken*. Edited by Charles A. Fecher. New York: Alfred A. Knopf, 1989.

Meyers, Jeffrey. *Hemingway: A Biography*. New York: Harper & Row, 1985.

Miller, James E., Jr. *T. S. Eliot: The Making of an American Poet*. University Park: Pennsylvania State University, 2005.

Modlin, Charles E., ed. *Sherwood Anderson Selected Letters*. Knoxville: University of Tennessee Press, 1984.

Monroe, Harriet. "Ezra Pound." *Poetry* (May 1925): 90.

Moody, A. David. *Ezra Pound: A Portrait of the Man and Work Volume I: The Young Genius 1885–1920*. New York: Oxford University Press, 2007.

Moorehead, Caroline. *Gellhorn: A Twentieth Century Life*. New York: Henry Holt, 2003.

Mort, Terry. *The Hemingway Patrols: Ernest Hemingway and Hunt for U-boats*. New York: Scribner, 2009.

Mullins, Eustace. *This Difficult Individual, Ezra Pound*. New York: Fleet, 1961.

Norman, Charles. *Ezra Pound*. New York: MacMillan Co., 1960.

O'Connor, William Van, and Edward Stone, eds. *A Casebook on Ezra Pound*. New York: Thomas Y. Crowell Co., 1959.

Oldsey, Bernard, ed. *Ernest Hemingway: The Papers of a Writer*. With an introduction by the editor. New York: Garland, 1981.

Olson, Charles. *Charles Olson and Ezra Pound: An Encounter at St. Elizabeths*. Edited by Catherine Seeyle. New York: Grossman, 1975.

O'Rourke, Sean. *Grace Under Pressure: The Life of Evan Shipman*. Los Angeles: Harvardwood, 2010.

Overton, Grant, ed. *Mirrors of the Year: A National Review of the Outstanding Figures, Trends and Events of 1926–7*. New York: Frederick A. Stokes, 1927.

Page, Tim, ed. *Selected Letters of Dawn Powell, 1913–1965*. With an introduction by the editor. New York: Henry Holt, 1999.

Patmore, Brigit. *My Friends When Young: The Memoir of Brigit Patmore*. London: Heinemann, 1968.

Poli, Bernard J. *Ford Maddox Ford and the Transatlantic Review*. Syracuse: Syracuse University Press, 1967.

Polizzotti, Mark. *Revolution of the Mind: The Life of André Breton*. New York: Da Capo, 1997.

Pound, Ezra. *ABC of Reading*. 1934. New York: New Directions, 1960.

_____. *Antheil and the Treatise on Harmony*. 1927. New York: Da Capo, 1968.

_____. *The Cantos of Ezra Pound*. 7th printing. New York: New Directions, 1979.

_____. *Gaudier-Brzeska: A Memoir*. 1916. New York: New Directions, 1970.

_____. *Guide to Kulchur*. New York: New Directions, 1938.

_____. *Impact: Essays on Ignorance; The Decline of American Civilization*. Edited by Noel Stock. Chicago: Henry Regnery, 1960.

_____. *Jefferson and/or Mussolini*. 1935. New York: Liveright, 1970.

_____. *The Letters of Ezra Pound, 1907–1941*. New York: Harcourt, Brace, 1950.

_____. *Pavannes and Divagations*. New York: New Directions, 1958.

_____. *Personae: The Shorter Poems of Ezra Pound*. Revised edition prepared by Lea Baechler and A. Walton Litz. New York: New Directions, 1990.

_____. Pound Manuscript Collection. Lilly Library, Bloomington, Indiana, University of Indiana. Pound Mss. 1919–24; Pound Mss. II 1900–73; Pound Mss. III 1910–27; Dorothy Pound, 1943 and 1947–73.

_____. "Pound on Prizes." *Poetry* (December 1927): 155–56.

Pound, Omar, and Robert Spoo, eds. *Letters from Captivity, 1945–1946*. Annotated by the editors. New York: Oxford University Press, 1999.

Putnam, Samuel. *Paris Was Our Mistress: Memoirs of a Lost and Found Generation*. New York: Viking, 1947.

Quinn, Sister Bernetta. *Ezra Pound: An Introduction to the Poetry*. New York: Columbia University Press, 1972.

Rachewiltz, Mary, A. David Moody, and Joanna Moody, eds. *Ezra Pound to His Parents: Letters 1895–1929*. New York: Oxford University Press, 2010.

Rainey, Lawrence. *Ezra Pound and the Monument of Culture: Text, History, and Malatesta Cantos*. Chicago: University of Chicago Press, 1991.

Ray, Man. *Self Portrait*. Boston: Little, Brown, 1963.

Read, Forrest, ed. *Pound/Joyce: The Letters of Ezra Pound to James Joyce, with Pound's Essays on Joyce*. With commentary by the editor. New York: New Directions, 1967.

Reck, Michael. *Ezra Pound: A Close-Up*. New York: McGraw-Hill, 1973.

Reid, B. L. *The Man from New York: John Quinn and His Friends*. New York: Oxford University Press, 1968.

Reynolds, Michael. *Hemingway: The Paris Years*. New York: W. W. Norton, 1989.

_____. *Hemingway: The 1930s*. New York: W. W. Norton, 1997.

_____. *Hemingway: The American Homecoming*. Cambridge: Blackwell, 1993.

_____. *Hemingway: The Final Years*. New York: W. W. Norton, 1999.

Rideout, Walter B. *The Radical Novel in the United States 1900–1954: Some Interrelations of Literature and Society*. New York: Hill & Wang, 1956.

_____. *Sherwood Anderson: A Writer in America Volume 1*. With an introduction by Charles E. Modlin. Madison: University of Wisconsin Press, 2006.

Ringle, Fred J., ed. *America as Americans See It*. New York: Literary Guild, 1932.

Sawyer-Laucanno, Christopher. *E. E. Cummings: A Biography*. Naperville, Illinois: Sourcebooks, 2004.

Scott, Thomas L., *et al*., eds. *Pound/The Little Review, The Letters of Ezra Pound and Margaret Anderson: The Little Review Correspondence*. New York: New Directions, 1988.

Simpson, Louis. *Three on a Tower: The Lives and Woks of Ezra Pound, T. S. Eliot and William Carlos Williams*. New York: William and Morrow, 1975.

Souhami, Diana. *Gertrude and Alice*. London: Pandora, 1991.

_____. *Wild Girls, Paris, Sappho and Art: The Lives and Loves of Natalie Barney and Romain Brooks*. New York: St. Martin's Press, 2005.

Spanier, Sandra, and Robert W. Trogdon, eds. *The Letters of Ernest Hemingway Volume 1 1907–1922*. Cambridge: Cambridge University Press, 2011.

Spanier, Sandra, Albert J. Fefazio, and Robert W. Trogdon, eds. *The Letters of Ernest Hemingway Volume 2 1923–1925*. Cambridge: Cambridge University Press, 2013.

Spivak, Lawrence, and Charles Angoff, eds. *The American Mercury Reader*. Philadelphia: Blakiston, 1944.

Staley, Edgcumbe. *Heroines of Genoa and the Rivieras*. New York: Charles Scribner's Sons, 1911.

Stansell, Christine. *American Moderns: Bohemian New York and the Creation of a New Century*. New York: Metropolitan Books, 2000.

Stearns, Harold. *Confessions of a Harvard Man*. With a preface by Kay Boyle. Santa Barbara, CA: Paget Press, 1984.

Stein, Gertrude. *The Autobiography of Alice B. Toklas*. New York: Modern Library, 1993. First published in 1933.

Stendhal. *The Red and the Black*. 1830. New York: Penguin Books, 2002.

Stock, Noel. *The Life of Ezra Pound*. Expanded Edition. San Francisco: North Point Press, 1982.

Surette, Leon. *Pound in Purgatory: From Economic Radicalism to Anti-Semitism*. Chicago: University of Chicago Press, 1999.

Sutton, Walter, ed. *Pound, Thayer, Watson, and the Dial: A Story in Letters*. Gainesville: University Press of Florida, 1994.

Tannenbaum, Edward R. *The Fascist Experience: Italian Society and Culture 1922–1945*. New York: Basic Books, 1972.

Tavenier-Courbin, Jacqueline. *Ernest Hemingway's "A Moveable Feast": The Making of a Myth*. Boston: Northeastern University Press, 1991.

Thompson, Lawrence, ed. *Selected Letters of Robert Frost*. New York: Holt, Rinehart & Winston, 1964.

Thomson, Virgil. *Virgil Thomson by Virgil Thomson*. New York: Alfred A. Knopf, 1966.

Time. "An American Storyteller." December 13, 1954.

_____. "The Civilian Bag." May 14, 1945.

_____. "Confucius to Pound." September 13, 1954.

Torrey, E. Fuller. *The Roots of Treason: Ezra Pound and the Secrets of St. Elizabeths*. New York: McGraw-Hill, 1984.

Trogdon, Robert W. *Ernest Hemingway: A Literary Reference*. New York: Carroll & Graf, 2002.

_____. *The Lousy Racket: Hemingway, Scribners, and the Business of Literature*. Kent Ohio: Kent State University Press, 2007.

Tytell, John. *Ezra Pound: The Solitary Volcano*. New York: Anchor Press, 1987.

Warren, Donald. *Radio Priest: Charles Coughlin, The Father of Hate Radio*. New York: The Free Press, 1996.

White, William, ed. *Dateline Toronto: The Complete* Toronto Star *Dispatches, 1920–1924*. New York: Charles Scribner's Sons, 1985.

_____. *Ernest Hemingway, Dateline Toronto: His Complete Dispatches for the Toronto Star, 1920–1924*. New York: Simon & Schuster, 1985.

Wickes, George. *Americans in Paris*. With a new foreword by Virgil Thomson. New York: Da Capo, 1980.

Wilhelm, J. J. *Ezra Pound in London and Paris, 1908–1925*. University Park: Pennsylvania State University Press, 1990.

_____. *Ezra Pound: The Tragic Years 1925–1972*. University Park: University of Pennsylvania Press, 1994.

Williams, William Carlos. *The Autobiography of William Carlos Williams*. New York: Random House, 1951.

Wilson, Edmund. *Axle's Castle: A Study of the Imaginative Literature of 1870–1930*. New York: The Modern Library, 1996.

_____. *The Collected Essays of John Peale Bishop*. With a new introduction by Edmund Wilson. New York: Scribner's Sons, 1948.

_____. *The Sixties: The Last Journal, 1960–1972*. Edited, and introduction, by Lewis M. Dabney. New York: Farrar, Straus & Giroux, 1993.

Wilson, Robert Forrest. *Paris on Parade*. Indianapolis: Bobbs-Merrill Co., 1925.

Winter, Ella, ed. *Letters of Lincoln Steffens Vol. II: 1920–1936*. Westport, CT: Greenwood Press, 1966.

Witmeyer, Hugh, ed. *Pound/Williams: Selected Letters of Ezra Pound and William Carlos Williams*. New York: New Directions, 1996.

_____. *William Carlos Williams and James Laughlin: Selected Letters*. New York: W.W. Norton & Co., 1989.

Yeats, W. B. *A Vision*. 9th edition. New York: Collier Books, 1977.

Index